Ireland and Cultural Theory

The Mechanics of Authenticity

Edited by

Colin Graham
Lecturer in English
University of Huddersfield

and

Richard Kirkland
Lecturer in English
Keele University

palgrave

First published in Great Britain 1999 by
MACMILLAN PRESS LTD
Houndmills, Basingstoke, Hampshire RG21 6XS and London
Companies and representatives throughout the world

A catalogue record for this book is available from the British Library.

ISBN 0–333–67596–7 hardcover
ISBN 0–333–67597–5 paperback

First published in the United States of America 1999 by
ST. MARTIN'S PRESS, INC.,
Scholarly and Reference Division,
175 Fifth Avenue, New York, N.Y. 10010

ISBN 0–312–21290–9

Library of Congress Cataloging-in-Publication Data
Ireland and cultural theory : the mechanics of authenticity / edited by Colin Graham and Richard Kirkland.
p. cm.
Includes bibliographical references and index.
ISBN 0–312–21290–9 (cloth)
1. Ireland—Civilization—Theory, etc. 2. English literature– –Irish authors—History and criticism—Theory, etc. 3. National characteristics, Irish, in literature. 4. National characteristics, Irish. 5. Ireland—In literature. 6. Irish—Great Britain. 7. Culture. I. Graham, Colin, 1967– . II. Kirkland, Richard.
DA925.I63 1998
941.5—dc21 97–32314
CIP

This book is printed on paper suitable for recycling and made from fully managed and sustained forest sources.

Printed and bound in Great Britain by
Antony Rowe Ltd, Eastbourne
Transferred to digital printing 2001

Contents

Notes on the Contributors

Claire Connolly lectures in the School of English Studies, University of Wales, Cardiff. She is a member of Cardiff's Centre for Critical and Cultural Theory, and is writing a book on gender and nation in the novels of Maria Edgeworth and Lady Morgan. She has edited Maria Edgeworth's *Letters for Literary Ladies* (Everyman, 1995) as well as two volumes of the Pickering collected Maria Edgeworth (1996).

Colin Graham is a lecturer in English at the University of Huddersfield. He studied at the Queen's University of Belfast and the University of Bristol and was formerly Junior Research Fellow at the Institute of Irish Studies at Queen's, Belfast. He has published articles on post-colonial theory and Ireland, post-nationalism, the subaltern, Derek Mahon and Maria Edgeworth. He has edited the poetry of Elizabeth Barrett Browning and of Robert Browning and is author of *Ideologies of Epic* (Manchester University Press, 1998).

Tom Herron is a lecturer in English at the University of Aberdeen, where he is completing a doctoral thesis on *The Field Day Anthology of Irish Writing*. He has published essays on Ciaran Carson and Irish/Northern Irish nationalism, on the Field Day Anthology and post-colonial theory, and on the Anthology as communicative space/act. He is currently working on two projects: the first on masculinity in Frank McGuinness's drama, and the second on interrogations of social pathology within national narratives in the novels of Patrick McCabe and Colm Tóibín.

Eamonn Hughes lectures in the School of English, Queen's University of Belfast, Northern Ireland, specializing in Irish writing. He is the editor of *Culture and Politics in Northern Ireland 1960–1990* (Open University Press, 1991) and has published widely on Irish writing.

Richard Kirkland is a lecturer in English at Keele University. He has published widely on Northern Irish poetry, fiction and culture and is the author of *Literature and Culture in Northern Ireland since 1965: Moments of Danger* (Longman, 1996). Before coming to Keele he was Teaching Fellow in the School of English, Queen's University of Belfast.

Jim Mac Laughlin, a graduate of Syracuse University, New York, is a political geographer at University College Cork. His current research interests are in nationalism, ethnic conflict, political regionalism and racism. He has published extensively on these and related topics and on ideology in the social sciences. His most recent works include *Ireland: The Emigrant Nursery and the World Economy* and *Travellers and Ireland: Whose History, Whose Country?* His teaching interests are in Latin American studies, emigration and political geography.

Lance Pettitt was an Irish/United Kingdom Government Exchange Scholar at University College, Dublin. He is Director of Irish Studies at St Mary's University College, Strawberry Hill. His research interests include: the British media and Ireland, Irish cinema, sexuality in popular culture and Irish migrant writing. Publications include articles in *Irish Studies Review, The Sunday Tribune* and *South Atlantic Quarterly*. His essay on gay representation in contemporary Irish film appears in *Sex, Nation and Dissent* (Cork University Press, 1996). He has been the editor of the British Association for Irish Studies Newsletter since 1994.

Shaun Richards is Head of Literature at Staffordshire University. A graduate of the Universities of Wales, Sussex, York (Toronto) and Essex he has published widely on the cultural politics of twentieth-century Irish Drama with articles and chapters on, among others, Yeats, Synge, Shaw, O'Casey, Deevy, Murphy, Field Day, Parker and Heaney. He is co-author (with David Cairns) of *Writing Ireland: Colonialism, Nationalism and Culture* (Manchester University Press, 1988) and is currently working on a book on twentieth-century Irish drama.

Gerry Smyth was born and educated in Dublin. He worked as a professional musician in Spain and England before returning to full-time education. He has a BA in Literature, Life and Thought from Liverpool John Moores University, an MA in Cultural Studies from the University of Lancaster, and his Ph.D. research, from which Chapter 3 of this book is adapted, was undertaken at Staffordshire University. He has published articles on Matthew Arnold, Neil Jordan's *The Crying Game*, Irish cultural criticism, and is author of *The Novel and the Nation: Studies in the New Irish Fiction* (Pluto, 1997).

Bronwen Walter is Senior Lecturer in Geography at Anglia Polytechnic University. Her longstanding interest is contemporary Irish migration to Britain, her recent research focusing on Irish women's experience in Britain and America. She has published in academic journals and London Irish community group reports. She is co-author, with Mary Hickman of the Irish Studies Centre, University of North London, of a report for Racial Equality on anti-Irish discrimination, which was completed in 1996.

Acknowledgements

The editors would like to thank Shaun Richards of Staffordshire University for the advice and support he offered during the compilation of this volume.

The editors and publishers are grateful to the following for permission to reprint copyright material:

Reprinted by permission of Faber and Faber Ltd: excerpts from *Door into the Dark* by Seamus Heaney. Copyright 1969 by Seamus Heaney; excerpts from *Field Work* by Seamus Heaney. Copyright 1979 by Seamus Heaney; excerpts from *North* by Seamus Heaney. Copyright 1975 by Seamus Heaney; excerpts from *Station Island* by Seamus Heaney. Copyright 1984 by Seamus Heaney; excerpts from *Fivemiletown* by Tom Paulin. Copyright 1987 by Tom Paulin; excerpts from *Liberty Tree* by Tom Paulin. Copyright 1983 by Tom Paulin; excerpts from *A State of Justice* by Tom Paulin. Copyright 1977 by Tom Paulin; excerpts from *The Strange Museum* by Tom Paulin. Copyright 1980 by Tom Paulin; excerpts from *Walking a Line* by Tom Paulin. Copyright 1994 by Tom Paulin; excerpt from *Our Exagmination Round His Factification For Incamination Of Work In Progress* ed. by Samuel Beckett. Copyright Faber 1961.

Reproduced by permission of Frederick Warne and Co. (Penguin UK): excerpt from *Imaginary Homelands: Essays and Criticism 1981–1991* by Salman Rushdie (Grant/Penguin Books, 1991). Copyright 1985, 1991 by Salman Rushdie.

Reprinted by permission of The Gallery Press: excerpt from *The Rough Field* by John Montague. Copyright 1989 by John Montague.

Reprinted by permission of A.P. Watt Limited and Michael and Anne Yeats: excerpt from *Fairy and Folk Tales of the Irish Peasantry* by W.B. Yeats.

Reprinted by permission of Raven Arts Press: Michael O'Loughlin poems from *Another Nation, New and Selected Poems* by Michael O'Loughlin, published by New Island Books in Ireland and Arc Publications in Britain.

Reprinted by permission of Farrar, Straus and Giroux, Inc.: excerpts from *Field Work* by Seamus Heaney. Copyright 1981 by Seamus Heaney; excerpts from *Poems 1965–1975* by Seamus Heaney. Copyright 1980 by Seamus Heaney; excerpts from *Station Island* by Seamus Heaney. Copyright 1984 by Seamus Heaney.

Reprinted by permission of Macmillan Press: excerpts from 'In a Wood' by Thomas Hardy.

Reprinted by permission of Lucas Alexander Whitley Literary Agents and Michael Longley: excerpts from 'The Linen Workers' and 'On Slieve Gullion'. Copyright 1986 Michael Longley.

Every effort has been made to trace all the copyright holders but if any have been inadvertently overlooked the publishers will be pleased to make the necessary arrangement at the first opportunity.

1

Introduction

Colin Graham and Richard Kirkland

> [. . .] what I find useful is the sustained and developing work on the mechanics of the construction of the Other; we can use it to much greater analytic and interventionist advantage than invocations of the *authenticity* of the Other.[1]
>
> (Gayatri Chakravorty Spivak)

> Authentic culture is not a matter of ourselves alone.[2]
>
> (Richard Kearney)

The idea for this collection of essays was inspired by the belief that the study of Irish culture was in the process of transformation, with new critical practices and theoretical frameworks almost inevitably challenging the orthodoxies of how Ireland is read and what is read as 'Ireland'. The points of focus in cultural theory which have arisen at the intersections of post-colonial theory, cultural studies, postmodernism and deconstruction – identity, commitment, locality, race, ethnicity, gender, cultural interaction – seemed to resonate through already established areas of Irish criticism and some momentum in the theorization of the study of Ireland looked to have begun.

At the beginning of this project the intervention of David Lloyd's work, for example, appeared to open the possibilities of a sophisticated and contentious post-colonial analysis of Irish culture, while Field Day's anthologizing act of bravura had had the effect of cataloguing Ireland in a way which, perhaps inadvertently, made a long overdue (if largely implicit) challenge to the supremacy of 'high' cultural texts in defining the parameters of 'Ireland'.[3] However, Lloyd's theoretical disruption of the 'ourselves alone' strategy of solely 'internal' explanations of Irishness has not yet led to major reassessments of Irish critical practice. Certainly, the determined use of 'theory' in Lloyd's work is put into a wider context by the publication of Luke Gibbons's collection of essays *Transformations in Irish Culture*, a work which further brings together the assumptions of cultural studies and post-colonial criticism in the context of Ireland.[4] The work undertaken by Gibbons and Lloyd needs to be balanced, though, against a continuing series of critical debates (mainly that between historical revisionism and 'nationalism') which have excluded the very possibility of theory – alternatively cultural theory can easily place itself or become placed within the parameters of these debates, and thus lose a large degree of its impetus. What appears to be a new application of theoretical knowledge has too often covered older critical practices restated; Declan Kiberd's *Inventing Ireland*, for example, arguably stagnates in its own stated use of a post-colonial model; Kiberd's belief that citing Albert Memmi and Frantz Fanon (or even Edward W. Said and C.L.R. James) is to engage with 'recent work' in colonial theory is symptomatic of the need to bring cultural theory into the context of Irish studies.[5] Most worryingly, in retrospect the invited intervention of major cultural theorists in the Field Day pamphlets seemed to reveal that established Irish studies had the ability to impose its strictures on those conceptual forces which come to it from the outside.[6]

From its inception then this collection has changed from being a putative focal point for a gathering momentum in Irish cultural studies to become a reflection of the varied ways in which Irish studies has moved towards its own theoretical agendas. Reviewing the philosophical bases for cultural studies and post-colonial theory, Lawrence Grossberg has pointed to 'three immediate and serious challenges' to cultural theory; how it understands issues of identity and difference, 'articulation as both a political and descriptive practice', and globalization.[7] If this were as far as cultural theory had been able to move then Irish studies of most descriptions could afford to be complacent in having discussed and identified these as central factors in 'reading' Ireland. But Grossberg's expansion on these areas, even when made as a summary of a more detailed position, reveals some of the stark conceptual gaps which exist between the underpinnings of Irish criticism and those of cultural theory. Summing up 'political struggles organized around notions, however complex, of identity and difference'[8] Grossberg asserts that the logic of identity politics makes the political act a synecdochal act of representation – for Irish studies any challenge to the notion of identity, the part for whole logic of the use of 'Irish', is a long way from being effected.[9] Grossberg is able to set for cultural/post-colonial studies the task of challenging 'culture's equation with and location in an identity'.[10] Where might a parallel assertion come from in established 'radical' Irish critics? Declan Kiberd, Seamus Deane, Terry Eagleton, even Luke Gibbons and David Lloyd in their particular ways, seem to resist such severe questioning of the basics and value of 'Irishness'.

The identity synecdoche leads inevitably to the process of articulation (who speaks as part for whole?), in the same way that disturbing the bases of identity formation leads to an analysis of the authority which is invested in the academic word. The increasing institutionalization of the practices of Irish studies seems likely to cement rather than diffuse the critical assumptions through which Ireland has been understood until now. Thus, curiously, while the academic acceptance (and departmentalization) of Irish studies develops, its ability to absorb or be disrupted by 'external' theorizations may be reduced. Knowing whether the 'subaltern can speak' through the academic may become an arcanely particularized and intense question for Irish cultural critics. Beyond debates around 'Dublin 4' or revisionist anti-nationalism lie the same problems Grossberg sees in cultural theory: 'questions about the agencies, effectiveness and modalities of articulation remain largely unexamined'.[11]

In a sense Irish studies has always studied globalization, the third of Grossberg's points of reference. Both the diasporic nature of 'the Irish' and the relationship with Britain have enabled the study of Ireland to be opened out to alignment with most definitions of globalization, whether they be simply 'to render world-wide', or based on techno-cultural change, economic migration patterns or capitalism and imperialism. The bringing together of post-colonial theories with emigration and diaspora studies is thus crucial to furthering the widest possible theoretical perspective on the construction of Irishness.

There can and should be no sole outcome of the application of cultural theory to Irish culture – cultural theory is itself contested from within and is in a continual state of dispute and flux. Where and how 'Ireland' steps into cultural theory will, as this collection illustrates, be carried out with concomitant diversity. Much suspicion of post-colonial criticism in Ireland is based on the mistaken notion that its application assumes and underwrites the triumph of the independent post-colonial nation. However, as this collection reveals, the use of a cultural theory informed by post-colonial criticism in fact denies and/or complicates such teleological frameworks. In turn, it locates moments of transience, instability and inauthenticity; a process designed not so much to buttress the existence of a new state but rather to question the frame in which ideas of the state are articulated. For this reason *Ireland and Cultural Theory* offers itself as part of a process of rereading; a process realized in varying ways by the individual essays.

The subject of authenticity itself is the concern of Colin Graham's essay '" . . . maybe that's just Blarney": Irish Culture and the Persistence of Authenticity' which reads the defining concept as haunting Irish culture across the process of colonization and its aftermath through its ability to reapply and reshape itself according to markets and audiences. By analysing authenticity in this way, the identitarian ideologies that it masks are recontextualized through a materialist reading as moments of transition and crisis. This focus on Irish identitarianism is reflected in Gerry Smyth's essay 'Decolonization and Criticism: Towards a Theory of Irish Critical Discourse' which reads oppositional forms of discourse in colonial struggles as dependent on the dominant colonial matrix. The essay's focus on critical rather than creative practice as the valorizing activity of the nation posits a model capable of rethinking the endless replication of identitarian readings based on primary or creative works.

Smyth's focus on the nineteenth-century roots of the struggle for national hegemony is developed by Jim Mac Laughlin's essay '"Pestilence on their backs, famine in their stomachs": the Racial Construction of Irishness and the Irish in Victorian Britain' which draws a crucial distinction between race and ethnicity in order to examine Victorian notions of the Irish both in terms of an unruly stereotype and as a labour pool for the capitalist revolution in manufacturing. The implications of this process in the twentieth century are developed by Bronwen Walter's essay 'Gendered Irishness in Britain: Changing Constructions'. In this essay the perceived racial difference of the Irish in Britain is seen as a gendered phenomenon that denies the process of social assimilation despite British society's emphasis on 'whiteness'. In turn, this process is seen to render Irish women as invisible and 'limited to a symbolic role'.

Shaun Richards's essay 'Breaking the "Cracked Mirror": Binary Oppositions in the Culture of Contemporary Ireland' analyses the many examples of binarist ideology, and the 'violent hierarchy' in which they exist, that dominate the cultural terrain of Ireland. Out of these oppositions Richards traces a shift in representations of the rural and the past in Irish culture that suggests a dialectical rather than regressive function. Lance Pettitt's essay, 'Troubles, Terminus and *The Treaty*' concerns itself with another violent hierarchy, the intersection of 'fact' and 'fiction' in drama-documentaries. In doing this it returns to the subject of authenticity and considers the strategies of its production in terms of a specific case study: the RTÉ/Thames co-production of *The Treaty* in 1991. This is placed in the context of the British government's secret communications with Sinn Féin during the same period, while the drama-documentary's reliance on verisimilitude is perceived as allowing a direct interventionist strategy.

The textual strategy of Thady's narrative in Maria Edgeworth's *Castle Rackrent* is the concern of Claire Connolly's essay 'Reading Responsibility in *Castle Rackrent*'. Various critical and theoretical appropriations of the novel are analysed in terms of their relationship to its 'untranslatability'. As a result of this, the text is seen as sharing and disseminating the political ambivalences prevalant at the moment of the text's production.

In Eamonn Hughes's essay, '"Could anyone write it?": Place in Tom Paulin's Poetry', the focus is similarly on ambivalence; in this case the ambivalence of the concept of 'home' in Northern Irish poetry. By tracing an important distinction between Seamus Heaney's invocation of 'nation' and Paulin's sense of 'state', Hughes demonstrates how aestheticization of landscape in Northern Irish poetry can be galvanized to allow for resistant affiliative readings.

Tom Herron's essay 'The Body's in the Post: Contemporary Irish Poetry and the Dispersed Body' demonstrates how the relationship of Northern Irish poetics to social violence can be galvanized through the application of Foucauldian cultural theory. The role of poetry as testimony, and with this, its relationship to political murder, is recontextualized through a focus on the site of the body as a contested and troubled space. Completing the collection, Richard Kirkland's essay 'Questioning the Frame: Hybridity, Ireland and the Institution' charts the fortunes of the concept of 'hybridity' as it becomes an accepted part of Irish critical discourse. The essay considers a number of recent critical interventions within Irish studies and analyses the elision that takes place between the institutional status of the critical utterance and the radicalized perception of the object of study.

As a collection these essays function as a summation of disciplinary and conceptual currents, movements and futures for the study of Irish culture within a theoretical framework. As Gayatri Spivak suggests in the quotation heading this Introduction, cultural theory implies a turn towards the mechanics of cultural construction rather than complete reliance on the value of ideological versions of culture as simultaneous means and end in analysis. It may be one of the peculiarities and advantages of the Irish situation that an engagement with cultural theory, in all its forms, will enable the mechanics of the authenticity invoked in 'Ireland' to be articulated and questioned.

Notes

1. G.C. Spivak, 'Can the Subaltern Speak?' in *Colonial Discourse and Post-Colonial Theory: A Reader*, eds P. Williams and L. Chrisman (London: Harvester Wheatsheaf, 1993), p. 90.
2. R. Kearney, *Transitions: Narratives in Modern Irish Culture* (Manchester: Manchester University Press, 1988), p. 7.
3. See D. Lloyd, *Anomalous States: Irish Writing and the Post-Colonial Moment* (Dublin: Lilliput, 1993); S. Deane, ed., *The Field Day Anthology of Irish Literature*, 3 vols (Derry: Field Day, 1991).
4. L. Gibbons, *Transformations in Irish Culture* (Cork: Cork University Press, 1996).
5. D. Kiberd, *Inventing Ireland: The Literature of the Modern Nation* (London: Jonathan Cape, 1995), p. 5.
6. These pamphlets (by Edward Said, Fredric Jameson and Terry Eagleton) are collected in S. Deane, ed., *Nationalism, Colonialism and Literature* (Minneapolis: Minneapolis University Press, 1990).
7. L. Grossberg, 'The Space of Culture, the Power of Space' in *The Post-Colonial Question: Common Skies, Divided Horizons*, eds I. Chambers and L. Curti (London: Routledge, 1996), pp. 169–88.
8. L. Grossberg, 'The Space of Culture, the Power of Space', p. 169.
9. Even David Lloyd, having deconstructed the identity politics of Heaney's poetry, talks about the 'past twenty-five years of *our* history', D. Lloyd, *Anomalous States*, p. 125.
10. L. Grossberg, 'The Space of Culture, the Power of Space', p. 169.
11. L. Grossberg, 'The Space of Culture, the Power of Space', p. 169.

2

'. . . maybe that's just Blarney': Irish Culture and the Persistence of Authenticity

Colin Graham

> On the side of the colonizer, it is the inauthenticity of the colonized culture, its falling short of the concept of the human, that legitimates the colonial project.[1]
>
> (David Lloyd)

> The Story of Ireland's heritage is a new reason for visiting Ireland. It is told in a modern but authentic style and mirrors European culture preserved in an island which makes it possible to visit centres from neolithic to 19th Century, even on a short visit.
>
> (Heritage Island marketing brochure)

INTRODUCTION

Somewhere between colonization and post-colonialism, domination and independence, the in/authenticity of the colonized is overturned. The role of authenticity alters from being a signifier of the colonized's cultural 'incapacities', to being a marketable sign of value. If authenticity is not only a product of colonialism but central to its ethics, then we need a clearer grasp of its definitions, of the means by which it comes to be elevated to the status of an evaluative ethic and of how it contorts with changes in the colonial situation. And as David Lloyd and 'Heritage Island' seem to suggest, authenticity may have both a typical and particular function in the context of Irish culture and the chronologies embedded in it.

This essay explores various dynamics of authenticity in the context of Irish culture, arguing that the definition of the authentic in Irish culture is central to claims for value. If the colonizer denies authenticity, then for Irish culture it becomes crucial that the 'birth of authenticity is rooted in revolution'.[2] Authenticity and claims to authenticity underlie the conceptual and cultural denial of dominance. The nation's very reason for being, its logic of existence, is its claim to an undeniable authenticity as a pure expression of the 'real', the obvious, the natural. In the Irish context, claims for authenticity move from the 'revolutionary' (in all its aspects) to the dominant, following the path of the nation. And just as the nation in Ireland becomes questioned and ironized, so too the 'jargon of authenticity'[3] becomes critiqued *as* jargon. This essay follows that process in Irish culture to its conclusion in a popular, advertising postmodernism which can be seen to make its own claims to authenticity through ironic rereadings of established versions of authentic Irishness.

The essay begins with an examination of authenticity as it is discussed in writings by Jacob Golomb and Theodor Adorno, stressing how authenticity attempts to defy definition through its ambiguous stresses on origins and teleologies of completeness fused with continual change. Gareth Griffiths suggests that the authorization of authenticity can still be undertaken by the colonizer after decolonization as a hierarchizing form of control in the post-colonial period.[4] This possibility needs to be addressed in the Irish context before going on to look at the categories of Irish authenticity which I have provisionally entitled Old Authenticities, New Authenticities and Ironic Authenticities. These distinctions are based not on the colonial/post-colonial chronology, but on the point at which an 'authentic' Ireland becomes more or less available apparently outside or in defiance of colonial dominance; thus the Old Authenticity discussed is found in Yeats, the New Authenticity in the tourist marketing of 'Heritage Island', and the Ironic Authenticity in a television advertisement for Smithwick's beer. My intention here is to begin a reassessment of the role of post-colonial cultural theories in Ireland by using 'authenticity' as a marker of the effects of the progress of colonialism in Irish culture – but a marker which unsettles certain of the teleologies of post-colonialism by virtue of its changeability and capacity for self-preservation. Authenticity is claimed and disclaimed in Irish culture, functioning as a standard of worth and a cultural core value. The origins of this cultural necessity may indeed lie in what David Lloyd (as quoted above) sees as the labelling of Irish culture as 'inauthentic' by the colonizer. But authenticity has not simply rolled along behind 'Irishness' in history; authenticity has affected the basic discourses of Irish culture and identity politics in its prevalence, and has thus attained a status near to that of a shared currency. Authenticity's origins in the colonial processes as well as its radiation from the colonial context need to be comprehended and disentangled from various Irish cultural contexts. Authenticity may then function not only as a complicating ideological trope in Irish culture, but as a way for an Irish cultural studies to bind together its approaches to cultural events and texts.

THEORIZING AUTHENTICITY

> All agree in principle that any positive definition of authenticity would be self-nullifying.[5]

Jacob Golomb's *In Search of Authenticity: From Kierkegaard to Camus* constitutes a major attempt to read authenticity as an integral part of Western philosophical, humanistic traditions and to place the 'search' for the authentic, if not the authentic itself, at the centre of energies directed against the undermining of our 'true' selves by the vagaries of the postmodern. Golomb concludes his crusading revival of the need for authenticity with the words: 'Only the return to our authentic pathos can prevent the betrayal of what is dearest to each of us: our own selfhood'. Against this is set 'the decline of the ethic of subjectivity in the postmodern era, and the suppression of individuality encouraged by the mass media and multinational markets'.[6]

Authenticity is thus at least partially 'lost' in postmodernity, in the contemporary. In the humanistic strategies at work here the 'selfhood' which protests its own benignity and logicality can only be defined by what it is 'other' than. Here the '*mass* media and *multinational* markets' deny the full existence of selfhood, drowning its self-expression, not through public discourse or capitalism, the market or the media, but through their postmodern reconfiguration into 'mass' events which stretch beyond the boundaries of class and nationality in which the notion of selfhood was fostered. Golomb is appropriately applying a nostalgia to a version of authenticity which itself relies on nostalgias for its definition – indeed by the end of Golomb's book, and through the poetics of authenticity he describes, it is possible to see such 'pathos' expressed about the fate of the authentic as in fact a simple *restatement of the authentic*, retreading the paths of decline and difficulty on which authenticity depends.

Golomb's notion that authenticity is disintegrated by postmodernity needs some thought – as I have already suggested, this may be merely a strategy of authenticity rather than an analysis of its fate. In order to understand the ways in which authenticities are challenged, rewritten or recharged in Irish culture it is necessary to turn to Golomb's notion that 'multinational markets' are at odds with the authentic, since this not only allows us to see why authenticity may need to 'return' in the face of the postmodern, but offers a possibility in beginning to politicize Golomb's definition of (the search for) authenticity.

Since the authentic, in Golomb's analysis, is articulated in the philosophies of Kierkegaard, Nietzsche, Heidegger, Sartre and Camus, it seems unlikely that when 'multinational markets' deface authenticity they do so because of their ideology of the market – if authenticity can (as ever, *almost*) arise in the work of these philosophers then, whatever authenticity's relationship with capital, it can hardly be thought to be suppressed by the existence of capitalism. It is presumably then the 'multinational' that is stifling authenticity, or that is perhaps itself 'inauthentic'. This is a vital recognition, since it allows Golomb's text to be read against itself, uncovering an alternative genealogy for authenticity to the one Golomb himself establishes. In the Irish context, and in the broader philosophical imaginings discussed by Golomb, it becomes clear that authenticity overlaps with nationalism's self-projections in crucial ways. Golomb may seek to avoid an explicit politics of authenticity, but the uses of authenticity in Irish culture reveal it to be a profoundly political pretext for evaluation. Authenticity may be traditionally reliant on the existence of the nation as the basis for political thought to the extent that it cannot, in some of its formats, be reimagined beyond nationalism – alternatively, reviving a form of authenticity validated by the nation may be a way of resisting multinationalism, post-nationalism and any other contortion or disruption to the centrality of the nation as a political unit.

Authenticity, Golomb notes, is bound to notions of authority, and in Heidegger's version of authenticity the authority underpinning the authentic changes from an 'authoritative God' to 'the historical dimension of the people in which one is rooted':

> One is historically authentic when one creates one's own history by utilizing and recreating one's past and the past of one's people, projecting them with anticipatory resoluteness towards one's future [. . .]. [Authenticity] is the loyalty of one's self to its own past, heritage and ethos.[7]

Authenticity here, to employ Golomb's vocabulary, becomes rooted in 'the people' and in the bond between the self and the group; and additionally, authenticity relies on the ability to 'utilize' and culturally employ such 'loyalty' – authenticity is thus constantly a cultural, textual phenomenon, defining, recreating and projecting. Authenticity may resist definition, but its materiality in textuality is undeniable. In this it shares with imaginings of nationalism an important reliance on its various media: what Benedict Anderson calls 'the technical means for "re-presenting" the *kind* of imagined community that is the nation'.[8]

Yet it is not just in its pervasively textual characteristics, or its espousal of connectedness with the past and a 'people', that authenticity overlaps with nationalism. Like nationalism, authenticity has an ambiguous relationship with 'origins'; reliant upon their antiquity *as* authenticity, yet disparaging of teleologies which destroy the mystique of authenticity through their rationalization of history. Golomb, early in *In Search of Authenticity*, argues that authenticity 'calls for no particular contents or consequences, but, rather, focuses on the origins and the intensity of one's emotional-existential commitments',[9] and later he suggests that Kierkegaard adds another meaning to authenticity, 'namely, the return to the genuine origins of ourselves, our feelings and our beliefs'.[10] That authenticity expresses a return seems to imply a reversal of thought or commitment along some established lines to an initial point. Yet elsewhere Golomb points out that Kierkegaard argues that the 'self is something that should be created and formed, not something possessing an intrinsic essence to be further developed'.[11] Like nationalism, it is the 'genuineness' of 'genuine origins' that authenticity highlights rather than the materiality of origins; and 'genuineness', in a perfectly circular resistance to theory, is known by its authenticity. As with the nation in Anderson's famous formulation, authenticity wishes to be conceived of as 'moving steadily up (or down) history',[12] and as with the nation, authenticity 'proves' itself through its simultaneous and contradictory textual existence and refusal to be defined. In its own best scenario authenticity is thus what Golomb calls 'a state of integrity between the innermost self and its external manifestations, whatever their form and content';[13] an integrity (or 'loyalty') which demands an unquestioning belief in a wholeness involving the individual and his/her social context.

If authenticity tends to a monologic unquestioning discourse concurrent with that of the 'nation', it arises also out of contexts in which the nation becomes an active arbiter between the past and a 'people'. Like the anti-colonial formation of nation, the 'quest for authenticity becomes especially pronounced in extreme situations', its 'birth' being 'rooted in revolution'.[14] Authenticity combines the prioritization of 'origins' with the 'pathos of incessant change' – again moving steadily through history. Its definition is a set of contradictions; static but changing; conservative but adaptable; originary but modern.

Golomb's book ends with a plea for the saving of a disintegrating sense of authenticity; one of the rare moments when authenticity allows its ideological susceptibilities to open out – Golomb's authenticity at this point reaches the limits of its ability to change, at the point at which the humanism, the nationalism, the play of rationality and love of the irrational it embodies, are consciously challenged. The pathos of its plea, so obvious when placed in the context of postmodernity, is made the centre of (Golomb's version of) authenticity's call for resurrection.

ADORNO AND BAUDRILLARD: SYSTEM TO SIMULATION

Although Golomb finishes with authenticity set against a vague and dark postmodernism, he is most vitriolic in his conclusions at the expense of 'the ratiocinations of Adorno and his followers'.[15] Adorno's *The Jargon of Authenticity* examines the points at which the authentic is socialized and popularized (that is, caught within Adorno's particular sense of the 'popular'); in Adorno the authenticities later traced by Golomb become materiality, culture and policy. Adorno's attempt to prick the bubble of authenticity is perhaps most effective in its analysis of authenticity *in and as a language and as an ideology*. Adorno sees 'authenticity' as a jargon-ized system, falsely constructing itself as essence and origin: '[the language of authenticity] is a trademark of societalized chosenness, noble and homely at once – sub-language as superior language'[16] – an almost de Valerean concept, coming from 'below', against the once-dominant (see de Valera's 'cosy homesteads [. . .] sturdy children [. . .] athletic youths [. . .] comely maidens'[17]). Adorno's irritation with the jargon is furthered by its exclusionism, identifying what is outside it:

> 'inauthentic', where something broken is implied, an expression which is not immediately appropriate to what is expressed [. . .]. 'Inauthentic' [. . .] becomes a 'critical' term, in definite negation of something merely phenomenal.[18]

Authenticity is thus the inherent factor in the creation of an organicism which is ideologically-charged, exclusivist, evaluative and almost a definition of the transcendentally heroic. Adorno thus sees the authentic as not only a cultural ideology but a way of thinking and being:

> Whoever is versed in the jargon does not have to say what he thinks, does not even have to think it properly. The jargon takes over this task and devalues thought. That the whole man should speak is authentic, comes from the core [. . .] . Communication clicks and puts forth as truth what should instead be suspect by virtue of the prompt collective agreement.[19]

Adorno's critique of authenticity hinges on disrupting the edges of its claims to wholeness and organicism, and its ability to become a self-sufficient ideology and way of speaking. Golomb's proposed search for authenticity, on the other hand, begins and ends with the self at the centre of authenticity, the site of definition and justification in which there is the continuously twisting paradox which suggests that authenticity and selfhood are both undefined until both can be defined by each other.

Before moving on to see how authenticity figures in Irish culture, it is useful to introduce Jean Baudrillard's perspective on authenticity's role in simulation. While Adorno and Golomb can be placed in some sort of mutual dialogue which relies on agreement that authenticity is a dispute over possible truths, Baudrillard sees authenticity adopting a role in the fantasy of representation:

> When the real is no longer what it used to be, nostalgia assumes its full meaning. There is a proliferation of myths of origin and signs of reality; of second-hand truth, objectivity and authenticity [. . .] there is a panic-stricken production of the real and the referential, above and parallel to the panic of material production [. . .] .[20]

Authenticity here has ceased being a measurement of value (or even a proof of 'true' existence) and become a sign of the need for such values. In the midst of apparent disintegration, authenticity reverts to the (re)production of origins and of itself. Golomb's ending is perhaps a philosophical expression of what Baudrillard identifies; holding on nostalgically to a selfhood which justifies and is 'created' by being authentic. Golomb's strategy for the self in postmodernism thus overlaps with Baudrillard's identification of the processes of nostalgia and authenticity in postmodernism. To this extent we have reached a point where the authentic can be seen as a site of contestation across Golomb/Adorno, with Adorno identifying the authentic as a jargonized ideology travestying what it represents – and with Baudrillard seeing the authentic as evidence of a loss of, or change in, the 'real'.

POST-COLONIALISM, IRELAND AND AUTHENTICITY

> There are real dangers in recent representations of indigenous peoples in popular discourse, especially in the media, which stress claims to an 'authentic' voice. For these claims may be a form of overwriting the complex actuality of difference equal but opposite to the more overt writing out of that voice in earlier oppressive discourses of reportage [. . .] .[21]

In his essay 'The Myth of Authenticity: Representation, Discourse and Social Practice', Griffiths suggests that the 'inauthenticity' once used to label the colonized, and which should have been subsequently 'reversed' by anti-colonialism, has transformed into an authenticity which is under the control of the 'West'. In other words, having rejected the 'inauthenticity' applied under colonialism, the once-colonized now suffer their authenticity to be prescribed and hierarchized by the colonizer:

> Whilst it is true that the various Australian Aboriginal peoples may increasingly wish to assert their sense of the local and the specific as a recuperative strategy in the face of the erasure of difference characteristic of colonialist representation, such representations, subsumed by the white media *under a mythologized and fetishized sign of the 'authentic'*, can also be used to create a privileged hierarchy of Australian Aboriginal voice.[22] (emphasis added)

Given that we have seen Lloyd (at the beginning of this chapter) apply the same prognosis to Irish culture under colonial rule, it must be seriously considered whether the certainties in expressions of authenticity in post-Independence Irish culture are prescribed or 'allowed' by the colonizer. Applied to the Irish situation, Griffiths' analysis of post-colonial power structures seems a little simplistic – the cultural interchanges between Britain/England and Ireland both during and after colonization were never as settled or monolithic as Griffiths suggests they were and are in Aboriginal experience. Because of proximity, geography, race and religion the position of the Irish in colonial discourse was and is, as I have suggested elsewhere, 'liminal'.[23] Irish culture, at once Western and colonized, white and racially other, imperial and subjugated, became marginal in the sense of existing at the edge of two experiences, with a culture that epitomizes the hybridity, imitation and irony latent in colonial interchanges. 'Authenticity' may play a key role in Irish culture, but, partly because of its liminality, the function of authenticity in colonial and post-colonial terms in an Irish context will not have its conceptual trajectory dictated by the colonizer in precisely the way that Griffiths outlines. Colonialism's initial denial of authenticity is at the root of the persistence of authenticity in Irish culture, but Ireland's colonially marginal, liminal status allows authenticity a less stable role subsequently – thus authenticity becomes embedded as a feature of discourses of Irish culture, but its provenance ultimately resists limitation and (typically) definition.

AN OLD AUTHENTICITY

The teleology of colonialism suggests that authenticity will be reclaimed as part of the '[bringing] into existence [of the] history of the nation'[24] which Frantz Fanon sees as crucial in the process of decolonization. If authenticity is a tool for the justification of colonialism then, like (and as part of) the nation, it must be turned to face the colonizer. The history of nineteenth-century Irish cultural nationalism can be seen as such a process of reclamation, restaking the grounds for Irishness, 'proving' Irish authenticities.

Immediately we try to divide the tropes of Irish authenticities we are faced with contradiction and multiplicity. Is the predominant anti-colonial Irish authenticity of the de Valerean or Yeatsian version, for example? Folkish or rural? Irish-Irish, Anglo-Irish or global Irish? These strains, along with many others overlapping and contesting, could be identified in a longer study. For the moment I wish to focus on claims to authenticity in a text which allows for some distinction in authenticities directed against the colonial claims to 'inauthenticity' Lloyd mentions – W.B. Yeats's 'Introduction' to *Fairy and Folk Tales of the Irish Peasantry* (1888). My purpose here, as throughout the remainder of this essay, is not to draw a topography or history of authenticity in Irish culture, but to detail a broad series of recurrences of the 'authentic' in Irish culture and suggest an explanation for the nature and persistence of these recurrences.

Yeats's collection of Irish 'peasant' tales is in one sense part of a continued popularization of the antiquarianism which had begun in Ireland earlier in the century; Yeats's folk and fairy tales are not remarkable but typical in the way that they attempt to construct an Irishness which is from 'outside' the social and sectarian remit of the collector, who through the act of collection, cataloguing, publishing and accumulation of knowledge sees a potential for becoming 'of' what is collated. The Irishness of Yeats's collection is constructed as both other and part of him, and is thus doubly authenticated; discursively he attempts to act as intermediary between an Irishness which is 'authentic', and a *receiver* of claims to authenticity whose identity will never be fully articulated (Britain or Anglo-Ireland?). As medium for the authentic, his knowledge of authenticity and his ability to recognize it 'infect' him with authenticity too.

Yeats's 'Introduction' to *Fairy and Folk Tales of the Irish Peas-*

antry expresses as much concern with the authenticity attached to the gathering of material as it does about the material itself:

> In the *Parochial Survey of Ireland* it is recorded how the story-tellers used to gather together of an evening, and if any had a different version from the others, they would all recite theirs and vote, and the man who had varied would have to abide by their verdict. In this way stories have been handed down with such accuracy, that the long tale of Dierdre was, in the earlier decades of this century, told almost word for word, as in the very ancient MSS. in the Royal Dublin Society. In one case only it varied, and then the MS. was obviously wrong – a passage had been forgotten by the copyist.[25]

The material of authenticity is here 'handed down' unchanged through history. This Irishness is certainly projected 'with anticipatory resoluteness towards one's future';[26] its trajectory begins in antiquity and survives history. While Yeats is seeming to stress primarily the objectivity (even democracy) of the authentification of the Irishness of 'the people', this first level authenticity is encapsulated by two processes for authentification – both the story-tellers, and at a different level the collector reauthenticate the tales; in the terms we uncovered in reading Golomb, by becoming 'genuine' the tales become authentic. And for Yeats the genuine 'proves' his loyalty – the editorial ownership of authenticity may connect Yeats to his material but it also arguably anticipates the hierarchizing of subaltern authenticities which Griffiths describes. From this point Yeats can retrace with yet greater assurance the nature and production of Irish authenticity:

> [In Lady Wilde's *Ancient Legends* the] humour has all given way to pathos and tenderness. We have here the innermost heart of the Celt in the moments he has grown to love through years of persecution, when cushioning himself about with dreams, and hearing fairy-songs in the twilight, he ponders on the soul and on the dead. Here is the Celt. Only it is the Celt dreaming.[27]

As noted earlier, authenticity combines the prioritization of origins with what Golomb calls the 'pathos of incessant change' – for Yeats, going more closely to the origins of the 'Celt' ('humour has given way') leads to the ultimate, unquestionable authenticity of 'pathos and tenderness', which has been, as Golomb says, 'especially pronounced in extreme situations'.[28] The ultimate collector of authenticated Irishness, in Yeats's 'Introduction', is Douglas Hyde:

> He knows the people thoroughly. Others see a phase of Irish life; he understands all its elements. His work is neither humorous nor mournful; it is simply life.[29]

As Adorno suggested, against the 'inauthentic' as broken, is the authentic as 'whole' – Yeats's Irish authenticity, by being 'simply life', trails off as authenticity must into a refusal to be defined[30] and 'in definite negation of something merely phenomenal'.[31]

This Irish authenticity is thus complicated and usefully foreshadows the warnings given by Griffiths that authenticity may be continually authorized by the 'colonizer'. It cannot be simply assumed that Yeats is entirely fulfilling the role of colonizer – in fact the authenticity of the text only makes sense if Yeats's position is not taken as colonial but as liminal, in that this authenticity both vindicates the colonized while implicating and ethically elevating the collector of this authenticity in the vindication.

A NEW AUTHENTICITY

Griffiths's notion that post-colonial authenticity still lies in the hands of the colonizer accords partially with Yeats's version of the authentic, since Yeats can be seen to construct a 'colonized' authenticity from a marginal position of hierarchy. Griffiths places his argument over authenticity in a familiar sphere in post-colonial studies, questioning how and if the 'subaltern speaks'. To believe in an ability to utter authentically (a belief Griffiths himself seems unwilling to question) may be to fail to see the continuation of power structures existing as after-effects of colonialism – it is certainly to ignore the layerings, in terms of language, class and gender, of post-colonial discourses uncovered in, for example, the writings of Ranajit Guha, Partha Chatterjee and Gyanendra Pandey, Homi Bhabha and Gayatri Spivak.[32] In particular Spivak's wariness of the reintroduction of subjectivity, even as a recuperative critical strategy, overlaps with and questions any notion of the 'authentic' in a post-colonial context and should alert us that any attempt at an identification of authenticity will run the same risks which Derek Gregory identifies, through Spivak, in the attempt at a 'retrieval of subaltern consciousness'.[33]

In the Irish case we need to be aware both of the particular circumstances of colonialism in Ireland (in shorthand, its liminality) and more generally that Griffiths's one-way process of cultural control may be naive. Authenticity, after all, appears to reverse itself during the anti-colonial process, and in the complicated and unstable cultural circumstances of Ireland this is unlikely to be simply an 'appearance'. Given Independence, how will authenticity, which is 'rooted in revolution',[34] move away from its origins?

Yeats's ambiguous control over the authenticity of his material reveals in its triple level of authentification (tales, story-tellers, folk-tale-collectors) that authenticity thrives on the textuality and substance of its medium – as suggested above it is the 'mass', not the media, which authenticity finds difficult. Textuality seems to provide the material existence which authenticity needs in tandem with its resistance to definition – its mystique is maintained and *evidenced*, while what is actually 'authentic' is filtered through further authenticating processes (folk tales are themselves authenticated democratically by their tellers, then authenticated and reauthorized by their collectors/editors).

How nineteenth- and early twentieth-century Irish modes of authenticity (of which there are undoubtedly more than the Yeats example suggests – Daniel Corkery might be a useful contrast) are played out in contemporary circumstances would be an obvious area of research in further examining authenticity in Irish culture. Anecdotally, one might suggest that 'authenticity' has increased in its value as a marker of what is Irish as Ireland has (partially) moved out of its anti-colonial mode. Authenticity's ability to co-exist with the market has not only enabled it to survive after decolonization but has allowed it to become, in some circumstances, as Griffiths says, a 'mythologized and fetished sign'.[35] What Griffiths calls 'an overdetermined narrative of authenticity and indigeneity'[36] characterizes rebirths of the old authenticities, whether these are used to sell or purchase the 'authentic' once-colonized.

In the Irish context the tourist industry is an obvious site for the peddling of the authentic in an explicit and populist way. Luke Gibbons quotes Robert Ballagh on Bord Fáilte: '"you have Bord Fáilte eulogizing roads where you won't see a car from one day to the other: it's almost as if they're advertising a country nobody lives in"'.[37] As Gibbons points out, Bord Fáilte's advertising seems initially at odds with the Industrial Development Authority's (IDA) selling of Ireland economically, as a market place and site for expansion; yet almost immediately the imagery and language of tourism becomes part of the IDA's marketing strategy: '"The factories and the bustling towns and cities exist in harmony with the Ireland the tourists flock to see, a land of unsurpassed natural beauty"'.[38] Gibbons call this phenomenon the 'appeal of remote antiquity to today's filofax generation',[39] and it is an important feature of the ways in which older Irish authenticities have been retained and made coexistent dualities in Irish contemporaneity.

Heritage Island sells Ireland on the currency of its authenticity, marketing an organic vision of an Ireland layered with visible, visitable history.[40] What follows comes under the heading of 'Irish Heritage Retold' in their marketing brochure:

> The story of Ireland's heritage is a new reason for visiting Ireland. It is told in a modern but authentic style and mirrors European culture preserved in an island which makes it possible to visit centres from neolithic to 19th Century, even on a short visit.
> Heritage Island properties can be found throughout Ireland and range from restored castles and historic houses to state-of-the-art story telling of the legends and history of Ireland. All interpretation has been professionally researched and where there has been reproduction the style is authentic.[41]

Authenticity here relies on preservation; what is to be visited is not modern, new Ireland but authentic Ireland made modern and new. Thus Ireland is now 'modern *but* authentic' in *style*; *story-telling* is state-of-the-art, but uses legends and history. It is the media (style and story) which are able to embody this apparent dichotomy of old and new and which in the process preserve the authentic.

Golomb, as we have already seen, pits authenticity against 'mass media', and I have been stressing that the simple fact of changing media is not necessarily a threat to the authentic. Here the attempt to cope with the changed social/political context for Irish authenticity is embodied in the notion that 'modern but authentic' Ireland's style 'mirrors European culture preserved in an island'.

There is a nod here to Irish post-nationalism and a valorizing of the European context, and yet 'mirrors' retains a distance from the possible inauthenticities of what is outside Ireland undermining the indigenous authenticity of the 'national culture' (with which authenticity so closely equates itself). The word 'preserved' is crucial, implying not only that authentic Irishness is newly (and economically) available in Ireland, but that this haven of authenticity includes (but is not swamped by) an almost lost authentic European antiquity. Authenticity's claims may always tend to such extravagance.

Heritage Island is a reworking of the Yeatsian authenticities of the 'Introduction' to *Folk and Fairy Tales of the Irish Peasantry*, showing how authenticities are self-preserving through their willingness to reproduce themselves in new media and new discourses. The structures of authentification here are also those expressed by Yeats. Just as Yeats sees authenticity at a base level in the Irishness of tales themselves, at another level in the standardization by tellers and at a final level by their collectors/editors, so Heritage Island reassures its customers of Irish heritage's authenticity through the same three levels. Ireland's history/legends are the authentic material; but their (re-)telling is further proof of their authenticity since they are told in 'modern but authentic style' ('state-of-the-art'). And as a final affirmation that no inauthenticity has corrupted the 'stuff' of the authentic, the authoritative validator steps in, filling Yeats's role as collector/editor: 'All interpretation has been professionally researched'. Here the Yeatsian amateurism of editing has been transmuted through the 'market' to become a professionalized authenticating process in which the authentic is commodified, reproduced and retold.

In Griffiths's words, there is certainly a tendency here to 'an overdetermined narrative of authenticity and indigeneity';[42] Irish authenticity, in Yeats and Heritage Island, displays the same characteristics of definition – Heritage Island is however more aware of itself as a rewriting rather than a creation. Just as Golomb sees authenticity as at its best a 'search', and Adorno condemns authenticity as a 'jargon', we can now begin to see that Irish authenticity, through its very structures, is a series of claims to authenticity which persist both despite changing cultural circumstances and media and in full knowledge of what those circumstances and media are.

AN IRONIC AUTHENTICITY

If authenticity in Irish culture followed only the trajectory mapped out above then its ability to order Irish cultural experience would be almost unchallengeable. From the examples I have used it might be possible to see not only the authenticity of the folkish, rural and historical/legendary as nearly monolithically dominant, but to note that its repeated forms of self-sustenance and validation give it a layered texture which enables reinforcement of its desire for dominance. Is it then possible for this standardized authenticity to be challenged? And if it is challenged, how far is the notion of authenticity itself (as well as what is considered authentic) undermined?

Golomb's crusading restatement of the necessity for a search for authenticity is, as has already been noted, set against the postmodern, the 'mass' media and the 'attempt to dissolve the subjective pathos of authenticity'.[43] The vigour of Golomb's attack on these aspects of the postmodern may signal the way into reading 'against' authenticity as a central defining feature of, and plea for, cultural integrity. In the Irish case this would mean looking to new forms of culture as a means of disrupting the influence of old authenticities and their new forms – as Heritage Island shows, an apparently postmodern form (tourist advertising) does not guarantee such disruption.

To move towards a possible alternative formation of the authentic in Irish culture I want to discuss a television advertisement for Smithwick's beer, appropriately and significantly entitled 'Ireland' by its makers.[44] 'Ireland' takes as its theme the authenticity of advertising, the authenticity of Ireland, and the authenticity of advertising Irish beer. The 20-second advertisement ironically constructs and deconstructs the Irish authenticity examined so far, and can be read as a possible attempt to posit a revised, ironic authenticity as a replacement.

To summarize 'Ireland' completely would take an article in itself. Its format is deliberately complex; it is almost stereotypically a postmodern montage. 'Ireland' begins with the words 'GET' and then 'INTO' in white on red, with a Northern American voice-over saying: 'Get into . . . Ireland'. The complete screen then splits into a screen divided horizontally and vertically to make four squares, each of which has changing images and film clips throughout. The first four identifiable images are (clockwise from top left): a moving aerial shot of a rural landscape; a stained glass pattern with a shamrock; a Celtic cross (towards which the camera zooms); and a neon sign for 'Home Cookin' '.

Here already we can begin to establish the patterning of authenticity in 'Ireland'. The four-part structure is undoubtedly a jokey reflection of the four provinces of Ireland – or the four green fields, given the top left shot. Rurality and standard cultural imagery (shamrock, Celtic cross) allow the viewer to 'get into Ireland' in an unchallenging, familiar way. The product here is on the verge of being made authentic *because* of its Irishness. And yet the bottom left of the four hints at what is to come. Neon and 'Home Cookin' ' suggest an alternative cultural background to the 'authentic' (that is nostalgic) Irishness which is immediately dominant at this point of textual origin. (In parallel here the red words on white background allude to the iconic drinks marketing of Coca-Cola.) This is quickly reinforced by the next series of images (again top left clockwise): Ronald and Nancy Reagan drinking Guinness on a trip to Ireland; three pints of Smithwick's; a fiddler (a shot which fades into another of an Irish dancer); and Smithwick's advertising on a neon sign in Belfast. The neon and the lost 'g' in cooking, ironize 'home', which has become Americanized (signified also by Reagan).

The globalization and Americanization of the authenticity of Irishness is overemphasized in the next series: a boot kicking a ball; 'I [football, i.e., love] N.Y.'; John F. Kennedy speaking in Ireland (he can be heard to say the word 'haemorrhage' – a reference to Irish emigration to the United States); the Statue of Liberty overwritten by the word 'Donnelly'. Having made this point about Irishness in a global context, as an exporter of Irishness to the United States, as a culture existing in a global market and as a culture constructed *by* America, 'Ireland' reverts to its original authentic Irishness in order to carry out another deconstruction. So a mountain/shepherd/sheep, waves, a dancer and a woman carrying pints of beer become a map of Ireland with 293,140 unemployed (and money slipping off the map), a picture of a banana with the word REPUBLIC underneath, a diver, and a condom advertisement. Here old Irish authenticities are 'truly' challenged – a (post)modern, contemporary, urban Ireland takes over from an old authenticity and presents new realities of unemployment, sexual liberality and criticism of established state nationalism.

The advertisement, to which I have not done full justice here, ends with its lower two squares seeming to take on the possibility of reconciliation between north and south; a white dove flies across a plaque with a red hand (Ulster) and over a ceramic tile with a harp engraved on it (signifying Ireland in a more nationalistic sense). If this appears to replace an old authenticity with a new liberal politics, such a notion is undercut by a simultaneous but opposite movement in the top two squares. While the peace and reconciliation theme is played out from right to left in the lower squares, the top squares have, on the left, a shot of graffiti ('Who stole my bike') and on the right an image of a whitewashed (and rural) housefront across which (left to right) rides an old man in a long coat on a bicycle. The humour here is at the expense of the older political discourse of national politics (and the problem of Northern Ireland), raising again the prospect of an alternative focus, established through ironic versions of the past.

'Ireland' suggests that the older authenticities are simultaneously contradicted and yet established by Ireland's cultural representation in a context wider than the geographical (and conceptual) boundaries of Ireland. The United States is viewed both as a consumer and producer of Irishness, and its effects on the maintenance of Irishness are charted through the tongue-in-cheekness of the double representation of the American Presidential desire to affix an Irishness to the Presidency. Almost all the commentary to the advertisement is spoken in snippets of North American voices: 'It's great to be back here in mythical, mystical Ireland'; 'the most wonderful place in the world; home'. And yet 'home' has already been shown to be Americanized in the sign Home Cookin'; so 'Ireland' sees Ireland's attempts at established authenticated culture as pitifully denying the cultural matrix which preserves old Irish authenticities.

Does 'Ireland' then represent a form of culture which is anti-authentic, or is it more interested in the establishment of an alternative authenticity? Certainly the movement from the old rural authenticity of the shepherd, or the pub scene with the woman carrying pints of beer, to, respectively, the map with unemployment figures and a condom advertisement, would suggest that 'Ireland' is altering rural, folkish, 'tourist' authenticities in favour of urban, socialized, radicalized versions of Ireland (which are arguably simply reliant on the notion that they are more authentic than previous versions of Ireland). This challenging of old authenticities and their newer resurrections (in tourism, in exile stereotypes of Irishness) is noteworthy in itself. But 'Ireland' does not rest there; its irony is finally turned partially on itself. The only (Northern) Irish voice used in the commentary says: 'Are ye going for a pint . . . or what?'. A totally unrevealing comment? A stereotype? As another (North American) voice says: 'You just can't handle the truth' – in this Ireland the truth is impossible to pin down; competing claims to authenticity (claims which are allowed to compete in 'Ireland') have rendered their truths and their authentic origins obscure and unstable. 'Ireland' ends with the wonderfully ironic and destabilizing comment (again in North American voice): '. . . maybe that's just Blarney'. Finally the process of authentification, claims to authenticity, and the pathos of those claims are questioned and dismissed in a double-edged use of a stereotype ('Blarney') culled from the excesses of populist versions of restored Irish authenticity. 'Ireland' almost undoes its own undoing of the authentic through a near-sliding back into 'the jargon of authenticity'; and yet in doing so it both reveals the power and dissects the pathos of established Irish authenticity.

According to Baudrillard, '[when] the real is no longer what it used to be [. . . there] is a proliferation of myths of origin and signs of reality; of second-hand truth, objectivity and authenticity'.[45] 'Ireland', in its joyous uncovering of myths of origins *as myths*, and signs of reality *as signs*, is able to question the objectivity and authenticity of old and renewed claims in Irish culture – its processes uncover both the mechanics of authenticity and the cultural desire for authenticity. 'Ireland' toys with an alternative authenticity, but finally cannot rest on anything but its own ironic 'maybe that's just Blarney'.

CONCLUSION

The persistence of authenticity in Irish culture is best seen, then, as a series of claims, a desire for validation. There can be no doubt that this persistence arises from the cultural crises of colonialism and its de-authenticating of the colonized. Against this Irish authenticities can be read as movements against colonialism, (re-)establishing authenticity. And yet this anti-colonial authenticity is not purely formed; the Yeats example used above suggests that any Irish authenticity will be complex, layered and affected by the liminal space of colonialism in Ireland, never securely other than the colonized itself. While such old authenticities can be seen re-established after colonialism, they are rife for deconstruction by a globalized context and by any recognition of either Irishness as a claim to the authentic or of the authentic as a jargon. 'Ireland' may tend towards an authenticity which is urban and contemporary but its initial destabilization of an old authenticity means that it cannot trust claims to the authentic again. And still 'Ireland' is not an entire rejection of authenticity but an ironic acknowledgement of its persistence in Irish culture.

Reading Irish culture in terms of authenticity can allow cultural criticism to trace changes and consistencies in cultural production and reception arising out of the power structures of colonialism in Ireland. Authenticity as a focus potentially shifts Irish cultural criticism away from the often reified pre-existing terms of debates in literary studies, and allows cultural theory to enter Irish cultural criticism in a way which might, when necessary, deny the sacred status of established politicized readings of Irish culture.

Notes

1. D. Lloyd, *Anomalous States: Irish Writing and the Post-Colonial Moment* (Dublin: Lilliput, 1993), p. 112.
2. J. Golomb, *In Search of Authenticity: From Kierkegaard to Camus* (London: Routledge, 1995), p. 12.
3. T. Adorno, *The Jargon of Authenticity* (London: Routledge and Kegan Paul, [1964] 1986).
4. G. Griffiths, 'The Myth of Authenticity: Representation, Discourse and Social Practice' in *De-Scribing Empire: Post-Colonialism and Textuality*, eds C. Tiffin and A. Lawson (London: Routledge, 1994), pp. 70–85.
5. J. Golomb, *In Search of Authenticity*, p. 7.
6. J. Golomb, *In Search of Authenticity*, p. 205.
7. J. Golomb, *In Search of Authenticity*, p. 117.
8. B. Anderson, *Imagined Communities: Reflections on the Origin and Spread of Nationalism* (London: Verso, 1991), p. 25.
9. J. Golomb, *In Search of Authenticity*, p. 9.
10. J. Golomb, *In Search of Authenticity*, p. 39.
11. J. Golomb, *In Search of Authenticity*, p. 54.
12. B. Anderson, *Imagined Communities*, p. 26.
13. J. Golomb, *In Search of Authenticity*, p. 79.

14. J. Golomb, *In Search of Authenticity*, pp. 3 and 12.
15. J. Golomb, *In Search of Authenticity*, p. 204.
16. T. Adorno, *The Jargon of Authenticity*, p. 5.
17. Quoted in T. Brown, *Ireland: A Social and Cultural History 1922–1985* (London: Fontana, 1990), p. 146.
18. T. Adorno, *The Jargon of Authenticity*, pp. 7–8.
19. T. Adorno, *The Jargon of Authenticity*, p. 9.
20. J. Baudrillard, *Simulations*, trans. P. Foss, P. Patton and P. Beitchman (New York: Semiotext(e), 1983), pp. 12–13.
21. G. Griffiths, 'The Myth of Authenticity', p. 70.
22. G. Griffiths, 'The Myth of Authenticity', p. 71.
23. C. Graham, 'Liminal Spaces: Post-Colonial Theory and Irish Culture', *The Irish Review*, 8 (1994), 29–43.
24. F. Fanon, *The Wretched of the Earth* (Harmondsworth: Penguin, 1990), p. 40.
25. W.B. Yeats, *Fairy and Folk Tales of the Irish Peasantry* (1888) in *Fairy and Folk Tales of Ireland* (London: Picador, 1973), p. 4.
26. J. Golomb, *In Search of Authenticity*, p. 117.
27. W.B. Yeats, *Fairy and Folk Tales of the Irish Peasantry*, p. 7.
28. J. Golomb, *In Search of Authenticity*, p. 3.
29. W.B. Yeats, *Fairy and Folk Tales of the Irish Peasantry*, p. 7.
30. J. Golomb, *In Search of Authenticity*, p. 7.
31. T. Adorno, *The Jargon of Authenticity*, p. 8.
32. *Subaltern Studies I–VI*, ed. R. Guha (Delhi: Oxford University Press, 1982–9); *Subaltern Studies VII*, eds P. Chatterjee and G. Pandey (Delhi: Oxford University Press, 1992); H.K. Bhabha, *The Location of Culture* (London: Routledge, 1994); G.C. Spivak, *In Other Worlds: Essays in Cultural Politics* (London: Routledge, 1988), *The Post-Colonial Critic: Interviews, Strategies, Dialogues* (London: Routledge, 1990).
33. D. Gregory, *Geographical Imaginations* (Oxford: Blackwell, 1994), p. 187.
34. J. Golomb, *In Search of Authenticity*, p. 12.
35. G. Griffiths, 'The Myth of Authenticity', p. 71.
36. G. Griffiths, 'The Myth of Authenticity', p. 84.
37. L. Gibbons, 'Coming Out of Hibernation: The Myth of Modernity in Irish Culture' in *Across the Frontiers: Ireland in the 1990s*, ed. R. Kearney (Dublin: Wolfhound, 1988), p. 210.
38. L. Gibbons, 'Coming Out of Hibernation: The Myth of Modernity in Irish Culture', p. 211.
39. L. Gibbons, 'Coming Out of Hibernation: The Myth of Modernity in Irish Culture', p. 213.
40. Heritage Island, established in 1992, is a private company offering tourist marketing services 'to a select number of the best Heritage Centres in [Ireland]' (C. Finegan, 'Marketing Ireland's Heritage to the International Market', paper given at Tourism Development Conference, Killarney, 1996). I am grateful to Cartan Finegan, Managing Director of Heritage Island, for supplying me with a copy of this paper.
41. Heritage Island Marketing Brochure, *c.* 1994.

42. G. Griffiths, 'The Myth of Authenticity', p. 84.
43. J. Golomb, *In Search of Authenticity*, p. 204.
44. 'Ireland', McConnell's Advertising Limited, *c.* 1994. My thanks to McConnell's and to Guinness Ireland for their generous assistance in supplying information on this ad.
45. J. Baudrillard, *Simulations*, p. 12.

3

Decolonization and Criticism: Towards a Theory of Irish Critical Discourse

Gerry Smyth

I

Of all the violent exchanges which characterize the encounter between colonizer and colonized, perhaps the most significant is that colonialism, in the words of Ashis Nandy,

> creates a culture in which the ruled are constantly tempted to fight their rulers within the psychological limits set by the latter. It is not an accident that the specific variants of the concepts with which many anti-colonial movements in our times have worked have often been the products of the imperial culture itself and, even in opposition, these movements have paid homage to their respective cultural origins.[1]

In recent years Nandy's insight has been echoed in Irish cultural debate, with the critic David Lloyd pointing out that the conceptual coherence of the identity conceived as part of an Irish decolonizing strategy during the nineteenth century derived paradoxically from British imperialist discourse, thus propping up through its organizational assumptions that which it claimed to oppose. For Lloyd, in fact, identitarian discourse is not the solution to colonial violence, but the precise location of the problem; this because he imagines effective resistance to imperial domination residing more in haphazard, fragmentary and adulterated discourses than in fully rational politico-cultural initiatives which are always already undone by constituting themselves in response to (and therefore in collusion with) the oppositional logic of imperialism.[2]

Lloyd's mistrust of a 'reality' always on the side of Caesar recalls those strategies of resistance developed under the auspices of post-structuralist modes of thought, and I shall be touching upon the issue of the relationship between Irish cultural politics and a European theory with globalizing pretensions throughout this essay. Initially, however, I am more concerned with two related matters. I want first of all to trace the emergence of the initial colonial imposition and its violent, dualistic logic in the course of a narrative of Irish decolonization in the nineteenth century, a narrative which ensured that, in imitation of contemporary British practices, it was questions of national identity that set the limits on Irish cultural and political discourse. In this, I am in sympathy with contemporary post-colonial critics working within a broad post-structuralist framework.

Beyond this, however, I wish to suggest that in seeking to deconstruct the collusion of anti-colonialist practices with colonialist logic, such critics must attend to the oppositional logic which invariably structures their own interventions, if they are to avoid reinscribing at the level of method that which they claim to disdain at the level of history. I intend to relocate the strange conspiracy between Irish identity and English imperialism, therefore, in terms of a set of *critical*, as opposed to *creative*, practices. This is because the critical/creative opposition in history has been every bit as violent, as insidious, and as persistent as the opposition of colonizer/colonized; indeed, according to Jacques Derrida, it figures perhaps as the original imposition upon which all subsequent forms of discursive ambivalence, including colonialism, are based.[3] Nandy's point about a decolonization tempted to operate within the psycho-cultural limits of oppositional logic encompasses *post*-colonial interventions also, no matter how aware the critic may be of its insidious nature; and it is no use congratulating ourselves for deconstructing the paradoxes of colonial imposition if that liberatory gesture occurs within a discursive landscape mapped in advance by the colonial encounter. In recent years, post-colonial studies has taken to task any number of professional fields, revealing the roles they play in producing and reproducing colonial relations. The paradigmatic instance is of course Edward Said's work on orientalism.[4] About the crucial part played by an enabling metadiscourse such as criticism in resisting colonial imposition, however, post-colonialism has had relatively little to say. What follows, therefore, is a set of notes towards the restructuring of contemporary Irish cultural debate, in which it is suggested that criticism is the factory wherein the 'mechanics of authenticity' are set to work to produce both a coherent narrative of the decolonizing nation and a set of images of the national essence. This narrative and these images subsequently become available for activation and development throughout the emerging nation, including the crucial practices of cultural and political nationalism.

II

With regard to the representation of the colonial subject, Homi Bhabha has called for 'a theoretical self-consciousness of those critical practices which in claiming to restore the "natural" and "reasonable" meanings of texts, are in fact engaged in strategies of naturalization and cultural assimilation which make our readings unwillingly collusive and profoundly uncritical'.[5] This is interesting for two reasons. In the first place, it signals a crucial shift in emphasis, away from practices traditionally considered 'primary' or 'artistic', and towards the systematic analysis of 'secondary' or 'critical' forms of discourse, as well as the ideology which produced this hierarchy of practices. I say 'crucial' because literary criticism needs to be recuperated from the parasitical terms in which it has been traditionally characterized, and seen instead as the discourse in which both colonial and anti-colonial strategies gain their force and their coherence. To understand this it is necessary to look briefly at the emergence of the modern institution of Anglophone literary criticism.

As it developed from specific English cultural and political concerns during the eighteenth and nineteenth centuries, literary criticism imagined for itself a democratic-rationalist function, which was to demarcate a specific form of social activity (writing) and to translate this activity into descriptive and evaluative languages. Figures such as Joseph Addison and Richard Steele had imagined an emancipatory role for criticism in its appeal to reason and its potential for wide dissemination. Ever since Plato decided to expel the imaginative writer from his ideal state, however, criticism's self-professed secondary and revelatory role has masked a much more active and discriminatory agenda in which the meanings of imaginative texts were not so much *discovered* and subsequently disseminated by the critic, as these same texts were *covered* in terms of the critic's ideologically-determined agenda.[6] Rather than demonstrating a rationalist principle of universal enlightenment, therefore, literary criticism in eighteenth-century England quickly became a policing exercise designed to demarcate an area of privileged activity, and to help to constitute the subjects engaging in, and excluded from, this activity. The new reading classes wished to gain something from their skill, and what is discovered very early is the fact that criticism *is* an ideology in its own right, and that because of various social and political issues with which it is inextricably bound – literacy, print capitalism, leisure, and so on – criticism is an interested discourse from its inception. It has a use value which can be exploited and an effective function which can be harnessed. What occurs in England at this time, then, is that the spaces and practices of literary criticism are appropriated by interested groups within society seeking to convert its ostensible communicative rationality into an instrumental rationality. Thus the magazine and the newspaper become more and more partisan until they are openly polemical; the essay and the review become tools of attack, and the promise of rationality and enlightenment initially held out by literary criticism is denied.[7]

Like colonialism, therefore, the modern institution of criticism is from its inception a highly ambivalent discourse, encompassing both emancipatory and repressive agendas. Moreover, not only does it function in a structurally similar way to colonialism; during the eighteenth century, with the consolidation of a new Anglo-Irish community and the beginnings of the modern phase of Catholic Irish resistance, literary criticism becomes the specific location for the production and contestation of colonialist representations. This interpretation helps to account for the endurance of a particular debate in both Irish and British modern cultural history – the function of criticism. One has only to think of some of the figures who have engaged in this debate – Burke, Johnson, Coleridge, Arnold, Wilde, Yeats, Eliot, Leavis – to appreciate not only the intellectual and academic importance of critical discourse, but also its wider implications for the other well-known issues preoccupying these writers. The point is that the question of 'the function of criticism' as it has been formulated since the nineteenth century has also always been a question of the function of the nation. If it has become a commonplace of contemporary post-colonial theory to claim that without the repeated 'acts' of the nation, especially the literary acts, there would in fact be no nation at all, then it is surely necessary to turn to that discourse which, far from merely identifying the links between culture and nation *after the creative event,* actually provides the spaces and the forms which allow these 'acts' to be performed.

When Irish intellectuals began to formulate a cultural politics in response to colonialist practices in the years after the Treaty of Limerick, it was the critical, rather than the artistic, text which became the prime location for these hegemonic encounters. This situation is complicated by the presence of a settler community attempting to negotiate a dual role vis-à-vis the remnants of Gaelic Ireland and, as the eighteenth century wore on, an increasingly unsympathetic mother country. But the critical controversies surrounding the status of texts discovered, created and translated during the First Celtic Revival from the mid-eighteenth century on is one obvious location for the formulation of discourses of resistance, and we shall be encountering more shortly.[8] A present-day shift in emphasis to critical discourse, therefore, signals a recognition that there can be no decolonizing literature, no national culture of resistance, before a prefiguring *critical* discourse creates a series of social and institutional spaces in which such a culture and its particular effects can function and have meaning; and even after this culture is established and the artist becomes self-conscious of his/her role as the 'narrator of the nation', literary criticism still performs a crucial function in validating, refining, and policing the cultural acts wherein the national narrative is performed.

What this means is that when one turns to modern Irish culture to observe the emergence of a narrative of decolonization, it is to critical rather than 'imaginative' or 'creative' discourse that one must initially turn, for criticism is already imaginative and creative in the oppositional role it constructs for itself. The repeated acts of literature in which the nation is performed throughout the nineteenth and twentieth centuries have themselves to be performed in a prefiguring critical discourse, a discourse which in its own forms and practices responds to the ongoing narrative of decolonization. Despite the claims of generations of both imperialist and nationalist critics, that is, Irish literature cannot express, reflect, or embody the decolonizing nation until it is so constituted by an enabling metadiscourse – literary criticism.

III

Bhabha's statement is interesting, secondly, for his identification of the manner in which the critical discourse of decolonizing formations is invariably outmanoeuvred by the violence of the initial colonial imposition, just as Nandy claims. Decolonizing criticism, that is, adheres to the oppositional logic insisted upon in colonial discourse, and operates in terms of what Bhabha calls 'image analysis',[9] in which cultural representations are considered in terms of their fidelity to a pre-existing reality – a reality, moreover, which in any encounter between the colonizer and the colonized always favours the former. Taking a cue from the colonialism which dominates the discursive landscape, the colonized subject learns to process phenomena in terms of a pre-established economy of similitude and difference, and this tendency gives rise within the decolonizing formation to two main critical strategies.

The first such strategy or *mode* of decolonizing criticism is called *universalism* by Bhabha, but for the purposes of this essay I shall call it *liberal*.[10] This liberal mode is one in which a subordinate colonial subject (whether native or settler) demands equality with the dominant metropolitan other; in the terminology of modern resistance theory it is characterized by the demand for 'equal access to the symbolic order' by the subordinate subject.[11] The flaw at the heart of this project, however, is that the 'equality' to be achieved is already overwritten by the values of the dominant subject, and the language in which equality can be achieved is thus always already inscribed with, because formed on the basis of, difference. Liberal, egalitarian, and universalist strategies, therefore, can be of only limited success because even 'victory' in these terms will necessitate a recognition on the part of the colonized subject of the inherent inferiority of pre-colonial culture. As Albert Memmi writes: 'The first ambition of the colonized is to become equal to that splendid model [the colonizer] and to resemble him to the point of disappearing in him',[12] where 'disappearance' amounts to continued native subservience to colonial domination. For the liberal critic trying to *raise* the experience of the colonized up to that of the colonizer, or to locate a non-ideological realm in which colonizer and colonized can converse in an innocent language, 'equality' ultimately signifies a denial of national validity and an adherence to that structure of differences which maintains the economy of power in favour of the colonizer.[13]

The second *mode* of decolonizing criticism is called *nationalism* by Bhabha. It might be more useful, however, to see nationalism as a late stage within a larger strategy – which I shall call *radicalism* – focusing on what is imagined as unique and different about native identity. This mode of critical decolonization involves the rejection of metropolitan discourse, a celebration of difference and otherness, and the attempted reversal of the economy of discourse which constructs the colonial subject as inferior. In modern Irish history, three factors have combined to make possible this radical strand of decolonization: i) the emergence of Anglo-Irish patriotism during the mid-eighteenth century; ii) the survival of a residual Gaelic presence on the margins of Ascendancy Ireland; iii) a British imperialist discourse producing in the wake of the American and French Revolutions simultaneous representations of Ireland as an integral component of a corporate British identity, and as violently other to that identity. In its more militant moments this second mode came to register as a need to cast off, violently if need be, the material and intellectual trappings of subordination, and embrace/construct instead a pristine prehistory which would serve as both Edenic cause and Utopian effect of nationalist activity.[14]

Inasmuch as this second mode was concerned with the often violent overthrow of English imperial domination, it has been predominantly associated in modern Irish history with the Gaelic – or what was referred to in the cultural debates of the early twentieth century as the Irish-Irish – element of the nation. Any Anglo-Irish subject wishing to embrace this politico-cultural option would always find it difficult to gain full access to those discourses and practices from which the radical decolonizing gesture emerged. In spite of this, some of the more significant moments in the genealogy of this radical mode are, as we shall shortly see, marked by the writings and activity of Anglo-Irish subjects.

It is also necessary to recognize, however, that this strategy is predicated on a crucial political and theoretical error, for at the same time as it affirms the value and validity of *otherness* the colonial critic confirms and implicitly accepts the regime of discourse which constructs the colonial experience as oppositional in the first place. As the Irish radical critic asserts cultural difference he/she merely confirms what the English reader 'knew' all the time: *They are not the same as us, therefore our domination is justified.*

IV

From the discussion so far, then, it can be seen that criticism undertaken within a decolonizing formation is a highly ambivalent practice. On the one hand it provides opportunities for subjects to speak their anti-colonialism in a choice of liberal and radical registers. On the other hand, its adherence to the dialectical mode of thought made available by the colonial power ensures that such creative discourse is always already overwritten with colonialist values. This dual critical orientation – simultaneously enabling and disabling – can be seen to operate throughout the history of modern Irish decolonization.

The critical discourse of Samuel Ferguson provides a typical liberal example. Ferguson represents a particular type of Anglo-Irishness – at once fiercely Irish, Protestant, nationalistic and loyal – a confused and confusing position which finds resonances throughout subsequent Anglo-Irish practices in the work of figures such as Hyde, Yeats and Synge. His criticism of James Hardiman's *Irish Minstrelsy* in the *Dublin University Magazine* of 1834 constitutes one of the most comprehensive statements of Anglo-Irishness, and at the same time one of the most skilful politico-cultural manoeuvres, of the nineteenth century.[15] During the course of his critique Ferguson constructed a position for the Anglo-Irish in which they would be fully integrated into the national community – in fact, they would be the natural leaders of that community by virtue of their greater access to metropolitan reason in the form of a rational Protestant religion. In other words, he made use of whatever was to hand – Irish history, English reason – to construct a powerful position for the national fraction he represented, a position which would maintain their former power in spite of Catholic Irish agitation and English reform. As an Irishman he defends a discourse – Irish literature in the English language – with which Ireland can begin to assert its historical validity in the modern world; as an Anglo-Irish Protestant, he is on hand to lead this new Ireland, for without him they will be condemned to the silence or effeteness which marked their former confrontations with the modern world. Ferguson, then, employs literary criticism to validate the Anglo-Irish identity and history he requires, and in a reciprocal motion achieves critical closure in terms of his political agenda.

Thomas Davis is a radical decolonizing figure from the same era, another Anglo-Irish Protestant who limited his interventions in the national debate to writing. Yet unlike Ferguson, Davis became an integral part of post-revolutionary mythology. Like Wolfe Tone, Robert Emmet and Patrick Pearse, after 1922 Davis was elevated into the nationalist pantheon where his writings, again like the violent sacrifices of these others, became valuable nationalist currency.[16] Indeed, despite the anti-military ethos of his nationalism, Davis was avidly appropriated by a later generation of radical nationalists, most notably Patrick Pearse, and converted into an apologist for blood sacrifice.[17] Davis was a radical decolonizing intellectual confronting head on the difficulties of constructing an Irish identity in terms made available by the imperial power he was attempting to throw off. One means of warding off the implications of this contradiction was through the construction of a critical ideology predicated on the interdependence of culture and geography. After Davis it would be very difficult for anyone to discuss Irish literature or Irish nationalism without being aware of the 'common-sense' linking these two seemingly symbiotic categories. The location of this ideological operation was Davis's own discourse, in which he employed the structures and codes of criticism to create the myth of a national tradition.

Despite the historical contingency of its own emergence, Irish nationalism after Davis started to believe as authentic the stories it told about its own origins, and began to find it more and more difficult to acknowledge alternatives to its own peculiar way of seeing. Despite its constitution as a specific *decolonizing* strategy, that is, this radical mode progressively denied colonial history and the indissoluble implication of England and Englishness in the historical emergence of the concept of Ireland and Irishness. At a certain point in Irish history, despite the best efforts of its liberal and left wings, radical decolonization was commandeered by a nationalist bourgeois elite which tried to arrest the process at the point where it assumed control of the state apparatus left vacant by the offshore power. The drive towards an essential national identity in the years after 1922 actually reinforced social and political hierarchies even as it claimed to be the agent of liberation from such hierarchies.

Both these critical modes, then, are ultimately inappropriate for the decolonizing critic. This is because, as Bhabha says, the debate between liberal and radical (or what he calls universalist and nationalist) critics which constitutes the major controversy surrounding the question of colonial culture is fought essentially on the same aesthetic ground – that of 'image analysis'. As critical strategies, the liberal and radical modes guarantee that the subaltern cannot speak, for speaking in these modes always entails an acknowledgement, however remote or tacit, of the agenda preset by the colonizing power. And even after independence has been achieved, the residue of liberal and radical critical discourse leaves the post-colonial subject, as so much commentary in Ireland since 1922 attests, still bound to the *other* against which it must constantly measure its 'freedom'. So, the question then becomes: once positioned as the *other* within a discursive economy of power and knowledge, how can individuals and groups strive for release from subjugation without at the same time accepting their designation as *other* and thereby reinforcing the structures of that economy? How can the colonized subject articulate differences without metamorphosing into the image of that which she/he opposes? Can the subaltern speak?[18]

It becomes necessary in the face of this impasse to postulate a *third* mode of resistance if the decolonizing subject is not to remain in thrall to ultimately disabling systems of thought. The possibility of such a third stage has been the subject of much debate amongst post-colonial intellectuals, indeed in most contemporary narratives of resistance.[19] But strategies to go 'beyond' or 'outside', or posit a discursive realm 'before', the law of oppositional logic again merely reaffirm the structure of colonial difference and the economy of power/knowledge on which it relies. In fact, there is no 'outside' or 'beyond' to which the colonial subject can escape, for although presence, essence and identity may be said to be at the root of the colonial problem, they remain the only available realm for decolonizing activity.[20] The question insists: how can the individual and the community deal with those oppositions given that there is no language they could speak, no activity in which they could engage, which could not somehow be narrativized and recuperated by this oppositional cast of mind?

For many, the most interesting and promising approach to these questions is predicated not on a rejection of, or alternative to, the identitarian discourse of liberal and radical modes, but on their *displacement* and *performance* in what Said has called an anti-authoritarian, anti-institutional, anti-narrative discourse.[21] There are many ways of imagining this discourse, but I want to focus here on two interdependent tactics common to all: a refusal of the concept of a non-ideological space beyond history and discourse, and an acceptance of the necessity of working within, albeit subversively, the dualistic terms of colonialism.

We have seen that the two modes discussed so far function in a simultaneous discursive economy at any one time in the narrative of Irish decolonization. They may be defined as necessary but insufficient, capable of throwing off metropolitan domination but only in such a way as to reconfirm, even in the moment of independence, the disabling dialectic in which they are located. However, like the colonial discourse to which they are opposed, to exist they have to be performed, repeatedly and publicly, each performance in fact reconstituting the category (the nation) and the identity (the subject) of which it (the performance) is supposed to be an expression. Now, this necessity for constant public repetition of the nation provides a space in which the colonial dialectic can be rethought, for there are ways in which this discourse can be performed and repeated which question the foundationalist message and identitarian politics of both colonialism and nationalism.

What is suggested instead is a politics of *displacement*, an operation whereby the given categories are (necessarily) performed, but in such a way as to question their givenness, their authenticity, their originality. This entails a strategy of parody, not in the sense of a comic imitation but in the sense of a subversive deconstruction of presence, essence and identity, of the very laws of symbolic representation – for present purposes, of the categories which make up the colonialist discursive economy. Judith Butler, one of the 'queer theorists' who has been instrumental in advancing this line writes: '[the] parodic repetition of "the original" [. . .] reveals the original to be nothing other than a parody of the *idea* of the natural and the original [. . .]. What possibilities of recirculation exist? Which possibilities of doing gender [nationality/

race] repeat and displace through hyperbole, dissonance, internal confusion, and proliferation the very constructs by which they are mobilized?'.[22] If one accepts the reasoning, it could be claimed that as repeatable, normative discourses with practical consequences for subjects, both colonialism *and* the collusive strategies of liberal and radical decolonization can be undone by means of a parodic, disruptive repetition showing itself to be a copy of which the 'originals' are already constructs – a copy, that is, of a copy.

This strategy finds parallels in the work of many leading theorists, but perhaps the most relevant example in this context is Bhabha's description of 'colonial fantasy', which he describes in the following way:

> To the myth of realist narrative – its grand syntagms and sequentiality, its pleasure, irony, comedy, characters and consolations, its historic utterances and easy identifications between you and I – colonial fantasy presents scenarios that make problematic both Authority and Intention. It registers a crisis in the assumption of the narrative priority of the 'first person' and the *natural* ascendancy of the First World. And this colonial fantasy – this specific historical formation of the 'subject' – demands another kind of reading, another gaze [. . .]. In shattering the mirror of representation, and its range of Western bourgeois social and psychic 'identifications', the spectacle of colonial fantasy sets itself up as an uncanny 'double'. Its terrifying figures – savages, grotesques, mimic men – reveal things so profoundly familiar to the West that it cannot bear to remember them [. . .] for they address that 'other scene' within ourselves that continually divides us against ourselves and others.[23]

What Bhabha is describing here is the 'scene' that emerges during every colonial encounter, but is either repressed or recast into narratives of exoticism, danger or fantasy by the dominant formation. It is the scene where the coherent, transparent subject developed by Western discourse comes under pressure in the precise moment of differentiation between identity and otherness on which colonial discourse turns. Decolonizing critics must not only know where and how to look for this disruptive scene; once located, it must be read differently, against the grain of a hermeneutics which in its interpretative assumptions – authority, intention, identity – always reproduces the 'reality' of colonialist discourse.

Returning to the narrative of Irish decolonization, these qualities of hyperbole, dissonance, discursive confusion and colonial fantasy raise the spectre of James Joyce, whose vision of Irishness haunts so many subsequent interventions. In fact, it is probably not going too far to say that much of the theoretical revolution that has overtaken Western intellectual discourse in the last 30 years or so is heavily influenced, through one line or another, by Joyce; and many of the issues which exercise the contemporary intellectual imagination – language, gender, exile, and so on – are anticipated in his writings. What Joyce's work demonstrates is that while liberal and radical modes of resistance are important and necessary in any narrative of decolonization they are insufficient, and to escape effectively the deadening hand of colonial domination (and its double – nationalism) one must go one step further and undermine the subject categories of colonizer and colonized. In undermining these subject positions, moreover, Joyce threatens to undermine all notions of authority – religious, political, cultural. Joyce's work is parodic as many have remarked, but it is a subversive parody in which he has seized the rules of dominant decolonizing discourse and disrupted what he sees as its flawed identitarian message. For present purposes, however, Joyce's most important threat is to the authority of Irish-related literary criticism and the twin assumptions upon which it rests: a natural link between imaginative writing and the nation, and a natural aporia between primary (imaginative) and secondary (critical) discourses.

The third mode of decolonization realized by Joyce represents, then, not an alternative to liberal and radical discourses but a staging of the rules, codes and languages which provides their conceptual coherence. These strategies of resistance are still possible; indeed, they are necessary stages within the narrative of decolonization, but the final trope in that narrative requires a performance of all previous decolonizing discourse so that the colonial subject can experience her/his symbolic identity as both pressing reality and staged event, as both the basis for decolonizing praxis and the fiction, the rhetoric, the myth which enables that praxis. Only in this way can the colonial subject 'break out of' the disabling symbolic dialectic, although as the scare quotes suggest, this 'breaking out of' will also entail a 'breaking into' as the colonial categories are maintained in performance even as their constructed nature is revealed.

V

There are a number of problems, however, with trying to incorporate such a strategy into a model of Irish decolonization and criticism as it has been outlined so far. Although *Ulysses*, for example, certainly gives the lie to criticism's traditional pretensions to master the artistic text from some secure extratextual location, it is difficult to imagine how such a profoundly ambivalent discourse could be harnessed to forms capable of practical critical intervention. This, of course, is precisely the point, as Bhabha would no doubt argue, but it does nevertheless leave potentially disruptive colonial scenes open to reappropriation by the liberal and radical narratives described above. Criticism's inevitable dedication to the revelation of meaning militates against the activation of the 'other' scene, no matter how understanding the critic or how disruptive the text. This was the difficulty confronted by Samuel Beckett who, in the opening essay of a Joyce-inspired critical collection focusing on *Work in Progress*, wrote:

> And now here am I, with my handful of abstractions, among which notably: a mountain, the coincidences of contraries, the inevitability of cyclic evolution, a system of Poetics, and the prospect of self-extension in the world of Mr Joyce's *Work in Progress* [. . .]. Must we wring the neck of a certain system in order to stuff it into a contemporary pigeon-hole, or modify the dimensions of that pigeon-hole for the satisfaction of analogymongers? Literary criticism is not book-keeping.[24]

What Beckett confronts here is the paradox of trying to criticize, even sympathetically, a text which refuses the institutional boundary between different kinds of writing, between inside and outside the text, between imaginative *writing* and critical *righting*, between Joyce and Beckett. But in what soon became a major scholarly industry, academics worldwide began to carve out careers by endlessly refining the main critical threads 'identified' at a very early stage in Joyce criticism – the transcendentalist Joyce of Eliot, the empirical Joyce of Pound, the humanist Joyce of Valery

Larbaud. Joyce's promise to forge in the smithy of his soul the uncreated conscience of his race somehow led him instead to the conference centres, lecture theatres and seminar rooms of the modern academic world, for the fact of the matter is that Joyce remains the preserve of a small intellectual elite, circulating as a name rather than as a practice.[25]

Beyond this, however, the idea of a third mode of critical decolonization – which might be called 'virtual' or 'dissident' – is itself the subject of much adverse criticism. In the first place, the affirmation of a realm of activity only tangentially and (allegedly) subversively linked with colonial reality is in constant danger of reconfirming the dialectical structure it purports to outmanoeuvre. A strategy based on the parodic disruption of 'normal' relations can quite easily become the *sign* of marginality, a psychotic, exotic realm of activity beyond meaning and intention, drained of any potential for practical intervention. In some critical circles, Joyce has indeed become the ultimate sign of Irish difference, and literary criticism has been able to redeploy itself to cover his work in precisely these terms. Richard Kearney, for example, has interpreted the impasse of liberal and radical decolonization as the 'orthodox dualist logic of either/or'.[26] He goes on to suggest that 'the Irish mind may be seen to favour a more dialectical logic of both/and: an intellectual ability to hold the traditional oppositions of classical reason together in creative confluence', and he traces the career of this faculty throughout the history of Irish writing in English – Swift, Sterne, Berkeley, Wilde, Shaw, Beckett, O'Brien, Behan, and so on. He then nominates Joyce as the seminal modern exponent of this creative, disruptive hermeneutics, the figure who more than any other in Irish cultural history challenges the disabling structure of colonial dependence. Such a model would appear to tie in with the 'dissident' critical politics described above. However, despite many riders and qualifications, Kearney cannot escape the possibility that this dialectical logic, which he opposes to classical dualistic logic, could itself become the *sign* of Irish otherness, thus once again becoming subsumed into the oppositional thought and identitarian politics of colonialist discourse. 'Joyce', in this reckoning, becomes the archetypal Irish writer precisely because he is the one furthest removed from reality, and just as every tactic employed by the patient to refuse the analysis can be explained by the analyst, so the refusal by the colonized to recognize the borders created by the colonizer can eventually be diagnosed as a typical colonial response, another brick in the wall forming the border between us and them. The concept of an 'Irish mind' which functions differently to the 'orthodox' mind thus allows a space for the reassertion of the logic of 'Us' and 'Them', and the effects of power which such a logic allows.

Besides this objection, there is always the potential for a discrepancy between the way an author's intentions are *encoded* within a text, and the way they are *decoded* by the society to which the text is addressed. Anyone armed with a battery of post-structuralist techniques and concepts can expose the myth of origins at the origin of both colonialism and nationalism, revealing the contradictions and ambivalences of texts founded upon the assumptions of identitarian discourse. But post-colonial theory has yet to come up with a convincing theory of how such texts are actually consumed at various points throughout society (although once again Bhabha has made interesting gestures in that direction[27]), preferring instead to mystify the process and the efficacy of antimimetic practices. *Ulysses* may refuse the idea of a critical metanarrative, but this has not stopped generations of critics searching out, and frequently discovering, coherent narratives in the text, for it is book enough to satisfy any number of critical initiatives. Meaning and interpretation, therefore, may have more to do with particular instances of what Tony Bennett calls 'reading formations' than with any radical strategy embodied in the text on the shelf.[28]

Furthermore, the optimism evinced by critics such as Bhabha and Butler with regard to the effectiveness of strategic attempts to actualize instability and fragmentation might be regarded as misplaced when confronted with a global system of image production which actually flourishes in conditions of change and flexibility. In fact, the critical politics of displacement, with its playful and ironic attitude towards traditional narrative, is particularly susceptible to appropriation and depoliticizing, 'not only', as one commentator puts it, 'because the principle of innovation is also the principle of the market in general but also because the postmodern obsession with antimimetic forms is always on the lookout for new modes of "self" fracture, for new versions of the self-locating, self-disrupting text'.[29]

Taken together, these objections constitute a serious problem for any 'virtual' critical strategy based on performance and contradiction. The endless revelation of an absence at the heart of modern Irish identity must surely become frustrating when it comes to the question haunting every critical discourse: *what is to be done*? The practical relevance of post-colonialism's central thesis – that the decolonizing subject has no validity and that the text's attempt to speak subalternity only serves to perpetuate the effects of imperialist discourse – is questionable when confronted with the banal but inevitable problem of making sense of the text. Until a lot more study has been undertaken on the ways in which critical and creative texts have actually been read in modern Irish history, therefore, one would be advised to introduce a radical hesitancy with regard to a decolonizing strategy based on sophisticated theories of disruption and dissonance.

It is worth mentioning in passing that one direction in which such research might go is towards a reformulation of the notion of the power relations between colonizer and colonized, which in recent years, and as this essay attests, has tended to be dominated by a Foucauldian paradigm. A model based on intimate and radically destabilizing exchanges between Ireland and England in the modern period, while still retaining sight of the realities of domination and subordination, might go some way to undoing the violent oppositional logic imposed (and critically superimposed) on the colonialist encounter.[30]

In the meantime, however, and in the absence of such a body of research, we are faced with a narrative of Irish decolonization and criticism which is, like so many narratives left over from the colonialist era, unfinished. Contemporary cultural critics continue to attempt, in the words of Seamus Heaney, either to 'cajole or ignore' Irish history, while initiatives to outmanoeuvre this spurious choice are compromised by their refusal of a 'real' language capable of winning hearts and minds. Again, *Ulysses* offers a suggestive analogy and the seeds of an alternative myth. Love, as Leopold Bloom knows and Stephen Dedalus suspects, may be 'the word known to all men',[31] but this word has to remain unspoken if it is to avoid being recruited for inevitably collusive narratives. Love's ineffability is both a strength and a weakness; a strength, because the word always exists as a potential, but a weakness because it is difficult, if not impossible, to articulate a word capable of signifying to each member of the community as well as to the community as a whole. In 'Act of Union', perhaps his most bitter and pessimistic poem, Heaney adopts the persona of a wistful, ageing England, assessing the fallout from youthful colonial adventures in Ireland and elsewhere:

> No treaty
> I foresee will salve completely your tracked
> And stretchmarked body, the big pain
> That leaves you raw, like opened ground, again.[32]

But perhaps hope lies somewhere in the word 'completely' which, in its simultaneous promise and postponement of a fully realized, final narrative of Irish identity, carries enough traces of 'the word that is known to all men' to shift, if ever so slightly, the politics of the possible. The realization of this possibility may be the task of Irish criticism in the years either side of the millennium.

Notes

1. A. Nandy, *The Intimate Enemy: Loss and Recovery of Self Under Colonialism* (Delhi: Oxford University Press, 1983), p. iii.
2. See D. Lloyd, *Nationalism and Minor Literature: James Clarence Mangan and the Emergence of Irish Cultural Nationalism* (Berkeley: University of California Press, 1987), and *Anomalous States: Irish Writing and the Post-Colonial Moment* (Dublin: Lilliput, 1993).
3. See J. Derrida, *Of Grammatology*, trans. G.C. Spivak (Baltimore: The Johns Hopkins University Press, 1976) where he traces the paradoxical relations between sign (literature) and supplement (criticism) – 'supplement' in the sense of something extra and in the sense of making complete. Derrida writes: 'Yet if reading must not be content with doubling the text, it cannot legitimately transgress the text towards something other than it, towards a referent (a reality that is metaphysical, historical, psychobiographical, etc.) or towards a signified outside the text whose content could take place outside of language, that is to say, in the sense that we give the word here, outside of writing in general' (J. Derrida, *Of Grammatology*, p. 158). In his essay 'The Order of Discourse' in *Untying the Text*, ed. R. Young (London: Routledge and Kegan Paul, 1981), Michel Foucault makes a similar point when he writes: '[by] a paradox which it always displaces but never escapes, the commentary must say for the first time what had, nonetheless, already been said, and must tirelessly repeat what had, however, never been said [. . .]. It allows us to say something other than the text itself, but on condition that it is the text itself which is said, and in a sense, completed' (M. Foucault, 'The Order of Discourse', pp. 58–9). I shall be expanding on these issues in section II.

4. E.W. Said, *Orientalism* (London: Routledge and Kegan Paul, 1978). See also S. Slemon, 'The Scramble for Post-Colonialism' in *De-Scribing Empire: Post-Colonialism and Textuality*, eds C. Tiffin and A. Lawson (London: Routledge, 1994), pp. 15–32.
5. Although see H.K. Bhabha, 'Representation and the Colonial Text: A Critical Exploration of Some Forms of Mimeticism' in *The Theory of Reading*, ed. F. Goldsmith (Brighton: Harvester, 1984), pp. 93–122.
6. See R. Barthes, 'Criticism as Language' in *Twentieth-Century Literary Criticism*, ed. D. Lodge (Harlow: Longman, 1972), p. 650.
7. T. Eagleton, *The Function of Criticism: From the Spectator to Post-Structuralism* (London: Verso, 1984).
8. On the critical politics surrounding the status of 'Celtic' texts such as MacPherson's *Ossian* and Brooke's *Reliques of Irish Poetry* during the eighteenth century see E.D. Snyder, *The Celtic Revival in English Literature 1760–1800* (Cambridge: Harvard University, 1923).
9. H.K. Bhabha, 'Representation and the Colonial Text', p. 99.
10. 'Liberal' and the terms which follow are borrowed from Julia Kristeva's model of feminist struggle. While I have found feminism useful in developing a model of colonial resistance I do not wish to be seen to 'read' one from the other as if colonial and gender (or other marginal) discourses were mapped onto each other in a totalizing critique of *otherness*. It seems clear, rather, that gender and race participate in contingent and uneven exchanges, creating a complex politics of marginality. For an analysis of this see J. Dollimore, *Sexual Dissidence: Augustine to Wilde, Freud to Foucault* (Oxford: Clarendon Press, 1991), *passim*.
11. T. Moi, *Sexual/Textual Politics* (London: Methuen, 1985), p. 12.
12. A. Memmi, *The Colonizer and the Colonized* (London: Souvenir Press, 1974), p. 120.
13. This first phase of decolonization finds analogies in many influential accounts, but see especially F. Fanon, *The Wretched of the Earth* (Harmondsworth: Penguin,1986) where he writes that: 'In this first phase, the intellectual native gives proof that he has assimilated the culture of the occupying power. His writings correspond point by point with those of his opposite numbers in the mother country. [. . .] This is the period of unqualified assimilation', pp. 178–9. Fanon's three-stage theory of colonial cultural resistance is not the same as the one described in this essay, limited as it is by his Freudian terms of reference. For a stinging critique on liberalism as a critical strategy in this context see C. Achebe, *Hopes and Impediments: Selected Essays 1965–87* (London: Heinemann, 1988), pp. 46–58.
14. The name *Sinn Féin* (Ourselves), for example – one of the dominant symbols of Irish radical decolonization – adumbrates the emphasis on the uniqueness of Irish national identity, although throughout the 1990s this emphasis has allegedly been undergoing a process of reformulation.
15. S. Ferguson, 'Hardiman's Irish Minstrelsy', *Dublin University Magazine*, Part One, 3:16 (1834), 465–77; Part Two, 4:20 (1834), 152–67; Part Three, 4:22 (1834), 447–67; Part Four, 4:23 (1834), 514–42.

16. In the foreword to a collection of Davis's work, Eamon de Valera wrote: 'The opinions and sentiments expressed and the ideals presented are independent of time and condition. They are, I believe, as potent to arouse the enthusiasm and to fire the zeal of the generous-hearted today as they were when the pieces were first written or delivered. [. . .] I urge that the essays and poems it contains be read and re-read by our "Young Ireland" until they are known by heart, and have become for them an abiding source of inspiration and an ever-present incentive to noble action'. Alluding to the Northern state and its unacceptable sequestration from the national trunk de Valera continues: 'Those who will be inspired by Davis's writings will dedicate themselves to the uncompleted task'. Anonymous (ed.) *Thomas Davis: Essays and Poems with a Centenary Memoir by Eamon de Valera* (Dublin: Gill and Son, 1945), pp. v–vi.
17. See P. Pearse, 'The Spiritual Nation' in *The Best of Pearse*, eds P. Mac Aonghusa and L. Ó Réagáin (Cork: Mercier, 1967), pp. 152–67. On Pearse's use of Davis see R.F. Foster, 'History and the Irish Question' in *Paddy and Mr Punch: Connections in Irish and British History* (London: Allen Lane, 1993), pp. 1–20, where Foster writes: 'Pearse's use of Irish history was that of a calculatedly disingenuous propagandist; it was this that enabled him, for instance, so thoroughly to misinterpret Thomas Davis', R.F. Foster, *Paddy and Mr Punch*, p. 14.
18. See the influential essay, G.C. Spivak, 'Can the Subaltern Speak?' in *Colonial Discourse and Post-Colonial Theory: A Reader*, eds P. Williams and L. Chrisman (Hemel Hempstead: Harvester Wheatsheaf, 1993), pp. 66–111. Spivak appears to reply to this question in the negative.
19. See P. Smith, 'Resistance' in *Discerning the Subject* (Minneapolis: University of Minnesota Press, 1988), pp. 56–69.
20. One of the chief tenets of many leading post-structuralist theorists is that there is no external standpoint from which to criticize the operation of power/knowledge effects. Narratives of change are only possible from within given discursive limits. As Derrida writes in an analogous context, '*there is nothing outside of the text*' (J. Derrida, *Of Grammatology*, p. 158).
21. E.W. Said, *Culture and Imperialism* (London: Chatto and Windus, 1993), p. 337.
22. J. Butler, *Gender Trouble: Feminism and the Subversion of Identity* (London: Routledge, 1990), p. 31.
23. H.K. Bhabha, 'Representing the Colonial Text', pp. 119–20.
24. S. Beckett, 'Dante . . . Bruno. Vico . . . Joyce' in *Our Exagmination Round His Factification For Incamination Of Work In Progress*, ed. S. Beckett (London: Faber, 1961), pp. 3–4.
25. On the Joyce industry see *Post-Structuralist Joyce: Essays from the French*, eds D. Attridge and D. Ferrer (Cambridge: Cambridge University Press, 1984). Perhaps the closest anyone has come to realizing the critical implications of Joyce's work is Jacques Derrida who, recognizing that the distinction between criticism and literature (like that between philosophy and literature) is a self-constituting effect produced from within the former discourse, argues against Western

criticism's drive towards conceptual closure, and for what one commentator has called 'the paradoxical potential of an a-decisive and a-critical form of criticism [. . .] a criticism under "erasure"', P. Smith, *Discerning the Subject*, p. 44.

26. R. Kearney, *The Irish Mind: Exploring Intellectual Traditions* (Dublin: Wolfhound, 1985), p. 296.
27. See H.K. Bhabha, 'Signs Taken for Wonders: Questions of Ambivalence and Authority Under a Tree Outside Delhi, May 1817', *Critical Inquiry*, 12 (1985), 144–64.
28. T. Bennett, 'Texts, Readers, Reading Formations', *Literature and History*, 9: 2 (1983), 214–27.
29. K. Sangari, 'The Politics of the Possible' in *The Post-Colonial Studies Reader*, eds B. Ashcroft, G. Griffiths and H. Tiffin (London: Routledge, 1995), p. 144.
30. Such a project might focus on a range of theoretical and methodological texts which take the peculiar intimacy of the colonizer and the colonized as the point of departure for historical and critical analysis, such as A. Nandy, *The Intimate Enemy*, R.F. Foster, *Paddy and Mr Punch*, and E.W. Said, 'Foucault and the Imagination of Power' in *Foucault: A Critical Reader*, ed. D. Couzens Hoy (Oxford: Basil Blackwell, 1986), pp. 109–22.
31. J. Joyce, *Ulysses* (Oxford: Oxford University Press, 1993), pp. 319 and 540.
32. S. Heaney, 'Act of Union' in *North* (London: Faber, 1975), pp. 49–50.

4

'Pestilence on their backs, famine in their stomachs': the Racial Construction of Irishness and the Irish in Victorian Britain

Jim Mac Laughlin

RACE AND ETHNICITY IN NINETEENTH-CENTURY POLITICAL DISCOURSE

The category 'race' was widely used not only to ascribe social inferiority to entire sections of the global population (particularly overseas colonial societies in the nineteenth century) but also to ethnic minorities in nation-building Europe and 'internal colonies' on the Celtic fringe of Victorian Britain.[1] As such, however, it was a category that was quite distinct from 'ethnicity', which signified a sense of belongingness and fostered quasi-biological constructs of peoples as self-conscious 'imagined communities' and nations in the metropolitan world.[2] Both these categories shared a common geography and a common history. They originated in Western Europe, particularly in Britain and France, and entered European academic and political discourse in the Darwinian half of the nineteenth century. There are, nevertheless, important distinctions between them which merit more detailed treatment, which they shall receive here. These distinctions are worth bearing in mind in any discussion on the position of Irish emigrants in their host societies since the nineteenth century. For present purposes, however, it is important to contrast the 'exclusiveness' of 'race' and the 'inclusiveness' of 'ethnicity'. Unlike 'race', 'ethnicity' was used, sometimes in conjunction with, but more often in preference to 'race' in order to legitimize the self-determination of Europe's more powerful *ethnically-defined* populations. It was also used to deny self-rule to racially 'inferior' peoples and ethnic minorities within Europe, in Great Britain and in the colonies. Whereas 'race' suggested a geography of closure which sought to keep the 'foreigner' and the socially inferior out of the nation-building metropolitan world, 'ethnicity' suggested inclusiveness and encouraged nation-building. As such it nurtured a geography of inclusion. It brought people together on the basis of shared cultural traits and common historical experiences. Thus 'ethnicity' did not so much imply a social aggregate (a group-in-itself); it more often than not referred to self-conscious social blocs and to groups-for-themselves. Unlike 'race', therefore, 'ethnicity' was not simply a 'classificatory category'. Like 'class', it was what E.P. Thompson calls an 'historical happening'.[3] More than that, it was an historical *geographical* phenomenon which entailed the notion of historical relationship and *geographical exclusion.*

Like 'class', 'ethnicity' was also embodied not so much in a 'structure' but in real people and in real contexts. It implied a process of individuation in that ethnic groups consciously selected their own cultural markers. They created their own sense of identity and constructed images of themselves as able people, as people capable of governing themselves. Indeed they were capable people because they were able to root themselves in their own history and in their own homelands. Ethnicity therefore 'happened' when and where people perceived themselves as possessing some degree of coherence and solidarity, and when they were at least latently aware of having common origins and common interests.[4]

'Race' on the other hand, particularly when used in a pejorative fashion, was much less a self-imposed social construct than an ideological construct. It was imposed upon people in order to justify their political domination and to legitimize their socio-political marginalization. In nineteenth-century political discourse, however, race was also used to categorize people, both according to their phenotypical characteristics and according to their cultural attributes. Aside from self-congratulatory images of Europeans as 'superior' white people – what Victor Kiernan calls 'the Lords of Humankind' – most usages of 'race' reflected negative tendencies of dissociation and exclusion.[5] As such the term was widely used to separate 'superior' from 'inferior' peoples. It outlawed any racial and cultural mixing that might occur across racial, or indeed *geographical* frontiers.

As applied to the Irish in Victorian Britain, 'race' signified a set of physical traits. It also suggested an amalgam of imaginary properties which 'fixed' the Irish as an 'inferior people' and set them apart from British Victorian society. This chapter analyses the racialization of the Irish in Britain in the nineteenth century, suggesting that the dividing lines of class and race coincided and *deepened each other* in that society, thereby contributing to the marginalization – some would say the 'brutalization' – of the Irish in the Victorian era. It explains how their 'Irishness' was used to legitimize the exclusion of Irish immigrants from mainstream British society and from 'respectable' Victorian communities. It also suggests that 'Irishness' was adopted as an explanation for the squalor and social degradation in which many Irish immigrants were compelled to live. It argues that, just when Irish nationalists were constructing positive images of 'Irishness' as an elevating force rooted in the cultural landscape of rural Catholic Ireland, nationalism in Britain fused with racism to exclude the Irish from the moral geography of the Victorian nation-state. This led to justifications for the socio-economic marginalization of the Irish in Britain on racial and ethnic grounds. The chapter traces the racialization and proletarianization of this minority population to quasi-biological racial and ethnic constructs of British Victorians as an 'Elect People'. The latter perceived themselves as in every way superior to the 'wilde' Irish in Ireland, and to the 'disorderly Irish' in Britain. The chapter concludes with a discussion of the geography of closure as it applies to the Irish in nineteenth-century Britain and to their concomitant construction as a 'dirty people'.

ANTI-IRISH RACISM AND NATIONALISM IN BRITAIN

Salman Rushdie has suggested that:

> To be a migrant is, perhaps, to be the only species of human being free of the shackles of nationalism (to say nothing of its ugly sister, patriotism). It is a burdensome freedom.[6]

Whatever the accuracy of this statement as applied to Britain's Indian intelligentsia in the post-war period, it certainly does not describe the experience of Irish emigrants in nineteenth-century

Britain. Rushdie could more accurately have argued that migrants are at once the victims of their own nation's effort at nation-building. For economic and/or political reasons, they are forced to emigrate and are subsequently 'shackled' by the nationalism and national patriotism of their host societies. 'Banished' from their own country, Irish emigrants have often found themselves 'outcasts' in the nation-building societies which have hosted them. Thus for example they were constructed as a 'dirty people' in Victorian Britain where they were widely perceived as not being entitled to a place within the institutions that constituted the material and moral structures of the English Victorian state. England's most influential newspapers and periodicals never allowed an occasion to escape them of treating the Irish in Britain as a kind of inferior race – as a kind of 'white negro'. A glance in *Punch* magazine is sufficient to show 'the difference between the plump and robust personification of John Bull and the wretched figure of lean and bony Pat'.[7] The 'essentialism' behind this type of race thinking blended with British nationalism in such a way as to define 'Britishness' and 'Irishness' in essentially hostile and oppositional terms. It suggested that Irish Celts possessed a number of qualities which marked them off as a race apart from those who claimed Anglo-Saxon, Danish, or Norman ancestry in the British Isles. More than this, and as L. P. Curtis has shown:

> Many members of the Victorian ruling class believed that Irish inferiority was a more or less permanent state of affairs, *the result of biological forces above and beyond the power of enlightened English administrators to control or ameliorate. Irish inferiority was seen as a function of Irish ethnicity,* which in turn represented the conjunction of so-called Irish mental and physical traits as these had passed from one generation to the next in accordance with the laws governing the transmission of hereditary characteristics.[8] (emphasis added)

The distinction between *wandering and migratory* Celts and *settled* Anglo-Saxons was a particularly long standing one in English political discourse. It is also fundamental to any discussion on British attitudes to the Irish in Britain since the nineteenth century. In the Darwinian half of the century it caused the Irish minority in Britain to be portrayed as an 'inferior' people because they were perceived as a 'rootless' people. From then onwards the British image of the Irish, not least those living in Britain, was also recast in racial, cultural and even biological terms. The standard image of the good-natured Irish peasant now gave way to that of a repulsive and threatening ape-like creature. Thus a satirical article on Irish immigration in *Punch* in 1862 described the Irish as 'the missing link' and referred to the 'hordes of Irish' invading England much in the same way as contemporary anti-immigrant discourse in Europe refers to 'hordes' of Asian, Black and Islamic immigrants invading 'Fortress Europe' today. The 'cultural baggage' which the Irish brought with them (their rural lifestyles, their peasant beliefs and customs, their Catholicism and their anti-individualistic gregariousness), together with that which they 'purchased' in the slums of the Victorian city were supposed to set the Irish apart from the Victorian British. Victorian England perceived itself as a well-integrated, cohesive and contented society and looked upon 'culture' as a refining and elevating force which was the achievement or 'invention' of 'settled' Victorians. Viewed thus 'culture' therefore was not just Victorian society's reservoir of the best that was known and thought, an Arnoldian palliative for neutralizing all that was savage and brutalizing about urban existence in the nineteenth and century.[9] It was a combative source of identity which brutalized and demonized outsiders like the Irish and set them apart from socially acceptable 'insiders' like the Victorian English. In this wider sense Victorian 'culture' was a viciously contested terrain wherein a wide variety of political and ideological causes engaged one another. This contestation in turn took place on a socio-political field wherein culture was not so much a placid realm of 'Apollonian gentility' but an essentially nationalistic and imperialist conflict wherein causes exposed themselves to the light of day and contended with one another in deadly competition.[10] Thus to the Victorian English 'their' culture was certainly superior to that of other cultures, especially that of the 'slum-dwelling' Irish. Other cultural practices, particularly those of the Irish in Britain, were to be denigrated and fought against because they were deemed inferior and out of place in Britain. The conservative political outlook of this Victorian Britain gave rise to a xenophobic opposition to Irishness based upon a purified national sense of identity, and a sense of themselves as an 'Elect People'. These stereotypes of Britishness and Irishness in turn were nurtured on the orderliness of the British and the social degradation and squalor in which the Irish in Britain were forced to live. Thus British historicism, together with English, Scottish and Welsh nationalism, emphasized the organic relationship between the imagined community of the Victorian nation and the territory that it inhabited. In conceiving of development as an organic and evolutionary process, the Victorians demonized the Irish and placed them at the hostile end of the continuum running from 'tradition' to 'modernity'. In conceiving of their culture as essentially elevating and ameliorative, the British looked on 'Irishness' as a demoralizing and degenerative force. Thus, for example, in J.W. Redfield's *Comparative Physiognomy*, published in 1852, the proverbial 'Irish eloquence' was equated with the 'barking of dogs'. Redfield wrote:

> Compare the Irish and the dog in respect to barking, snarling, howling, begging, fawning, flattering, backbiting, quarrelling, blustering, scenting, seizing, hanging on, teasing, rollicking, and whatever other traits you may discover in either, and you will be convinced that there is a wonderful resemblance.[11]

Viewed thus 'Irishness' was a form of social debasement. It was the ultimate source of physical and moral degradation, and a 'contagion' that could invade the body politic of Victorian Britain through emigration. It was also widely used to explain urban squalor in the Victorian city. Writing on the condition of the Irish working class as early as 1845, Friedrich Engels pointed to the fact that 'the worst quarters of all the large towns were inhabited by the Irish'.[12] An explanation for this urban squalor, and for disease, drunkenness and crime, was often found in the 'Irishness' of extremely deprived Irish districts of the Victorian city. The latter were seen to be apart from the urban landscape of Victorian gentility. They were instead perceived to be 'infested' by an 'alien' people who were the source of their own degradation. Thus racist discourse not only constructed Irishness as 'different' from Britishness – it stressed differences in 'origin' between the Irish and the British and did so in such a way as to locate the former culturally as well as biologically below the latter. Thus Mary Hickman suggests that:

> [. . .] documentary evidence of the nineteenth century reveals that both the type of jobs the Irish did in Britain and the

> conditions in which they were compelled to live were transmuted into corrobative evidence of their degenerative nature. Irish ghettoes became synonymous with disorderly conduct. This was usually attributed to the ingrained Irish habits of drunkenness and faction-fighting. The Irish, in particular the Irish Catholic working class, were constructed as both alien and inferior.[13]

By the latter half of the nineteenth century there was certainly no disagreement on the fundamental ontological difference between the Irish and the British. Neither was there any doubt about the borders that separated human spaces of 'Ireland' and 'Britain', and separated also Irish communities in Britain from British society at large. There was not a flicker of disagreement about the ontological differences between 'Little Irelands' in the Victorian city and Victorian society itself. Thus belief in the supremacy of the latter was not only accompanied by convictions regarding the supposed inferiority of the former. It was also associated with what Johann Fabian and Edward Said have termed 'a denial of coevalness' in time, and in a radical discontinuity in terms of human space.[14] Ireland, and especially 'offshoots' of it in Victorian Britain, were seen as places that had to be controlled and dominated by the British state because they were believed to be populated by a different species. It was not just that the English created 'representations' of Irishness the better to master and control the Irish. It made such representations in order to master and control the Irish, not least those in Britain. As Said has insisted, the dominating element in Western culture, especially in English Victorianism and in nineteenth-century French culture, distinguishes these from other cultures.[15] It also bestowed order and orderliness on Victorians and associated Irishness with republicanism and anarchy. Thus those who wrote on the 'Irish Question' in the late nineteenth century did not merely 'reproduce' Ireland as an 'outlying' territory adjacent to Britain. They worked these two racial categories out and animated them with an orderly species and a disorderly subspecies ever intent on invading Britain both from Ireland and from Irish ghettoes in 'mainland Britain'. They also insisted that the Irish in Ireland, and especially those in Britain, should be ruled because they were deemed 'inferior' to 'British people'.

The roots of anti-Irish racism are not only to be found in a late

Victorian social Darwinism. They are also traceable to a whole range of Victorian attitudes to culture and progress which linked these to orderliness, cleanliness, industry, temperance and deference to authority, and to the rootedness of Victorian ideals of self-improvement in Britain's social landscape. While the simianization of the Irish in Britain which this encouraged, particularly in the Darwinian half of the nineteenth century, emanated from the convergence of these deep-seated and powerful views on the nature of man and civilization in Victorian society, it also stemmed from ideas about the security of property and the 'worthiness' of Anglo-Saxon and aristocratic privilege in Victorian Britain. The latter, it was argued, was threatened by the influx of Irish immigrants, just as it was seen to be menaced by democracy, socialism, republicanism and Fenianism.[16] One convenient way of epitomizing these fears was to shift the burden of proximity to gorillas onto Irish immigrants; hence the Irish minority were portrayed as uncivilized 'outsiders' living inside British Victorian society.

There was a marked overlapping between anti-Irish sentiment and attitudes towards progress which went back to the circumstances in which Victorian Britain was conceived as a cradle for bourgeois respectability. The Irish were viewed as a stubbornly 'unmeltable' minority and seen as a threat to hegemonic notions of respectability and industry. They were considered gregarious social vagabonds and as such they were the bane of a settled modernity. They spurred political rulers and property-owners all over Britain into an 'ordering and legislating frenzy'.[17] As 'masterless vagabonds' it was feared that they might go on the loose and create havoc in the very heart of Victorian society. Thus when Henry Mayhew and John Binney published their report on criminals and English prisons in 1862 they described the children of the criminal Irish as beyond parental control and a threat to British civility. Here the Irish child grew up:

> [. . .] not only unacquainted with any industrial occupation, but untrained to habits of daily work, and long before he has learned to control the desire to appropriate the articles which he either wants or likes, by a sense of the rights of property in others, *he has acquired furtive propensities from association with the young thieves located in the neighbourhood.*[18]

Just when Victorianism made *civility* the order of the day, the 'disorderly' Irish arrived and threatened to 'contaminate' British society.

Anti-Irish racism of this genre was not an epiphenomenal diversion from more hegemonic forms of British racism. Neither was it an inchoate expression of social prejudice; it had all the characteristics of a Foucauldian discourse as defined by Michel Foucault in his *Archaeology of Knowledge* and in *Discipline and Punish*.[19] As such it was a strategy for marginalizing and dealing with the Irish. Thus this discourse did not simply identify the Irish in Britain as the 'other'; rather it treated them as the 'opposite' to the settled Victorians and viewed thus the Irish constituted a threat precisely because they were outside respectable society. They were, moreover, outsiders in a moral and a geographical sense. A politics of exclusion emerged and had given rise to a geography of closure in the course of the nineteenth century which excluded the Irish from 'respectable' communities. This geography of closure may be regarded as a Victorian variant of contemporary 'blood and soil' nationalism which is currently excluding Turkish and Islamic minorities from the mainstreams of European life and relegating them to the closed world of the ethnic ghetto.[20] The sheer 'clubbiness' of English, Scottish and Welsh society in the nineteenth century was one of their fundamental characteristic features. This made it all the more difficult for the Irish to 'fit in' here. Although they clearly occupied an important economic space in nineteenth-century Britain, the Irish were always forced to look on from the margins and from outside at most of Victorian society's social and cultural rhythms. Iain Chambers has suggested that British culture at this time was found, both in the temporal and symbolic sense, to exist beyond the mechanical rhythms and commercial logic of industrial society.[21] The 'unending moral clarity and purpose' of this Britain mapped it out as an essentially 'upright and decent' place where the Irish, both as economic refugees and as perpetrators of 'Fenian outrages', had great difficulty in constructing a place for themselves. The Manichean view of Britain which this perception of itself fostered portrayed it as a country of civilized 'insiders' invaded by 'hordes' of fearful and alien 'outsiders'. In a *Report on Poor Removal* in 1884 the Irish were described as flooding into England with 'pestilence on their backs, and famine in their stomachs'.[22] While the needs of rational capitalism dictated that Irish labourers could not be excluded from expanding British cities, particularly from the expanding industrial frontier towns in the north of England and lowland Scotland, anti-Irish racism here fused with a proprietorial sense of place to create quasi-biological constructs of communities as kith and kin from which the Irish were radically excluded. What made this all the easier to achieve was the fact that the Irish generally bypassed many of the older bastions of English Victorianism. They gravitated instead to the port cities, new towns and the expanding industrial heartlands of nineteenth-century Britain. By the third quarter of the century they were especially visible in the towns of central Scotland and in large urban centres like Liverpool, London, Manchester, Birmingham, Bradford, Leeds and Newcastle. They also settled, albeit in smaller numbers, in the south Wales towns of Swansea, Merthyr Tydfil and Newport. By the close of the century their numbers in London and Liverpool had dropped, if only slightly, and the Irish now began to be more dispersed throughout the urban hierarchy. From then on towns like Middlesborough, Bolton, Barrow, Halifax and Portsmouth all attracted large numbers of Irish immigrants.[23]

Not being any part of the 'Elect People', the Irish in Britain were also clearly outside the pale of a moralizing Victorian Evangelicalism. This creed of an Elect People, a principal element in late Victorian imperialism, had driven plebeian and cruder kinds of extravagance and profligacy underground. It also established a code of social and moral behaviour for all who wished to stand well with their fellows. The moralizing society which the Victorians constructed rendered social disapproval a force which only the boldest sinners might fear. Thus Evangelicalism:

> imposed upon English society, even on classes which were indifferent to its religious bias and unaffected by its economic appeal, its code of Sabbath observance, responsibility, philanthropy; of discipline in the home, regularity in affairs; it had created a most effective technique of agitation, of private persuasion and social persecution.[24]

The social history of the Irish in this Britain is largely one of rebellion against an Evangelical English mind-set. The Irish used all the energy at their disposal to rid their 'Little Irelands' here of all the restraints which Evangelicalism had laid upon the senses, upon the intellect, upon amusement and enjoyment, and upon plebeian culture, curiosity and criticism in Victorian society at large. Thus if Ireland was considered 'an uneasy place in the body politic' of Victorian Britain, the Irish in Britain were considered even more of an oddity. They could be neither forgotten, ignored nor assuaged. If the 'Irishry' in Ireland were considered irrational because they sought to 'misgovern' themselves as Catholics and smallholders, the Irish in Britain, through their association with 'disorder' and drunkenness, were a 'pestilence' which the government was determined to stamp out. The success of state policies relating to them depended upon what Said has termed 'a flexible positional superiority'. This gave the state control over them as 'foreigners'.[25] It also meant that the Irish in Britain often found themselves immersed in other populations, and in other people's communities. On the one hand they were an integral, albeit an ethnically distinct part of the labouring classes. On the other hand they were rigidly set apart from settled communities by their nomadic and migratory ways and by their 'foreign' Catholic ways.

IRISH IMMIGRANTS AS A 'MUTANT PEOPLE'

While this discourse portrayed Anglo-Saxons as rigidly and rightly rooted in the very soil of Britain, the Irish here were a 'hybrid' or 'rootless' people. They dwelt as much in 'imaginary homelands' of the mind, and in the safe domesticity of their own humble homes, as in any real places. They were products of emigration who were subsequently forged upon the anvil of anti-Irish racism in Britain. If mass emigration gradually created a new society in Ireland in the course of the late nineteenth century, mass immigration reproduced a 'hybrid' Irish people in late Victorian Britain. It thus created radically 'new types' of Irish people here, as well as in the United States.

J.A. Jackson has shown how background, the past and home were all congealed into one through emigration and built a landscape of the mind that was then inhabited by the Irish emigrant. The Irish were thus also forced to define themselves because other people constantly defined and denigrated them. As Rushdie suggests:

> To migrate is [. . .] to lose language and home, to be defined by others, to become invisible or, even worse, a target; it is to experience deep changes and wrenches in the soul.

He then goes on to argue that:

> [The] migrant is not simply transformed by his act; he also transforms his new world. Migrants may well become mutants, but it is out of such hybridization that newness can emerge.[26]

The economic and cultural displacement of the Irish in the nineteenth century certainly resulted in new forms of their social and political degradation both in Britain and in the United States. The Irish actively fought against all forms of such degradation. In the end they were forced to define themselves because others constantly defined them. They particularly defined themselves in terms of their 'otherness' and perceived themselves as a 'mutant people'. In their deepest selves strange fusions occurred, unprecedented unions between what they were and where they happened to find themselves.[27] What Rushdie says of the modern migrant's sensibility to cultural displacement is equally applicable to Irish emigrants at this time. The migrant, he argues,

> [. . .] *suspects reality*; having experienced several ways of being, he understands their illusionary nature. To see things plainly, you have to cross a frontier [. . .]. *Migrants must, of necessity, make a new imaginative relationship with the world, because of the loss of familiar habitats.*[28] (emphasis added)

As we have already seen, racist discourse constructed these 'hybrid' Irish as a potentially traitorous people. The Irish were also perceived as having all the characteristics which rendered them ever-prone to uncivilized behaviour. This discourse particularly stressed the 'shiftiness', the 'backwardness' and 'rootlessness' of the Irish in a sedentary, progressive society like late Victorian Britain. The very categorization of the Irish minority in Britain as 'rootless vagabonds', as the 'shock troops' of modern British capitalism, would have been quite familiar to the Donegal poet-navvy Patrick MacGill. His poetry and novels portray labouring Irishmen in late nineteenth- and early twentieth-century Britain as 'children of the dead-end'. Their abodes in 'the rat-pits' of

Victorian Britain grind them down into poverty and degradation. Nevertheless the Irish in his poetry and novels also 'conquer the wildernesses of Britain'. They are responsible for damming its turbulent waters, binding its torrents with bridges, battering down its mountain-cliffs, turning its wastes to a garden, and finally moulding its rocky landscape to one of towns and civilization. Indeed the labouring Irish in MacGill's writing construct the basis of a British capitalist economy, only to find themselves outcasts from Ireland and outcasts in British society. They are at once 'aliens' in Britain and alienated from the physical and industrial landscape which they helped to construct. His poem 'Serfs' is a particularly poignant portrayal of this 'outcastness' of Irish navvies in England and Scotland. Here the Irish live in 'primitive fastnesses' and are treated 'more like brutes than like men':

> They're huddled in rat-riddled cabins, stuck in the feculent fen,
> Where the red searing heat of the summer purges them drier than bone,
> Where Medusa-faced winter in turn stiffens their limbs into stone.
> Hemmed-up like fleas in the fissures, sweated like swine in the silt,
> So that your deserts be conquered, so that your mansion be built.
> Hair-poised on the joist or the copestone, and swept by the billowing gales,
> Handling their burdens of granite, bearing their mortar-piled pails,
> Pacing the tremulous gang-planks as the trestles are bent by the wind,
> With death and danger before them, and danger and death behind.

For MacGill the Irish in Britain are forced to endure a double exile – they are exiles from Ireland who are often forced to live in exile from English, Scottish and Welsh society. For MacGill these Irish emigrants are:

> [. . .] our serfs and our bondmen, slighted, forsaken, outcast,
> Hewing the path of the future, heirs to the wrongs of the past,

> Forespent in the vanguard of progress, vagrant, untutored, unskilled, [. . .]
> Building the homes of the haughty, rearing the mansions of worth –
> Wanderers lost to the wide world, hell-harried slaves of the earth,
> Visionless, dreamless, and voiceless children of worry and care,
> Sweltering, straining and striving under the burdens they bear –
> Stretches the future before them clouded and bleak as their past
> They are our serfs and our brothers, slighted, forsaken, outcast.[29]

No better portrait of the Irish as 'the wretched of the British earth' exists. Excluded from the moral geometry of nation-building Ireland, they were also radically excluded from the political and moral structures of nation-building Britain. The places where they lived were euphemistically called 'Irish towns', even 'Little Irelands'. These were never places in their own right. They were racial constructs built at the racist outer edge of British society, as much products of anti-Irish racism as expressions of Irish ethnicity. As racially constructed local worlds carved out in the narrow ground available to the Irish in Victorian Britain, they were a world apart from rural Ireland and from Irish nationalist ideals of Irishness. They were filled with immigrants for whom emigration had been a 'wrenching' experience which 'lifted' young adults from the hearts of rural communities and deposited them in alien urban environments where they were proletarianized into the lowest echelons of the industrial and agricultural labour force. In the apt phrase in the title of Ruth Ann Harris's recent study of labour migration from Ireland in the pre-Famine years, the Irish here lived in *The Nearest Place That Wasn't Ireland*.[30] John Berger describes the position of Irish emigrants in mid-nineteenth-century Britain thus:

> In their new situation they were without a trade. They had to accept low wages. They were mobile. They were disorganized. They were seen by the English working class as inferiors, and were accused by them of cutting wages. They lived in the worst slums, which became Irish ghettos. They worked as navvies,

> dockers, steel-workers, and they were indispensable to the building of the physical installations necessary for the expansion of British industry after the invention of the steam engine.[31]

Marx and Engels were among the first to examine the racialization and ethnicization of relations between the indigenous working class and new arrivals on the arena of working class politics in Victorian Britain. They particularly emphasized the links between the process of capital accumulation, core-formation and peripheralization, and the consequent internationalization of rural poor and working class communities in nineteenth-century Scotland and Ireland.[32] For Engels indeed:

> The rapid extension of English industry could not have taken place if England had not possessed in the numerous and impoverished population of Ireland a reserve at command. The Irish had nothing to lose at home, and much to gain in England; and from time to time when it became known in Ireland that the east side of the Irish Sea offered steady work and good pay for strong arms, every year brought armies of the Irish thither.[33]

Marx showed that the global division of labour which emerged throughout the latter half of the century suited the core areas of the world economy. It converted 'one part of the globe into a chiefly agricultural field of production for supplying the other part which remains a chiefly industrial field'.[34] He also stressed the importance of labour pools in rural Ireland and the Scottish Highlands to the development of the core areas of British capitalism. Thus he regarded the Highland clearances and the rural exodus from Ireland as serving identical ends – the creation of viable fields of agricultural production in post-peasant Scotland and Ireland and the simultaneous transformation into 'emigrant nurseries' where capital accumulation could proceed unhindered.[35]

THE POLITICAL GEOGRAPHY OF ANTI-IRISH RACISM IN BRITAIN

Robert Miles has argued that the social and economic inferiority of migrant workers in the metropolitan world often justified their classification as *unfree labour*. As migrants they were:

> citizens of proximate social formations, and therefore 'aliens' as far as the state of the social formation where they sold their labour was concerned. The state in the social formation of recruitment therefore had to devise a legal and administrative mechanism which would allow the entry and residence of persons defined as 'foreigners' and which would regulate their activities once having emigrated.[36]

This was also the case with Irish workers in Britain in the nineteenth century, since on entering the British social formation, Irish immigrants also entered a web of state-defined restrictions and regulated rights which affected the way they reproduced themselves and their families outside Ireland. The *scale* of Irish labour migration to Britain at this time, together with the *size* of the 'foreign' Irish working class in Britain suggest that 'unfree' Irish labour was not peripheral to the expansion and reproduction of capitalism in Britain. The Irish constituted between 15 and 20 per cent of the total population of cities like Liverpool, Glasgow and Dundee in the mid-nineteenth century. They were between one tenth and one sixth of the population of cities like Bristol, Birmingham, Newcastle and Edinburgh. Anti-Irish racism provided the ideological justification for the 'unfreeness' of this ethnically-defined working class. It also gave the state power to commodify the power of Irish labour and to rationalize restrictions on its upward mobility. This meant that anti-Irish racism was an important element in the formation and reproduction of free and unfree relations of production in nineteenth-century Britain. It in turn was responsible for the production and reproduction of particular cultural forms, and for social class formation and class factions both in Irish society in Britain and in British society. Whilst the Irish contributed to core-formation and the expansion of urban and rural capitalism in nineteenth-century Britain, their labour power was a hidden transfer of value from rural Ireland to industrial Britain. As such it was a form of 'development aid' from the colony to the colonizer.[37] There was a geography to this 'aid' which was reflected in the settlement patterns of Irish immigrants, most of whom located in low amenity urban areas in the north of England and lowland Scotland. They chiefly 'settled' in 'Irish towns' and 'Little Irelands' in expanding conurbations where the labour market was already ethnically-stratified and where opportunities for social advancement were few and far between.

The need for Irish labour in these areas reflected important qualitative and quantitative developments in British capitalism. The form of these developments was such that it led to increased reliance on Irish workers to perform particular tasks in the urban and rural landscapes of mainland Britain. One Manchester employer outlined the reasons for employing Irish labourers as follows:

> The Irish are employed in this town, not because they are preferred to the English, but because they are necessary, or perhaps because they are here. There are not English enough to supply the demand. The English from the country parishes would not be suited to the work of the towns; the Irish adapt themselves more speedily to it, and are more importunate: they thrust themselves forward more.[38]

Another commentator at the time claimed that the Irish were more migratory and had all the attributes of racially 'inferior' nomadic peoples who fortuitously lived at England's back door, and at English employers' 'beck and call'. Commenting on the scarcity of 'native workers' in the industrial heartland of mid-England, he further stated:

> The reason why no English come from the pauperized parishes in the southern counties is [that] the distress is more recent; in Ireland, the poverty is of long standing. Perhaps the greatest reason is the English are settled in their parishes, and the Irish are not.[39]

Prevailing attitudes towards race and the colonies suggested that Irish workers were best suited for the type of work and occupations that the economic expansion of British capitalism required. Thus, while the stage of capitalist development made it necessary for English and Scottish employers to transcend the boundaries of national labour markets, the nature of that development, and the prevalence of racial attitudes, suggested that Irish workers, and workers from other 'internal colonies' like the Highlands of Scotland and the Welsh valleys, were best suited for these jobs.[40] This meant that immigrants from Ireland were not only proletarianized into the British labour market. They had to accept conditions, and had to occupy positions deemed by the indigenous working class to be beneath them or against their interests.

'IRISHNESS' AND URBAN SQUALOR IN VICTORIAN BRITAIN

As we have already seen, anti-Irish racism was closely associated with the urban squalor in which many of the urban Irish poor lived. The concentration of the Irish in low-status, often migratory work, exacerbated this racism. Fear of this genre of 'low life' hung like a spectre over 'respectable' classes in Victorian Britain. Graham Davis suggests that this fear of a 'moral cess-pool' that could threaten, even destroy, the moral and political institutions of respectable society, was central to Victorian constructions of the Irish as an inferior people.[41] The *Report on the State of the Irish Poor in Great Britain* in 1836 regarded Irish migration to Britain as 'an example of a less civilized population spreading themselves as a kind of substratum beneath a more civilized community'.[42] The language used by sanitary reformers to describe the living conditions of the Irish was often indistinguishable from that which condemned them as morally corrupt. In this class-based, racist discourse, what begins as a description of the 'contagion' of disease and urban squalor, ends with an explanation of Irishness as the source of contagion. J.P. Kay, secretary to the Special Board for the Board of Health, writing at the height of a cholera outbreak in Manchester in 1832, described living in Irish districts of the city as follows:

> This unhealthy spot lies *so low* that the chimneys of its houses, some of them three storeys high, are *little above the level of the road.* About two hundred of these habitations are crowded together in an extremely narrow space, and they are chiefly inhabited by the *lowest Irish.* Many of these houses have also cellars, whose floor is *scarcely elevated* above the level of the water flowing in the [river] Medlock. [. . .] The district has sometimes been the haunt of hordes of thieves and desperadoes who defied the law, and is always *inhabited by a class resembling savages in their appetites and habits.* It is surrounded on every side by some of the *highest factories* of the town, whose chimneys vomit forth dense clouds of smoke, which *hang heavily over the insalubrious region.*[43]

The Irish also aroused deep hostility among the indigenous working class because of their role as 'checks on combination'. This was how one employer saw Irish workers in the first half of the nineteenth century:

> The Irish have, in those branches of industry which could be easily taught, either to children or adults, been a check on the combination of the English and Scotch of the western counties, as they could be brought over almost in any numbers, at short notice, and at little expense. Thus not only can the Irish be put into the place of the natives, if the latter turn out, but the natives sometime abstain from turning out, in the consciousness that their places can be immediately filled.[44]

Contrary to a dominant nationalist, and essentially racist discourse, the socio-economic and political subordination of the Irish in Britain did not reflect the racist essence of British society.[45] It did not stem from an inveterate hatred of 'the Irish' by 'the British'. It was instead a socio-political, historical, even geographical construction. As we have already seen it was thus central to the social and geographical expansion of capitalism in a wide variety of regional and social class contexts in nineteenth-century Britain. Ireland, as we have also seen, supplied cheap and abundant labour to the core areas of the British and North American economies. This meant that the historic relationship between colonizer and colonized which had traditionally linked Britain to Ireland since the opening years of the seventeenth century now gave way to new relationships between ex-colonial subjects and British employers within Britain. While migration from the colony to England clearly involved a change in the location of the relationship between colonizer and colonized, it did not involve any fundamental change in the nature of that relationship. Thus the Irish, like other 'unmeltable ethnics' such as the Scots and the Welsh, were expected to subordinate their identities to that of their host society. In this discourse indeed Ireland was portrayed as an overpopulated and impoverished country which poured forth its most destitute offspring on prosperous Britain. The Irish here were then scapegoats who served as a convenient explanation for the squalor and depravity of urban life in the Victorian era. They were everywhere regarded as a serious social evil. As one commentator stated:

> The Irish have taught the labouring classes of this country a pernicious lesson [. . .]. Debased alike by ignorance and pauperism they have discovered, with the savage, what is the minimum of the means of life, upon which existence may be

> prolonged [. . .]. As competition and the restriction and burdens of trade diminished the profits of capital, and consequently reduced the price of labour, the contagious example of ignorance and a barbarous disregard of forethought and economy exhibited by the Irish, spread.[46]

Not surprisingly, given these attitudes to the Irish poor in Britain, many in Victorian England accepted the legitimacy of labelling the Irish as 'foreigners' and 'barbarous' and their social inferiority was frequently legitimized in racial terms.

Stephen Castles has argued that the imposition of the citizenship of the colonizer on the colonized was an ideological instrument of domination in the age of empire.[47] For reasons that we have already discussed, the imposition of British citizenship upon Irish immigrants was fraught with difficulties not only because the Irish frequently lived a segregated life away from the centres of high Victorianism, but also because the geography of exclusion practised against them tended to exclude the Irish from the mainstreams of British life. From the point of view of employers however, Irish labourers could not, and would not be excluded from the economic landscape of Britain. As a highly mobile and expendable labour force, Irish workers were just what the new industrial system needed. Core-periphery *and* race relations between Ireland and Britain entered a new stage at this time. This added a new sharpness to anti-Irish racism in Britain. Larger and larger numbers of migrant workers from colonial Ireland were now exploited in Britain, rather than in Ireland. The history of their exile and presence in metropolitan Britain rightly belongs with the history of colonialism and neo-colonialism. The Irish here were the 'shock troops' of British capitalism. They not only provided cheap labour that undercut the wages of English, Scottish and Welsh workers – they acted as strike breakers who often obstructed the wider cause of British trade unionism and working class progress. While all this is quite familiar to students of British labour history in the nineteenth century, it deserves re-emphasis here if we are to counterbalance the exaltation of the Irish in British labour politics and in trade union organization by those writers who have ignored the anti-union activities of large numbers of Irish workers.

What made nineteenth-century anti-Irish racism all the more significant was the fact that revolutionary developments in the organization and functioning of communications had linked Ireland to the core areas of Britain, and to the world economy. This transformed the world wherein Ireland found itself from a functioning geographic unit composed of separate but interdependent economies, into a space of 'unified and monopolized communications in which, potentially at least, all populations were somehow immediately visible to, and in contact with, one another'.[48] This in turn exacerbated racial tensions between Irish workers and those of the host country and transformed racially and ethnically mixed inner city areas into contested domains where the 'foreign' Irish were seen as having no legitimate rights. Rodolpho Stavenhagen has argued that the stratifications arising from such status groupings were 'social fixations'. They were created by juridical means and maintained by specific social relations of production and social class relationships.[49] He further elaborates:

> Into these social fixations intrude other secondary, accessory factors (for example, religious, ethnic) which reinforce the stratification and which have, at the same time, the function of 'liberating it of its economic base changes'. Consequently, stratifications can be thought of as justifications or rationalizations of the established economic system, that is to say, as ideologies. Like all phenomena of the social superstructure, stratification has a quality of inertia which maintains it even when the conditions which gave it birth have changed. As the relations between classes are modified [. . .] stratifications turn themselves into *fossils* of the class relations on which they were originally based.[50]

In nineteenth-century Britain these racial stratifications arose out of the need to maintain core-periphery antimony between Britain and Ireland. While nationalism threatened to divide core from periphery in an intrazonal division of power, racial categorizations of the Irish in Britain reflected competition *between* native and foreigner in a racially and ethnically-ordered landscape and in an hierarchically-structured social order.[51] Similarly, while technical innovations in communication transformed the way the Irish and British economies increasingly functioned as one economy, they did not transform attitudes towards the Irish in Britain. Neither did they 'soften' British attitudes towards the Irish in Ireland and may in fact have hardened them. Discussing the origins of neo-racism in 'Fortress Europe' since the 1980s, Etienne Balibar has traced its roots to the changing relationships between the old colonial powers and the Third World. Thus he elaborates:

> the *'two humanities'* which have been culturally and socially separated by capitalist development – opposites figuring in racist ideology as 'sub men' and 'supermen', 'underdeveloped' and 'overdeveloped' – do not remain external to each other, kept apart by long distances and related only 'at the margins'. On the contrary, they interpenetrate more and more within the same space of communications, representations and life. Exclusion takes the form of *internal exclusion at world level*: precisely the configuration which, since the beginnings of the modern era, has fuelled not only xenophobia or fear of foreigners, but also racism as fear and hatred of *neighbours* who are near and different at the same time.[52] (emphasis in original)

This precisely describes the changing relationship between Britain and Ireland in the nineteenth century. The 'colony struck back' at the colonizer by arriving in larger and larger numbers on the shores of the colonizer's home country. This created a new deeply-contested multi-ethnic and multi-racial space wherein labour, capital, technology and racist constructs of 'insiders' and 'outsiders' freely circulated. Here was also a space wherein populations were subjected to the laws of supply and demand, and where 'foreign Irish workers' came into physical and symbolic contact with English, Scottish and Welsh workers, often for the first time. This fostered a highly ambivalent and deeply equivocal interiority-exteriority configuration which separated out Irish migrants from indigenous rural and working class communities. This formed one of the structuring dimensions of a modern anti-Irish racism which was reproduced, expanded and re-activated in a variety of socio-regional contexts throughout the nineteenth and well into the twentieth century. This interiority-exteriority configuration suggested that the 'inferiority' of the Irish in Britain was culturally and environmentally determined. It also had clear geographical connotations. Thus one description of Little Ireland in mid-nineteenth-century Manchester is as follows:

> The *physical ghetto consisted of both external and internal features.* Black smoke, polluted rivers, unpaved streets, the smell of pig sties, privies, open sewers, coupled with the filthy, cramped

> dwellings with *their barren, damp interiors, all created a miserable existence for the Irish of Little Ireland.*[53] (emphasis added)

Engels wrote of the inhabitants of these ghettos in the early 1840s in the following terms:

> *The Irishman loves his pig as the Arab his horse,* with the difference that he sells it when it is fat enough to kill. Otherwise he eats and sleeps with it, his children play with it, ride upon it, roll in the dirt with it, as anyone may see a thousand times repeated in all the great towns of England.[54] (emphasis added)

Another account of the Irish in Scotland described how human urine and their own excrement was used by the Irish for eventual sale as manure. Here indeed the Irish – born in Britain – are indistinguishable from the produce of their own dungheaps. They are:

> [. . .] worse off than wild animals, many of which withdraw to a distance to conceal their ordure [. The] dwellers in these courts had converted their shame into a kind of money by which their lodging was paid.[55]

In Charles Booth's survey of the London poor in the late Victorian period, the Irish were still living in social conditions similar to those that prevailed in the worst 'rookeries' of the city in the mid-nineteenth century. Thus Booth reported that:

> They live in the drains and haunt the canal barges and factories, wherever there may be anything they can eat, and on a summer morning after a shower they come out in their thousands.[56]

An account of the Irish in Glasgow in 1842 matched their living conditions with their social, moral and physical degradation such that the latter was the consequence of the former. Here indeed the Irish are portrayed as living and breeding like urban rabbits in 'warrens' of the lowest order:

> There are no privies or drains there, and the dungheaps received all the filth which the swarm of wretched inhabitants could give; and we learnt that a considerable part of the rent of the houses was paid by the produce of the dungheaps [. . .]. In

> [their] interiors these houses and their inmates correspond with the exteriors. We saw half-dressed wretches crowding together to be warm; and in one bed, although in the middle of the day, several women were imprisoned under a blanket, because as many of the others who had on their backs all the articles of dress that belonged to the party were out of doors in the street.[57]

Balibar suggests that this form of *interiorization of the exterior* marks the horizon against which the representations of 'race' and 'ethnicity' are played out against a background of apparently antithetical forms of exteriorization of the interior. The latter, he argued:

> cannot be separated from those which result from the formation – after the more or less complete departure of the colonizers – of states which claim to be national (but only become so very unequally) throughout the immense periphery of the planet, with their explosive antagonisms between capitalist bourgeoisies or 'Westernized' state bourgeoisies and wretched masses, thrown back by this very fact upon 'traditionalism'.[58]

CONCLUSION

The formation of a 'national' society under bourgeois nationalist hegemony in nineteenth-century Ireland was predicated upon large-scale emigration. Not the least of the ironies surrounding the study of the latter was the fact that emigration was traditionally portrayed, particularly by nationalists, as a 'blight' on Irish society, a 'blight', moreover, that was said to have been brought on by British 'misrule' in Ireland. This chapter has shown how Victorians also looked on Irish emigration to Britain as a 'blight', one that 'invaded' the body politic of Victorian society and was widely perceived as a threat to the social fabric of that society. It has portrayed emigrants as a 'hybrid' people who were 'double victims' of the nation-building process. On the one hand they were social class victims of structural changes in Irish society who were 'banished' from Ireland as a result of structural changes taking place in the Irish economy throughout the nineteenth century. On the other hand they were 'shackled' by the nationalism of Victorian Britain and this caused them to be treated as an inferior 'dirty people'.

In the Darwinian half of the century the idea of race was increasingly used to define the Irish in Britain, to explain their social behaviour, to essentialize their social and cultural practices and to legitimize their relegation to the outer edges of Victorian society. Thus just when 'ethnicity' was used, both in Ireland and in Britain, to construct positive, quasi-biological national societies, when applied as a classificatory category 'race' was used against the Irish in Britain. As such it reflected negative tendencies of dissociation and exclusion at national and community level. The racialization of the Irish minority here reflected widespread assumptions about their racial inferiority. It also suggested that their growth, regional distribution and social status should be carefully monitored if they were not to get out of control in Victorian Britain. This chapter has also been at pains to stress that the 'idea' of race is not a universal phenomenon. It emerges instead from specific national, regional, social, class and historical circumstances. History, and indeed historical geography, suggest that the 'idea' of race rarely remains at the level of pure theory or 'ideology'. The closure of the gap separating peripheral capitalism in Ireland from the core areas of industrial and rural capitalism in Britain was partially effected through emigration. This contributed to, and probably exacerbated, the racialization of the Irish in Britain and gave new political significance to race thinking in Victorian Britain. As Irish emigrants spilled across the borders separating Ireland from Britain, particularly when they asserted claims to social justice, a new and more aggressive form of anti-Irish racism emerged in British society. This was a racism of 'radical disavowal' in that the Irish here were now attacked because they sought to acquire rights and properties in Britain, and to espouse social values which British nationals felt were their prerogative. This genre of anti-Irish racism was indistinguishable from expressions of grassroots Victorian nationalism in nineteenth-century Britain.

Notes

1. M. Hechter, *Internal Colonialism: The Celtic Fringe in British National Development* (Berkeley: University of California Press, 1975); J. Mac Laughlin, 'Place, Politics and Culture in Nation-Building Ulster', *Canadian Review of Studies in Nationalism*, 20: 4 (1993), 236–57.

2. B. Anderson, *Imagined Communities: Reflections on the Origin and Spread of Nationalism* (London: Verso, 1983).
3. E.P. Thompson, *The Making of the English Working Class* (Harmondsworth: Pelican, 1968).
4. E.E. Cashmore, *A Dictionary of Race Relations* (London: Routledge, 1984), p. 97.
5. V. Kiernan, *The Lords of Humankind* (Harmondsworth: Pelican, 1972).
6. S. Rushdie, *Imaginary Homelands* (London: Penguin, 1992), p. 124.
7. L.P. Curtis, *Apes and Angels: The Irishman in Victorian Caricature* (Washington: Smithsonian Institution Press, 1971), p. 1.
8. L.P. Curtis, *Apes and Angels*, p. 95–6.
9. See M. Arnold, *Culture and Anarchy* (London: Macmillan, 1869).
10. E.W. Said, *Culture & Imperialism* (London: Verso, 1994), p. xiv.
11. J.W. Redfield, *Comparative Physiognomy* (London: Grenville, 1852), p. 78.
12. F. Engels, *The Condition of the English Working Class in 1844* (Stanford: Stanford University Press, 1959).
13. M. Hickman, 'The Irish in Britain', *Irish Studies Review*, 10 (1995), 16.
14. J. Fabian, *Time and the Other: How Anthropology Makes Its Object* (New York: Columbia University Press, 1983), p. 83; E.W. Said, *Culture and Imperialism*, p. 130.
15. E.W. Said, *Culture and Imperialism*, p. 231.
16. L.P. Curtis, *Apes and Angels*, p. 21.
17. S. Bauman, *Life in Fragments* (London: Blackwell, 1995).
18. H. Mayhew and J. Binney, *The Criminal Prisons of London* (London: Charles Griffin, 1862), p. 67.
19. M. Foucault, *Discipline and Punish: The Birth of the Prison* (New York: Vintage, 1979); *The Archaeology of Knowledge* (London: Routledge, 1989).
20. J. Mac Laughlin, 'Defending the Frontiers: The Political Geography of Race and Racism in the European Community' in *The Political Geography of the New World Order*, ed. C. Williams (London: Bellhaven Press, 1993), pp. 20–45.
21. I. Chambers, 'Narratives of Nationalism: Being British' in *Space and Place: Theories of Identity and Location*, eds E. Carter, J. Donald and J. Squires (London: Lawrence and Wishart, 1993), pp. 145–64.
22. *Report of Poor Removal* (London: William and Clowes, 1884), p. 305.
23. C. Pooley, 'Segregation or Integration? The Residential Experience of the Irish in mid-Victorian Britain' in *The Irish in Britain 1815–1939*, eds R. Swift and S. Gilley (London: Pinter, 1989), pp. 61–74.
24. G.M. Young, *Victorian England* (Oxford: Oxford University Press, 1969), p. 5.
25. E.W. Said, *Orientalism* (Harmondsworth: Pelican, 1991).
26. S. Rushdie, *Imaginary Homelands*.
27. S. Rushdie, *Imaginary Homelands*, p. 124.
28. S. Rushdie, *Imaginary Homelands*, p. 125.
29. P. MacGill, *Songs of the Dead End* (London: Yearbook Press, 1914), pp. 45–6.
30. R. Harris, *The Nearest Place That Wasn't Ireland* (Ames, Iowa: Iowa State University Press, 1994).
31. J. Berger and J. Mohr, *A Seventh Man* (Harmondsworth: Pelican, 1975), p. 108.

32. K. Marx, *Capital* (London: Lawrence and Wishart, 1961); K. Marx and F. Engels, *Selected Works* (Moscow: Moscow Press, 1975).
33. F. Engels, *Condition of the Working Class.*
34. K. Marx, *Capital*, p. 451.
35. J. Mac Laughlin, *Historical and Recent Irish Emigration* (London: University of North London Press, 1994); J. Mac Laughlin, *Ireland: The Emigrant Nursery and the World Economy* (Cork: Cork University Press, 1994).
36. R. Miles, *Capitalism and Unfree Labour* (London: Tavistock, 1987), p. 160.
37. R. Miles, *Capitalism and Unfree Labour*, p. 165.
38. *Report on the State of the Irish Poor in Great Britain* (London: Reports from Committee, 1836) Vol. 34, p. 39.
39. *Report on the State of the Irish Poor in Great Britain*, p. 84.
40. Hechter, *Internal Colonialism.*
41. G. Davis, 'Little Irelands' in *The Irish in Britain 1815–1939*, pp. 109–10.
42. *Report on the State of the Irish Poor in Great Britain*, p. 39.
43. G. Davis, 'Little Irelands', p. 110.
44. R. Harris, *The Nearest Place*, p. 153.
45. C. Phillips, *The European Tribe* (London: Faber, 1987), p. 178.
46. Quoted in G. Davis, 'Little Irelands', p. 110.
47. S. Castles et al., *Here for Good* (London: Pluto, 1984), p. 92.
48. E. Balibar and I. Wallerstein, *Race and Nation* (New York: Sage, 1991), p. 14.
49. R. Stavenhagen, *Agrarian Problems and Peasant Movements in Latin America* (New York: Doubleday, 1962), p. 99.
50. R. Stavenhagen, *Agrarian Problems and Peasant Movements in Latin America*, p. 101.
51. I. Wallerstein, *Geopolitics and Geoculture* (New York: Cambridge University Press, 1991), p. 82.
52. E. Balibar and I. Wallerstein, *Race and Nation*, p. 14.
53. Quoted in G. Davis, 'Little Irelands', p. 64.
54. F. Engels, *Condition of the Working Class*, p. 85.
55. *Report on the Sanitary Condition of the Labouring Population of Scotland* (London: HMSO, 1842), p. 24.
56. C. Booth, *Life and Labour of the People in London* (London: Macmillan, 1892), p. 47.
57. *Report on Sanitary Condition*, pp. 8–9.
58. E. Balibar and I. Wallerstein, *Race and Class*, pp. 43–4.

5

Gendered Irishness in Britain: Changing Constructions

Bronwen Walter

INTRODUCTION

The paradox of Irishness in Britain is that it is simultaneously outside and inside the national fold. On the one hand, the Irish have been constructed as 'other' for centuries, the longest-standing representation of what British people are not. On the other hand, the taken-for-granted inclusion of the Irish is central to recognition of 'the British Isles' upon which narratives of heroic independence are based, and from which more recent 'others' can be excluded.

Images of Irishness are not gender-neutral. Their representations are inscribed on bodies whose gender is integral to processes of construction of national identities. This chapter explores continuities and transformations in constructions of gendered Irish identities in Britain, and their material consequences for emigrant women.

RACIALIZED CONSTRUCTIONS OF IRISHNESS

The Irish have been racialized as inferior for centuries.[1] In the twelfth century Geraldus Cambrensis compared Irish dirt, vice and superstition with English civilization, and in the sixteenth century moral depravity and barbarism were used to justify the Cromwellian conquests.[2] However these representations assumed their most extreme forms in the later nineteenth century. L.P. Curtis[3] traces the growth between 1860 and 1880 of the monstrous images used to depict the Irish in cartoons aimed at middle- and upper-class English readers. Their currency was closely related to increasing political unrest in Ireland which threatened to undermine the Union. Attempts to keep the Irish 'in their place' relied on representations which drew on a variety of gendered imagery.

Racialization based on explicitly physical bodily characteristics was supported by the rise of scientific racism in the second half of the nineteenth century. Measurements of 'nigrescence' and the 'facial angle index' proved the 'white negro' status of the Irish, and provided 'a scientific basis for assuming characteristics of violence, poverty, improvidence, political volatility and drunkenness'.[4] Depictions of Irish people in both Ireland and Britain were almost exclusively male images, reproduced visually as depraved human and sub-human figures. *Punch* cartoons often showed Irish men as apes. Since only males were entitled to the public space of citizenship and formal political activity, they could represent national identity more generally. In the public sphere therefore Irish men stood at the boundary of the nation and their otherness was emphasized. This was especially necessary when they intermixed in Britain as a result of emigration.

But gendered representations were ambivalent. Different layers of racialization simultaneously depicted the island of Ireland, and by association its inhabitants, through Victorian stereotypes of femininity. The attribution of feminine characteristics to the so-called Celtic 'race' is traced back to Matthew Arnold's model for the relationship between Teuton and Celt which is likened to the roles of husband and wife in a Victorian marriage.[5] Feminine qualities of aesthetic appreciation, sensitivity and unreliability required control and protection. Ashis Nandy relates this strategy to broader issues of colonialism, epitomized in British representations of India. Nandy points to parallels in patriarchal and imperial power which indeed draw on male desires, the 'homology between sexual and political dominance'.[6] In extreme contrast to the ugly, pugnacious, ape-like cartoon figures of individual Irish men, Ireland is depicted by beautiful, delicate, young Hibernia. 'Indeed, the only Celt to be flattered and admired by *Punch*'s cartoonists was "Hibernia", the intensely feminine symbol of Ireland, whose haunting beauty conveyed some of the sufferings of the Irish people'.[7] In a well-known *Punch* cartoon of 1866 this contradiction is brought out starkly. Both male and female images

Figure 1 'The Fenian Pest', *Punch*, 3 March 1866; by permission of the Syndics of Cambridge University Library

appear at the same time, Hibernia being protected by Britannia from the ape-like Fenian [Figure 1].[8]

A key element of Irish contestation of British rule in the late nineteenth and early twentieth century was the development of an oppositional internal masculine representation of Irishness.[9] The Gaelic revival stressed masculine team sports and physical prowess, approving images of rugged rural men such as Robert Flaherty's *Man of Aran*.[10] But this was also an adoption of the language of the aggressor. Just as the feminization of Celts was a strategy to place Irish men in a weak position rather than a celebration of female virtues, so Gaelicization continued to leave Irish women out of the frame. Consequences for women of an Irish culture identified with male strength and independence have been profound.

The brutalization of representations of Irish men and the passive femininity of Ireland itself encapsulate the paradox of simultaneous exclusion and inclusion of the Irish in Britain. Use of gendered images to convey these images has repercussions on the material experiences of Irish men and women. Whereas Paddies are highly visible, nameless women are hidden from view.

In the nineteenth century therefore the Irish were racialized in two distinct ways, each strongly gendered. Masculine images were of uncontrolled subhumans incapable of self-government. Feminine images were of weakness requiring protection. Both representations justified continued British rule whilst bolstering images of the ruling centre as the antithesis of these negative characteristics.

CONTINUITIES AND TRANSFORMATIONS

Visual images which have been widely circulated retain their power over long periods. Curtis argues that the *Punch* cartoons had lost their currency by 1914, and ape-like Irishmen made only a fleeting reappearance during the bitter guerrilla war in the early 1920s.[11] However identical images were revived with extraordinary ferocity when the British press wished to express outrage and incomprehension at the outbreak of the 'troubles' in Northern Ireland in 1968. John Kirkaldy traces changes in newspaper images over the period 1968 to 1970 as the conflict intensified.[12] A generally positive image, that of the traditional stage Irishman, was replaced by the negative representations of the late nineteenth century. Striking growth in the virulence of anti-Irish imagery in *Punch* can be identified:

> Here, in a slightly more sophisticated form, are many of the crudities of Victorian imagery which could easily have come from the pages of the same magazine a century or so before. The Irish, or particular Irish groups, are seen as mad ('there is always one round the bend'), stupid ('it is their substitute for thinking'), reactionary ('notice their habit of taking ten steps backward for every one step forward') and lethargic ('you must watch closely as movement is almost imperceptible'). It is interesting to note that the Northern Irish are treated as aliens, despite their constituting part of the United Kingdom, and that Protestants, as well as Catholics, are included in the hostile stereotypes.[13]

Kirkaldy advances five hypotheses to explain this large-scale reversion to old hostile English stereotypes. These include suppressed guilt over the imperial relationship with Ireland in the past, the use of images of Irish 'insanity' to absolve England of responsibility for the current situation and a desire to cover up the contradiction between the claim that this was an Irish affair whilst English intervention was increasing. In addition, the images could be interpreted as having a cathartic effect, allowing the English to deal with their engagement in a situation they could not fully control, and as conditioning of the British public for yet further involvement in order to 'improve' matters.

Once again bodily images were used to represent the Irish as inferior. Rightwing newspapers reverted directly to cartoons portraying subhuman, simianized figures and animals whilst even liberal journalists showed their condescension and distaste. Kirkaldy describes a well-known *Sunday Times* writer as 'almost obsessed with the smallness and inferiority of the Irish and the largeness and commonsense of the English'. He lists many instances of male Irish politicians being described as 'little' together with some other unflattering adjectives – 'foxy', 'cunning', 'dumpy', 'slightly ridiculous'.

However some of the strongest ridicule and anti-Irish imagery was called forth in response to the young woman Member of Parliament, Bernadette Devlin, who was elected in 1969:

> Almost the entire British Press refused to take her seriously, ignoring her views or representing them as something of a joke. Fleet Street treated her like some kind of clockwork doll, an amusing diversion from the mainstream of parliamentary life: the general coverage of her early days as an MP combined sexism with patronising trivialisation and a refusal to see her in any other terms than 'swinging youth' and the then fashionable mini-skirt.[14]

Images of Irish inferiority, contrasted with English rationality, patience, toleration and moderation, have thus been revived and mutated to meet contemporary conditions. During the conflict Irish men continued to be represented as physically and mentally inferior. The only Irish woman to be portrayed could not be taken seriously at all. Images of a feminine Ireland in need of protection were being transformed as British uncertainty over its remaining territorial claim grew. In July 1972 *The Daily Mail* cartoonist Emmwood depicted an IRA/UDA confrontation over the prone mini-skirted figure of Ulster with the caption 'faceless, senseless – brainless' [Figure 2].[15]

Denial of difference has also continued in new forms. In the nineteenth century it was linked to the firm intention that Ireland should remain within the Union. In the later twentieth century the fact of Irish Independence has been conceded, at least for the 26 counties, although the British view in 1949 remained that Ireland was 'not a foreign country'.[16] The declaration of the Republic appeared to make no difference at all to British definitions of 'the British Isles'. School and university geography courses have continued to use this description of the archipelago. Even at the height of the conflict in Northern Ireland during the early 1970s an English newspaper mused over whether the Republic was a 'foreign country' which should be boycotted as hostile by British tourists.[17]

The Irish were therefore anomalously excluded from the provisions of the Immigration Acts of the 1960s although they were neither British passport holders nor even members of the British Commonwealth. Automatic entitlement to vote in British elections on arrival is a further indication of the special status of Irish immigrants. Although this has been questioned from time to time by small groups of Conservative MPs, there has been no serious challenge to the right.

Figure 2 'Faceless, Senseless – Brainless', Emmwood, *Daily Mail*, 12 July 1972; by permission of Solo Syndication

Side by side with British unwillingness to distance Irish people politically is a resistance to acknowledging problems raised by ethnic difference. Although a strong claim for recognition as an ethnic group was made in 1984 to the Greater London Council Ethnic Minority Unit,[18] local authorities and other resourcing bodies have been very slow to include the Irish in ethnic monitoring procedures and have frequently rejected proposals outright.[19] Grounds cited often relate to assumed equality of membership in the 'British Isles'. Indeed when Birmingham City Council recognized the Irish as an ethnic group in 1986, a claim was put forward on behalf of Scots in the city who felt that they were similarly entitled.[20] When a case of discrimination at work against a Northern Irish Protestant man was brought by the Commission for Racial

Equality in 1994 and upheld, national newspapers instantly raised this issue, often on the front page:

> The CRE's decision to classify those of Irish national or ethnic background as a distinctive group under the Race Relations Act immediately raised questions whether Scots or even Essex girls could also claim they had been victims of racial discrimination.[21]

> The Irish joke's on us: White Essex male is the most abused minority in Britain today.[22]

> Tory MP Sir Paul Beresford, a New Zealander of Irish origin, said the CRE had a serious job to do but was running 'a high risk of discrediting itself' in pursuing such a case.
> 'Where will it stop?' he asked. 'Will it cover the Scots when they are south of the border and the English when they are in Scotland?'
> 'When the All Blacks are playing in Wales will I be able to claim £6000 for racist taunts?'[23]

These strong reactions to the principle of acknowledging Irish difference, since only a small sum of money was involved, emphasize the importance attached to the preservation of British homogeneity. Underlying the equation of Irish ethnicity with Scottish, Welsh and even English county identities, is shared whiteness. In order for black immigration to be isolated as a particular threat to British integrity, the plurality of the remainder must be denied.[24] Similarities in the patterns of migration from Ireland and other sources of migrant labour, including the West Indies, India, Pakistan and Bangladesh, are ignored. Although considerable evidence of racism and discrimination against black migrants and their British-born descendents has been collected, to date no sustained research has been published on the experiences of Irish people within workplaces and neighbourhoods. However the first step was taken in 1994 when the Commission for Racial Equality announced funding for a project exploring the nature and extent of anti-Irish discrimination in Britain.[25]

Anti-Irish jokes rarely refer to Irish women. They name Irish*men* and involve male activities. In the case mentioned above they were also targeted against an Irishman, though women are by no means protected from their effects. Irish men are made to stand in for the population of Irish people in Britain in verbal as well as visual public representations. 'Paddies' and 'Micks' subsume both genders, but are overtly male in stereotype.[26] The content of the stereotype includes two main strands. Perhaps the strongest is stupidity, especially misunderstanding as a result of low intelligence and poor language skills. A second important component is violence, also associated with stupidity since it is often depicted as 'mindless', either resulting from drunkenness or from incomprehensible political beliefs. Both strands extend into irrationality and even insanity. Other elements invoked at different times include laziness, superstition, dishonesty and dirtiness. Ways in which Irish women are connected with these constructions, both in representations and in their material lives will now be explored.

CONSTRUCTIONS OF OTHERNESS: RELIGION, CLASS AND POLITICAL DEVIANCE

Irish women share in the racialized exclusion of Irish people who continue to be constructed as 'other', as anti-Irish jokes confirm. They are identified by their voices; accents trigger anti-Irish attitudes regardless of gender. Voices are of course attached to bodies so that although skin colour does not signify Irish people as inferior, their ways of speaking do. The slippage between the two forms of physical signification is illustrated by remarks made in an ethnographic survey by Mary Kells of young Irish middle-class migrants in London: 'The thing about being Irish in England, Martin told me, reporting a joke he had enjoyed, is that they don't realize you're black until you open your mouth'.[27]

Body images are drawn on because this is the dominant mode of racial visibility in post-war Britain. In fact:

> in pursuit of natural symbolisms of inferiority, racist discourses have never confined themselves just to body images. Names and modes of address, states of mind and living conditions, clothes and customs, every kind of social behaviour and cultural practice have been pressed into service to signify this or that racial essence. In selecting these materials, racist codes behave opportunistically according to an economy of means; they choose those signs which do the most ideological work

in linking – and naturalising – difference and domination within a certain set of historical conditions of representation. To make issues of in/visibility depend on physical appearance is to bracket out precisely these historical realities.[28]

As a result Irish people often monitor themselves. Yvonne Hayes, born in England, describes life in London in the 1970s for her parents:

> For Irish people, there's nothing that distinguishes them from being English, as long as they keep their mouths shut. And if you are trying to bring up a family and build a home, you just try and fit in with the establishment and don't put yourself out on a limb too much, so you don't get into trouble.[29]

Irish women may be identified more readily than men because their voices are more often heard in isolation. Many Irish men still work in predominantly Irish groups, one quarter being engaged in construction work in 1991, and socialize in clearly defined 'Irish pubs'. By contrast women's work brings them into contact with British people. Nearly 20 per cent are nurses and 35 per cent in the domestic service sector, which like most women's jobs involve personal interaction.[30] Miriam Jones left her job as a telephone operator because her employer was prejudiced against her accent:

> After a while I learned to operate the switchboard and I used to relieve the girl that was on the telephone but the boss didn't like my accent, so I wasn't allowed to answer the telephone any more. I had been in the job about three or four years, but he didn't like the idea of having an Irish accent at the end of his telephone. Most of his customers and friends seemed to like talking to me, but I think it wasn't good for his image to have an Irish woman on the telephone. That was the first occasion on which I was rejected as an Irish person, and it was a very salutary lesson. I didn't like it. I was very annoyed and I did complain. 'What's wrong with my voice?' I spoke perfectly good English, I was perfectly polite, and I was reassured – 'Oh no, it's nothing like that. It's just your accent. Mr. Sweetman doesn't like your accent'.[31]

Mothers have to negotiate state services on behalf of families, areas where their rights may be called into question and the hazards of identification assume added significance.[32] They also interact with neighbours to a greater extent than men. In Manchester, Anne Higgins's family 'mixed mainly with other Irish people. I suppose it was our accents, but mainly our religion which set us apart from the rest'.[33]

A major reason for the continued exclusion of Irish people in Britain is the adherence of the majority to the Catholic church. Although Britain is an increasingly secular society in which church attendance is declining and spirituality seen as an individual choice, the Established Church retains its symbolic importance for national identity. In the recently-revised National Curriculum for schools, its priority over multi-cultural religious activity has been reaffirmed. It is within this context of national allegiance that Catholicism has been seen as a threat since the sixteenth century.[34] Expressions of anti-Catholic prejudice have continued into the twentieth century in particular areas.[35]

Although women are excluded from the formal public structures of the Catholic church, they play a central role in maintaining and reproducing its support. Women participate more actively than men, a survey in 1994 finding that 63 per cent of Irish Catholic women compared with 51 per cent of men had attended Mass that week.[36] They also ensure that children are brought up in the faith.[37] For older women the church provides a supportive Irish community within which to socialize, often on a daily basis.[38] Of course, not all Irish women are Catholic, though the great majority have Catholic backgrounds. But the strength of association between Catholicism and Irishness means that Protestant Irish women in Britain find that they are regarded first and foremost as Irish, and their shared religion is given little weight.[39]

Irish women have been negatively stereotyped as having oversized families in obedience to Catholic teaching. At a time when British women were limiting family size in order to achieve consumer aspirations and take on paid work, large families were regarded as improvident and a drain on state resources as well as a sign of rural backwardness.[40] However whereas in 1971 there was still a significant difference between fertility levels of mothers born in the Irish Republic (average family size 3.5) and the total British population (2.4), family sizes have since converged.[41] Higher rates of growth of the second generation were viewed with alarm by government demographers, so that women were directly implicated in racist fears about Irish settlement in Britain.[42]

Irish people in Britain are usually stereotyped as 'working-class Catholics'. Whilst Catholicism clearly marks out those of Irish origin and descent, their class location might appear to link them into the dominant society. But the position is an ambivalent one. Britishness continues to connect most strongly with the ruling classes, represented by the monarchy and widespread acceptance of the authority of 'Queen's English'.[43] Even middle-class Irish people may be stigmatized as working-class because their accents 'place' them in the Irish stereotype. Rachel Harbron, who came from a professional Protestant family in Dublin, experienced this:

> It's a feeling I have, especially among upper middle-class English people, that they don't regard you in the same light as themselves. We are sort of second-class citizens, which you feel strongly. They might make jokes ragging your accent or whatever but the thought is still there, that in a general way they regard themselves as better.[44]

In the later nineteenth century the 'respectable' (British) working classes were admitted to the nation, but the 'rough' and dissidents remained outside.[45] The respectable working classes developed their own notions of Britishness based on territoriality, which again excluded Irish people especially where they threatened labour power. In the 1930s in Islington, North London, chauvinism derived from intense localism. According to Jerry White, who interviewed longstanding residents in the 1970s about their earlier experiences: 'Anti-Irish sentiment was common, even though many Campbell Road families could have claimed Irish descent: "You never get no Irishmen round there [. . .]. They've give the Paddies all the pubs – but *you* try and get one"'.[46] Women have not shared in this positioning to the same extent as men, as domestic roles have kept them 'off the street' and provided an approved caring role. But Irish mothers have been held responsible for their sons' behaviour.

Both religion and class have important geographic variations in Britain so that their salience as factors of exclusion varies sharply. They reinforce each other most strongly in South East England, the heartland of Britishness. Proportions of Catholics in the population are relatively low and of more direct Irish extraction than in areas such as North West England where immigration has been at high levels for at least six generations. Anglicanism, the Established Church of England and deeply entwined with English national identity, is the dominant form of Protestantism in the South East. South East England is also the core of 'Standard English' pronunciation, the badge of middle-class membership which places Irish accents as deviant.[47]

Irish women have been at the forefront of exposure to Protestant, middle-class English attitudes in the South East. Of all parts of Britain, this region has recorded the highest levels of demand for Irish women's domestic labour since the mid-nineteenth century. Such demand reflects widespread employment of private servants in middle-class households, subsequently augmented by the catering and cleaning needs of the rapidly expanding service sector. In London women have outnumbered men in the Irish-born population since 1841, the total being as high as 60 per cent greater in 1921.[48] As other women in paid work moved into clerical occupations from the later nineteenth century, demand for Irish women as domestic servants grew rapidly. They continue to find ready employment in many forms of public and private personal service, and have lower than average unemployment rates in London (8.1 per cent in 1991, compared with the average of 9.1 per cent). Irish-born men, by contrast have rates of 17.1 per cent, much higher than the average of 13.5 per cent for all men.[49]

In the South East, therefore, a distinctive Irish identity is retained by Irish migrants and their children. Mary Hickman found that children of Irish descent in Catholic secondary schools described themselves as 'London Irish' and were knowledgeable about, and proud of, their background. They were aware of the racist content of anti-Irish jokes and contested them.[50]

This recognition of difference and exclusion contrasts with Irish experience in the North West of England. The long history of immigration into Lancashire has given the Catholic church a wide measure of acceptance alongside other denominations, many members having by now lost all trace of their Irish origins.[51] Irish women have been integrated into the economy on the basis of shared class, rather than in the subordinate relationship of servants. In the past many were recruited for mill work in the textile industry. In Bolton in 1861, for example, 85 per cent of Irish-born girls (under 20) and 54 per cent of older Irish-born women were cotton trade workers, but only 134 were recorded as servants.[52]

Although Irish people retain a strong awareness of their origins, the need to assert difference takes different forms in the North West. On the one hand traditions of Protestant-Catholic conflict have been overt, reflecting the rival status of the religious groups within the working class, rather than their association with markedly dominant and subordinate groups.[53] On the other, second and subsequent generation Irish people have readily accepted a local regional identity.[54] Hickman found that schoolchildren of Irish descent in Catholic schools almost unanimously described themselves as 'Liverpudlian'.[55]

Experiences in Scotland and Wales are again of a different order and result in an ambivalent relationship. In both nations, nonconformist Protestant religion is deeply interwoven into claims for a national identity independent of England.[56] Protestant-Catholic rivalry has again been intense in parts of Scotland, notably Glasgow.[57] In Wales anti-Irish hostility erupted in the nineteenth century both as a result of workplace tensions arising out of competition and communal violence following pub brawls.[58] At the same time the Celticized 'fringes' share exclusion from full membership in the British nation:

> the 'Englishness' of a certain class can come to represent itself via racism as 'Britishness' against those ethnicities that it subordinates – such as those of the Irish, Scottish, Welsh, black British, or the ethnicities of the formerly colonized world.[59]

Thus shared resistance to English domination may result in feelings of greater closeness. In a survey carried out by the University of Bradford in 1994, 40 per cent of Scots questioned said they felt closer to the Irish than to the English, while 18 per cent gave the opposite answer. Figures for the Welsh were 33 per cent and 21 per cent respectively.[60]

A third aspect of Irish otherness is political deviance. Not only have the Irish retained a form of religion whose rejection symbolized England's declaration of independence from Rome in the sixteenth century, but they openly rejected the British monarchy in their choice of republicanism. Curtis argues that political challenges to British rule in Ireland in the nineteenth century were classified as 'Special Crimes' in an attempt to link them with defects in the Irish character rather than legitimate aspirations.[61]

In Britain the 'code of breeding' which excluded the Irish from belonging in the British nation in the nineteenth century brought together the two strands of racial inferiority and political dissent. This represented a potential alliance between '*all* the alien populations and ideas which the British ruling class most feared'.[62] Moreover the irrational aggression which was central to the Irish stereotype played a central role in confirming the rationality and non-violence of British policy and traditions.[63] This denial of the intrinsic violence of imperial control and expansion 'leaves a blank in the place of knowledge of the destructive effects of wielding power'.[64]

In the twentieth century fears about threatening alternative political ideologies were raised again by IRA opposition to direct British rule in Northern Ireland after 1972. These were dealt with by strict control of information about Republican views, especially in the media, and suppression of debate, particularly by use of the Prevention of Terrorism Act.[65] A prime purpose of this Act was to intimidate the Irish population in Britain into silence.[66]

In the absence of debate and balanced news coverage, the stereotype of sympathic support for mindless violence was extended to all Irish people in Britain. A survey of Irish nurses in London carried out in 1988 included a number of comments on the British people's assumption of their guilt by association for acts of political violence by the IRA.[67]

> We're all painted with the same brush – political activists.
> (Ward sister from Westmeath, arrived 1976)

> We have a 'bad name'. We are branded with the bad publicity of the IRA.
> (Student nurse from Kerry, arrived 1985)

> Association with the IRA. If anything happens we're all blamed.
> (Student nurse from Dublin, arrived 1987)

These elements of otherness inform taken-for-granted attitudes towards Irish people in contemporary Britain. Images from past centuries have been naturalized and are available for current use when required. Thus stereotypes of the Irish still define what the British are not, emphasizing the continuing importance of 'internal' others to the construction of British identity.

CONSTRUCTIONS OF BELONGING: GEOGRAPHY, WHITENESS AND CHRISTIANITY

At the same time denial of difference to the Irish in Britain is fiercely upheld. It is demonstrated in the continuing refusal to acknowledge the racism involved in anti-Irish humour. *The Daily Telegraph,* for example, whilst appearing to accept the validity of the discrimination case described earlier, gratuitously incorporated six (anti-) 'Irish jokes' into its report.[68] Such treatment of acknowledged (that is black) minority ethnic groups would be unthinkable in the 'quality press'. Earlier in 1994 the announcement of the research grant by the Commission for Racial Equality for a project to explore the extent and nature of anti-Irish discrimination in Britain received a similar outpouring of consternation and ridicule. 'Disbelief over grant to research prejudice' was the headline in *The East Anglian Daily Times.*[69]

A refusal to sever ties incorporating the island of Ireland into the British state is unthinkingly demonstrated in naming and mapping practices. Apart from continued reference to 'the British Isles', phrases in common use include 'mainland Britain' in discussions of Northern Ireland (implying that it is 'offshore Britain'), and 'the Celtic fringe' (of the absent centre, England). The confusion, and also its consequences, are highlighted by the presentation of a recent report on findings on ethnic minority disadvantage in London. A number of tables in the report included data on the category 'born in Ireland' and indicated significant levels of disadvantage. But places of origin were mapped under the title 'Communities over 10,000 who were born *outside the British Isles* and now live in London' (emphasis added).[70] The largest ethnic minority by migration is thus excluded from visual representation, without any apparent logic.

British national identity depends on the notion of unity. The Englishness at the heart of Britishness would be 'cut back to size' if the 'breakup of Britain' were to take place.[71] Nationalist demands in Scotland have advanced significantly in the last 30 years, whilst the attachment of Northern Ireland appears increasingly tenuous. As James Anderson points out, the very need to claim 'unitedness' of the Kingdom hints at its imperfect unity.[72] In the face of these threats, emphasis on the geographical integrity of the islands helps to naturalize notions of unity, even though it requires an international border to be disregarded.

Display of unity is also an attempt to hide the real plurality of British society. Robert Miles describes the 'myth of British homogeneity' which has been fostered in the post-war period to represent black people as unassimilable and inevitably alien. A key element of this homogeneity is 'racial' similarity.[73] In contrast to nineteenth-century representations of superior 'Anglo-Saxon' and inferior 'Celtic' characteristics, therefore, they are made to appear close and complementary. Together they constitute 'The Island Race', a powerful image which was invoked by Margaret Thatcher in 1982 to rekindle British patriotic self-esteem at the time of the Falklands War. Paul Gilroy argues that the image blurs the distinction between 'race' and nation and relies on this very ambiguity for its effect.[74]

Exclusionary ideas about 'race' lie at the heart of British national identity. Such boundaries can only be sustained if the island of Ireland is included. This helps to explain why immigration from Ireland is generally overlooked when the 'numbers question' of settlers from outside is being considered. The term 'immigrants' has a racialized meaning which makes it synonymous with black skin colour. An important added advantage to Britain is that Ireland can be allowed to remain a source of 'reserve' labour fluctuating according to British needs, whereas the economic connection between demand and supply of labour from other ex-colonial areas was severed by the Immigration Acts of the 1960s.

Shared whiteness is thus a central reason for Irish inclusion. The power of racialized exclusion on grounds of skin colour would be seriously weakened if similar divisions within the white population were exposed. The presentation of Census data in 1991 underlined this categorization. The dominant group was classified first as an undifferentiated 'white' group, against whom all 'others' were either implicitly or explicitly labelled 'black' and then fragmented by their geographical origins.[75]

Underlying this emphasis on whiteness lies the growing divide between the Muslim and non-Muslim worlds, against which splits within Christianity assume a much smaller importance than in the past. This was underlined by the 1988 Education Reform Act which required all state schools in England to have a daily act of Christian worship, replacing the multi-faith assemblies which many had adopted. As Gita Saghal and Nira Yuval-Davis point out 'Christianity, therefore, is given an affirmed legal status as the ideological cement of national culture'.[76] Although regional nationalisms are assuming greater salience, trends towards transnational Europeanism are also visible.[77] Catholicism is now a European norm and its continued embrace of patriarchal family structures chimes closely with conservative social democratic values.

The discourse of assimilation ensures that difference can be denied to the Irish but retained for other migrant groups.[78] Many historians of the Irish in Britain have chosen interpretations of nineteenth-century patterns which emphasize gradual acceptance over time and the reduction of disparities between the Irish and British populations.[79] It is assumed that the same model applies to twentieth-century Irish experience.[80]

CONCLUSIONS

British constructions of the Irish can be seen as 'nothing but the same old story'.[81] But the story is adapted to meet present day needs. Stereotypes of the Irish continue to allow the British nation to be defined by its opposites; as peaceful, just, rational, calm, industrious and sober, whilst remaining unexamined as the powerful 'absent centre'.

At another level these differences are played down and contained as 'jokes'. Thus 'the previously excluded become included in the context of the signification of the new "intruder"'.[82] Moreover references to the past imply a pre-existing homogeneity, broken for the first time in the post-war period by alien 'immigrants'.

Gender is central to these representations. Irish men carry the weight of ridicule and contempt, both for their aggressive masculinity and their feminized weakness. Irish women are limited to a symbolic role and rendered invisible as real bodies, allowing their material needs to be ignored.

Acknowledgement. This research was supported by ESRC research grant R000234790.

Notes

1. L.P. Curtis, *Anglo-Saxons and Celts: A Study of Anti-Irish Prejudice in Victorian England* (Connecticut: University of Bridgeport, 1968); N.

Lebow, 'British Historians and Irish History', *Eire-Ireland*, 6 (1973), 3–38.
2. M.J. Hickman, *Religion, Class and Identity: The State, the Catholic Church and the Education of the Irish in Britain* (London: Avebury Press, 1995).
3. L.P. Curtis, *Apes and Angels: The Irishman in Victorian Caricature* (Washington: Smithsonian Institution Press, 1971).
4. L.P. Curtis, *Apes and Angels*, p. 21.
5. T. O'Brien Johnson and D. Cairns, eds, *Gender in Irish Writing* (Milton Keynes: Open University Press, 1991), p. 38.
6. A. Nandy, *The Intimate Enemy: Loss and Recovery of Self Under Colonialism* (Oxford: Oxford University Press, 1983), p. 3.
7. L.P. Curtis, *Apes and Angels*, p. 31.
8. *Punch*, 3 March 1866, p. 89.
9. C. Nash, 'Remapping and Renaming: New Cartographies of Identity, Gender and Landscape in Ireland', *Feminist Review*, 44 (1993), 39–57.
10. *Man of Aran*, dir. R. Flaherty, 1934.
11. L.P. Curtis, *Apes and Angels*, p. 4.
12. J. Kirkaldy, 'English Newspaper Images of Northern Ireland 1968–73: An Historical Study in Stereotypes and Prejudices' (Ph.D. thesis, University of New South Wales, 1979).
13. J. Kirkaldy, 'English Newspaper Images of Northern Ireland 1968–73', p. 63.
14. J. Kirkaldy, 'English Newspaper Images of Northern Ireland 1968–73', p. 56.
15. *The Daily Mail*, 12 July 1972, p. 11.
16. *Ireland Act*, 1949.
17. 'Is a Holiday in Ireland Safe?', *The Sunday Times*, 4 June 1972, p. 44; cited in J. Kirkaldy, 'English Newspaper Images of Northern Ireland 1968–73'.
18. *Report on the Prevention of Terrorism Act and Report on Consultation with the Irish Community* (London: Greater London Council, Ethnic Minorities Unit, 1984).
19. 'Recognition of Irish Ethnicity', *The Irish Post*, 3 June 1995, p. 2.
20. 'Scots of Second City Suffer an Ethnic Setback', *The Guardian*, 15 February 1986, p. 3.
21. 'Industrial Tribunal Rules Irish Jokes Racist', *The Guardian*, 8 June 1994, p. 1.
22. The Irish Joke's On Us', *The Sun*, 9 June 1994, p. 9.
23. 'Who's Taking the Mickey?', *The Daily Mail*, 8 June 1994, p. 1.
24. R. Miles, *Racism After 'Race Relations'* (London: Routledge, 1993), p. 109.
25. The project was carried out by Dr Mary Hickman and Dr Bronwen Walter, and was based at the Irish Studies Centre, University of North London. It was completed in March 1996. Reports on welfare issues relating to anti-Irish discrimination have been initiated by Action Group for Irish Youth, including: J. O'Flynn, *Identity Crisis: Access to Benefits and ID Checks* (London: Action Group for Irish Youth, 1993); U. Kowarzik, *Developing a Community Response: The Service Needs of the Irish Community in Britain. A Charities Evaluation Services Report*

Commissioned by Action Group for Irish Youth and the Federation of Irish Societies (London: Action Group for Irish Youth and Federation of Irish Societies, 1994).
26. B. Walter, 'Irishness, Gender and Place', *Environment and Planning D: Society and Space*, 13 (1995), 35–50.
27. M. Kells, *Ethnic Identity Amongst Young Irish Middle Class Migrants in London* (London: University of North London Press, Irish Studies Centre Occasional Paper Series 6, 1995), p. 33.
28. P. Cohen, 'The Perversions of Inheritance: Studies in the Making of Multi-Racist Britain' in *Multi-Racist Britain*, eds P. Cohen and H. Bains (London: Macmillan, 1988), pp. 9–118.
29. M. Lennon, M. McAdam and J. O'Brien, *Across the Water: Irish Women's Lives in Britain* (London: Virago, 1988), p. 219.
30. B. Walter, 'Gender and Recent Irish Migration to Britain' in *Contemporary Irish Migration*, ed. R. King (Dublin: Geographical Society of Ireland Special Publications 6, 1991), pp. 11–20.
31. M. Lennon, M. McAdam and J. O'Brien, *Across the Water*, p. 65.
32. J. O'Flynn, *Identity Crisis*.
33. M. Lennon, M. McAdam and J. O'Brien, *Across the Water*, p. 146.
34. R. Swift, 'Crime and the Irish in Nineteenth-Century Britain' in *The Irish in Britain 1815–1939*, eds R. Swift and S. Gilley (London: Pinter, 1989), pp. 163–82.
35. M. Lennon, M. McAdam and J. O'Brien, *Across the Water*; F. Neal, *Sectarian Violence: The Liverpool Experience 1819–1914* (Manchester: Manchester University Press, 1988).
36. 'Catholic Loyalty at a High Level Still', *The Irish Post*, 26 December 1992, p. 7.
37. B. Walter, 'Ethnicity and Irish Residential Segregation', *Transactions of the Institute of British Geographers*, 11 (1986), 131–46.
38. M.J. Hickman and B. Walter, 'Deconstructing Whiteness: Irish Women in Britain', *Feminist Review*, 49 (1995), 5–19.
39. M. Lennon, M. McAdam and J. O'Brien, *Across the Water*; M. Kells, *Ethnic Identity Amongst Young Irish Middle Class Migrants in London*.
40. S. Mackenzie and D. Rose, 'Industrial Change, the Domestic Economy and Home Life' in *Redundant Spaces? Social Change and Industrial Decline in Cities and Regions*, eds J. Anderson, S. Duncan and R. Hudson (London: Academic Press, 1983), pp. 155–200.
41. B. Caulfield and A. Bhat, 'The Irish in Britain: Intermarriage and Fertility Levels 1971–1976', *New Community*, 9 (1981), 73–83.
42. R.S. Walshaw, *Migration to and from the British Isles* (London: Jonathan Cape, 1941), p. 75.
43. T. Nairn, *The Enchanted Glass* (London: Radius Press, 1988), pp. 62–71.
44. M. Lennon, M. McAdam and J. O'Brien, *Across the Water*, p. 205.
45. P. Cohen, 'The Perversions of Inheritance', p. 71.
46. J. White, *The Worst Street in North London: Campbell Bunk, Islington Between the Wars* (London: Routledge and Kegan Paul, 1986), p. 105.
47. J. Osmond, *The Divided Kingdom* (London: Constable, 1988), p. 166.
48. B. Walter, 'Gender and Irish Migration to Britain', *Anglia Geography Working Paper* 4, 1989.

49. D. Owen, 'Irish-Born People in Great Britain: Settlement Patterns and Socio-Economic Circumstances', *University of Warwick: Census Statistical Paper*, 9 (1995).
50. M.J. Hickman, 'A Study of the Incorporation of the Irish in Britain with Special Reference to Catholic State Education: Involving a Comparison of the Attitudes of Pupils and Teachers in Selected Secondary Schools in London and Liverpool' (Ph.D. thesis, University of London Institute of Education, London, 1990).
51. B. Walter, 'Tradition and Ethnic Interaction: Second Wave Irish Settlement in Luton and Bolton' in *Geography and Ethnic Pluralism*, eds C. Clarke, D. Ley and C. Peach (London: George Allen and Unwin, 1984), pp. 258–283.
52. Census Enumerators' books, Great and Little Bolton, 1861.
53. F. Neal, *Sectarian Violence*.
54. B. Walter, 'Tradition and Ethnic Interaction'.
55. M.J. Hickman, 'A Study of the Incorporation of the Irish in Britain'.
56. J. Osmond, *The Divided Kingdom*; D. McCrone, *Understanding Scotland: The Sociology of a Stateless Nation* (London: Routledge, 1992).
57. T. Gallagher, 'The Catholic Irish in Scotland: In Search of Identity' in *Irish Immigrants and Scottish Society in the Nineteenth and Twentieth Centuries*, ed. T.M. Devine (Edinburgh: John Donald, 1991), pp. 19–43.
58. P. O'Leary, 'Anti-Irish Riots in Wales', *Llafur: Journal of Welsh Labour History*, 5 (1991), 27–36.
59. A. Brah, 'Difference, Diversity and Differentiation' in *'Race', Culture and Difference*, eds J. Donald and A. Rattansi (London: Sage, 1992), p. 143.
60. 'How Close are the British to the Irish?', *The Irish Post*, 17 December 1994, p. 7.
61. L.P. Curtis, *Apes and Angels*, p. 21.
62. P. Cohen, 'The Perversions of Inheritance', p. 74.
63. M.J. Hickman, 'A Study of the Incorporation of the Irish in Britain', p. 7.
64. C. Pajaczkowska and L. Young, 'Racism, Representation and Psychoanalysis in *'Race', Culture and Difference*, eds. J. Donald and A. Rattansi, p. 202.
65. J. Kirkaldy, 'English Newspaper Images of Northern Ireland 1968–73'; P. Hillyard, *Suspect Community: People's Experience of the Prevention of Terrorism Act in Britain* (London: Pluto Press, 1993).
66. *Report on the Prevention of Terrorism Act*.
67. B. Walter, *Irish Women in London: The Ealing Dimension*, Second edition (London: Women's Unit, London Borough of Ealing, 1989).
68. 'Question: Why Can't They Make Icecubes in Ireland?', *The Daily Telegraph*, 9 June 1994, p. 17.
69. 'Disbelief Over Grant to Research Prejudice', *The East Anglian Daily Times*, 24 January 1994, p. 9. See note 25.
70. M. Storkey, *London's Ethnic Minorities: One City Many Communities: An Analysis of 1991 Census Results* (London: London Research Centre, 1994), p. 17.

71. T. Nairn, *The Break-Up of Britain: Crisis and Neo-Nationalism* (London: New Left Books, 1977).
72. J. Anderson, 'Nationalisms in a Disunited Kingdom' in *The Political Geography of Contemporary Britain*, ed. J. Mohan (London: Macmillan, 1989), pp. 35–50.
73. R. Miles, *Racism After 'Race Relations'*.
74. P. Gilroy, *There Ain't No Black in the Union Jack* (London: Hutchinson, 1987).
75. Office of Population Censuses and Surveys, *1991 Census Ethnic Group and Country of Birth* (London: Her Majesty's Stationery Office, 1993), pp. 51–52.
76. G. Saghal and N. Yuval-Davis, *Refusing Holy Orders: Women and Fundamentalism in Britain* (London: Virago, 1992), p. 13.
77. F. Anthias and N. Yuval-Davis, *Racialized Boundaries: Race, Nation, Gender, Colour and Class and the Anti-Racist Struggle* (London: Routledge, 1992), p. 55.
78. M.J. Hickman and B. Walter, 'Deconstructing Whiteness'.
79. For example, S. Gilley, 'English Attitudes to the Irish in England 1780–1900' in *Immigrants and Minorities in British Society*, ed. C. Holmes (London: George Allen and Unwin, 1978), pp. 81–110; G. Davis, 'Little Irelands' in *The Irish in Britain 1815–1939*, pp. 104–33; C. Pooley, 'Segregation or Integration? The Residential Experience of the Irish in Mid-Victorian Britain' in *The Irish in Britain 1815–1939*, pp. 60–83.
80. E. Rose and associates, *Colour and Citizenship* (Oxford: For Institute of Race Relations by Oxford University Press, 1969); C. Peach, ed., *Ethnicity in the 1991 Census*, Volume 2 (London: HMSO, 1996).
81. L. Curtis, *Nothing But the Same Old Story: The Roots of Anti-Irish Racism* (London: Information on Ireland, 1984).
82. R. Miles, *Race After 'Race Relations'*, p. 117.

6

Breaking the 'Cracked Mirror': Binary Oppositions in the Culture of Contemporary Ireland

Shaun Richards

At the self-revelatory climax of *Hear My Song*, a 1991 Ealingesque Comedy with an Irish angle, the protagonist, Mickey O'Neill, is held petrified over the Cliffs of Moher on the Atlantic coast of County Clare where he is interrogated by Josef Locke, the man he has sought to bring back to England to perform a concert which will save Mickey from financial ruin. With the sea roaring beneath him, Mickey is asked why he is doing it. 'For Nancy', he replies and, after a moment, 'the girl I – love'.[1] There, on the darkened coast, Mickey finally voices 'the simple truth' of the word he could not speak; a word whose absence has led to their break-up. Pulled back from the cliff edge he lies on the grass, his face upward to the stars, and smiles. Even in the amiable sentimentality of a 1990s commercial feature 'moving away from civilization' has replaced 'the anxiety of men who are eager for gain' by what Synge referred to as 'strange archaic sympathies with the world', a state in which, as he recorded in *The Aran Islands*, 'I could not see or realize my own body, and seemed to exist merely in my perception of the waves and of the crying birds'.[2] *Hear My Song* has no overt aspirations to cultural commentary yet it reveals the redemptive trope of 'the west' as enduring into the 1990s and, along with it, the 'other' in this binary opposition, the fallen, urban, modernized east where, as imaged in Roddy Doyle's 1994 TV drama *Family*, Charlo weaves his drunken and destructive way.[3]

Such binary oppositions, as argued by Jacques Derrida, exist in a 'violent hierarchy' in which one of the terms occupies a dominant position; the only effective escape for the subordinate in such a structure being an inversion 'which brings low what was high'.[4] The 'cultoromachia' of the Irish Revival was, in effect, an enactment of this inversion through which the previously denigrated Irish peasant, for example, was celebrated as the well-spring of the nation; as Douglas Hyde observed at an address in Dublin's Mansion House in 1926, '[they] will save the historical Irish Nation for [they] preserve for all time the fountain-source from which future generations can draw for ever'.[5] The corollary of the rural west of peasant purity was a rejection of the pernicious infiltration from the east of fallen, English values; Ireland, in George Moore's words, was not 'to be girdled with Brixton' as it refuted 'gross naturalism' and 'scientific barbarism'.[6] This inversion, however, effective as it was in providing much of the dynamic behind the struggle for independence and, ultimately, the creation of the Free State itself, was to be countered in its turn, and this time from within Ireland itself as, in Richard Kearney's analysis, Irish literature and culture worked through a polarity predicated on a choice between a form of politics which mythologizes and views the present in terms of the sacred tradition of the past, and one which demythologizes and looks beyond the present in terms of a secular progress towards a pluralist future.[7] The Literary Revival's inversion, and subsequent prioritization of the rural became open to attack as what was once regarded as Irish authenticity became seen as a regressive 'backward look' found wanting in comparison with a progressive, and frequently 'European' agenda. What has marked cultural debate within Ireland over the past decade is an ever more explicit engagement with the varying inflections of these basic binary oppositions; the question is whether, to adapt Seamus Heaney's response to the binary oppositions of the North, one can 'break the cracked mirror of this conceit';[8] and at what cost.

Patrick Pearse had laid down the dictum that '[the] Gael is the high priest of nature. He loves nature, not merely as something grand and beautiful and wonderful but as something possessing a mystic connection with and influence over man'[9] and it was this 'rural' side of the binary opposition which came to inform policy within the new nation state at the widest and deepest of levels. The Free State fusion of Revival imagery with Fianna Fail policy produced a situation in which the west was consolidated as 'the symbol of pure, Catholic, native Ireland'.[10] De Valera's Ireland was one whose destiny was to slough off the accretions of Anglicization and return to a source, denied through colonization and abandoned through modernization, which was located at the furthest historical and geographical distances from contemporary cultural pollution; accordingly the subsistence economy peasantry of Ireland's western coastline were apostatized as the living embodiment of the uncontaminated race. It was in this context that the 1934 première of Robert Flaherty's *Man of Aran*, full of seaweed gathering and (anachronistic) shark fishing, was attended by de Valera and members of his cabinet and lauded in her *Irish Times* review by his confidante, Dorothy Macardle: 'We have become almost resigned to being traduced in literature [but not] three generations of protesting could do as much to rehabilitate the Irish people in the imagination of the peoples of other countries as this faithful and beautiful motion picture will do'.[11]

This archaizing tendency was strenuously contested from its first articulation, notably by John Eglinton in a 1899 debate with W.B. Yeats where he dismissed a literature which looked back to 'the forms and images in which old conceptions have been embodied – old faiths, myths, dreams'.[12] But while it is 'Eglinton' who, in *Ulysses*, regards celtic rapture as the result of an over-infusion of peatsmoke it is 'Russell' who captures the mood of the Revival: 'The movements which work revolutions in the world are born out of the dreams and visions in a peasant's heart on the hillside. For them the earth is not an exploitable ground but the living mother'.[13] Luke Gibbons recently observed that 'a version of Eglinton's argument has gained credence in Irish cultural debate, taking the form of a steady chorus of complaints against the disabling influence of the past [. . .] the pastoral image of the countryside'.[14] While its credence has grown, its presence has been constant: Frank O'Connor in 1942 decried de Valera's 'dream of a nonentity state entirely divorced from the rest of the world'[15] while the same year saw Sean O'Faoláin declaring that 'the new generation can get no help from the aloof and subjective Yeatsian self-dramatisation'.[16] The impulse behind these denunciations is found in the opening editorial of *The Bell*, the journal founded by O'Faoláin in 1940. The old words, heroes and images were dead, he declared; '[these] belong to the time when we growled in defeat and dreamed of the future. That future has arrived and, with its arrival, killed them'.[17] It is clear that for O'Faoláin the hoped for future was open rather than insular, its inspiration less Yeats than Joyce for, as he wrote in *The Irish*, '[looking] back now at 1920–50 my most profound regret is that it had not been possible for us all to have read cold Joyce in our warm teens'.[18] The reference to Joyce is freighted with significance for, as further explored by Thomas Kinsella in a positive reformulation of the previous binary opposition of authenticity and modernity, 'the Irish writer, if he cares who he is and where he comes from, finds that Joyce and Yeats are the two main objects in view, and I think he finds that Joyce is the true father'.[19] While expressed in moderate terms by Kinsella, Yeats now becomes the negative pole who lacks the authentic contact with the culture, while it is Joyce, Irish and European, who forges links which 'simultaneously [revive] the Irish tradition and admits the modern world';[20] Irish authenticity then becomes outward, progressive and European rather than conservative and insular; indeed, as Yeats is the arch-articulator of these features they are rendered suspect precisely because of his multiple points of divergence from 'the people'.[21]

Kinsella's intervention is as much political as cultural, being publicly presented (1966) and then published (1970) in the crucial interim between T.K. Whitaker's *Economic Development* report of 1958 and Ireland's entry into the EEC in 1973. What followed Kinsella was a repositioning of 'Irishness' in which one side of the binary opposition, namely a modernity shorn of its negative English associations, was now the Irish good, while the rural, emanating from the suspect Yeats, was a regressive and debilitating drag on the nation's development and psychic health. With the destructive dimensions of the resurgence of the Northern troubles becoming daily more apparent, critics following Kinsella felt impelled to continue this reformulation of binary oppositions, not least because, as Seamus Deane noted in 1984, the conflict between the Civil Rights movement and Unionism was but 'a more recent example of the battle between a cosmopolitan liberalism and consolidated native loyalties'.[22] Deane demonstrably plays a variant on Kinsella in that the authentic Irish protest of Civil Rights is 'cosmopolitan liberalism' while Unionism becomes 'native loyalties'; a move which, in conflating the nominally 'Yeatsian' demand for the native with (non-cosmopolitan, non-liberal) Unionism, establishes both as inauthentic positions within the modern moment. As Deane observed, this pull of tradition had to be transcended: 'It is time to change ground before it opens up and swallows us'[23] as 'if you look not forward, but back, to a lost wholeness and then seek to regain that, then you have not only a conservative politics but you also have a romantic literature'.[24]

This rejection of the past and the rural orientation in official Irish culture was echoed by many in the 1980s but it was Declan Kiberd, in an article published simultaneously with Deane's, who scorched old pieties in an excoriating attack on 'the pull of the past': 'Once a rude imposition the pastoral Ireland of Yeats and de Valera has now become a downright oppression [. . .] a sentimentalisation of backwardness in Ireland, a surrender to what Marx once called "the idiocy of rural life"', above all, claimed Kiberd, what was being denied was 'the heroism of urban life'.[25] The impulse was then to celebrate that which had previously been denied, to embrace as progressively Irish the previously denied urban and modern pole of the oppositions. When Fintan O'Toole addressed the 1985 Yeats International Summer School the agenda was explicit, as he denounced the 'false opposition of the country to the city which has been vital to the maintenance of a conservative culture in the country'.[26] In O'Toole's formulation the rural image has rendered Ireland impotent to cope with far-reaching economic changes: 'By retaining a notion of a real, true Ireland of nature and landscape and sturdy peasantry, it has been possible to modernize the countryside, to turn it into a profitable base for American multinational industry and EEC capitalist farming, while still believing that the heart of the nation remains pure'.[27] Rather than literary-rural rhetoric what was wanted was a literature which engaged with, and so equipped its audience to see, the too long elided modern and urban reality of contemporary Ireland.

Following on from Kiberd's elevation of the 'heroic' urban life O'Toole concluded: '[it] is only now that an urban literature from within the modern city is beginning to develop, perhaps most clearly in the work of the Finglas writers Dermot Bolger and Michael O'Loughlin. It is no accident that the first task they have set themselves is the reclaiming of modern Irish history by those who have been written out of it'.[28] That 1985 position was reiterated three years later with the claim that '[writers] such as Bolger, O'Loughlin or Quinn, are creating a literature out of the new realities, confirming that the Irish young are part of the subculture of Europe, drifting in and out of the shifting army of industrial gastarbeiters in Germany or Amsterdam. Sex, drugs and rock and roll are more important in their work than religion, nationalism and land'.[29] This conscious inversion of Daniel Corkery's famous definition of the tripartite signifiers of Irish authenticity redefines Irishness as locatable within an urban European culture, but the work of those heralded as ushering in the decisively new dawn is less progressively European than regressively Irish; the dystopian urban images in their texts often simply legitimizing Hyde's Revival rejection of that fallen world from which emanated 'the garbage of vulgar English weeklies'.[30]

What has then replaced the rural kitsch into which the worst excesses of post-Revival ruralism had degenerated is an image of the urban so determinedly devoid of sustenance as to render suspect the viability of the Republic itself. As imaged by Bolger in the opening paragraph of *The Woman's Daughter*:

> There is a city of the dead standing sentinel across from her window. Through the gulley between them a swollen rivulet is frothing over smooth rocks brimming with the effervescent waste of factories. Within its boundaries grey slabs of granite are flecked with shards of mud as sheets of rain churn up the black pools that nestle in the webbed tyre tracks. Above its crumbling lanes and avenues stooped ivy trees shiver over the homes where no soul moves.[31]

Bolger's work is determinedly dystopian; whether in plays such as *The Lament for Arthur Cleary* where Dublin is 'like some honky-tonk provincial plaza. Everywhere closed except the burger huts, all the buses gone, everyone milling around drunk, taking to the glittering lights like aborigines to whiskey'[32] or *The Journey Home*, where the protagonist Hano, sheltering with his girlfriend in a deserted country cottage, reads both the rural and the urban as lost to the dispossessed Irish young: 'I used to think of here as the past, a fossilized rural world I had to fight to be rid of. I got the conflict wrong of course. [. . . This] crumbling house in the woods is our future, is our destination, is nowhere [. . .] soon it will be all that's left for the likes of you and I to belong to. City or country, it will make little difference, ruins, empty lots, wherever they cannot move us from'.[33] Bolger's Ireland is then a lost cause, and while it may be argued that he works to encourage the audience/reader to desire that self and national realization which, once promised, is demonstrably not delivered, the absence of any sign of redemption imposes a severe limitation on this as a possibility. To a lesser extent the same comment could be made of the early work of Michael O'Loughlin, another of O'Toole's 'dogs of the city'. In poems from the 1977 collection, *Stalingrad: The Street Directory*, O'Loughlin captures the resolutely anti-Revival note of that and the subsequent decade which involves a rejection of the mythic past and those aspects of the present which carry its association, most notably the language. In 'Cuchulainn' the ancient Irish hero is set as an irrelevancy in the modern world where his name means 'Less than Librium, or Burton's biscuits / Or Phoenix Audio-Visual Systems'.[34] The same anti-essentialist iconoclasm is found in 'The Irish Lesson' where he rejects his teachers' entreaties for him to learn Irish: 'I don't want to learn their language / It wasn't mine'; 'I didn't want to know their nation's heritage / It wasn't mine'.[35] It is the poem 'On Hearing Michael Hartnett Read his Poetry in Irish' from the 1985 collection *The Diary of a Silence*, however, that is paradigmatic of a more general critical-cultural shift as the repressed and derided dimension of the culture reasserts itself as, literally, a potentially sustaining centre: 'I hear our history on my tongue, / The music of what has happened!', 'tonight, for the first time / I heard the sound / Of the snow falling through moonlight/ Onto the empty fields'.[36] The lines irresistibly invoke the epiphany of Joyce's Gabriel Conroy in 'The Dead' as he moves from his fixation on Continental Europe and embraces, albeit in a dream state, the too long denied otherness of the western/rural reality of his own culture. For the contemporary critic and creator, however, an 'innocent' return is an impossibility; indeed any return can fall prey to the perils of nostalgia. A trap exemplified in all its seductive but disabling allure by the 1992 film *Into the West*.[37]

Into the West dramatizes the journey westward as a fabulous return to the source; a means of healing and redemption by which Papa Reilly is released from the 'settled' life in Dublin's decaying North Side into a return to the traveller's life he abandoned after the death of his wife in childbirth. From the opening credits in which the film's title emanates from the body of the white horse as it courses its shimmering path across the moonlit strand, the horse – named Tir na Nog (the land of the young) – carries a redemptive power. Papa's youngest son, Ossie, is relieved of his asthma attack by proximity to the horse and can make the animal obey his every command; he has 'the gift' is the judgement of his traveller grandfather who has brought the horse from the west into the desolation of Dublin, while Papa has 'lost the gift' and has become 'a fallen man'. The film's dramatic and thematic concern is with a redemptive return to the authentic source of the west and a rejection of the east where travellers live on social security fraud amid a desolation of derelict cars and high-rises, their only entertainment the television which runs a perpetual diet of westerns. It is this which opens up the film's thematic heart.

As Papa's two sons set out to the west on Tir na Nog, the horse's future threatened by a corrupt liaison between a Gardai and business man for whom the horse's show-jumping prowess promises rich rewards, their constant reference is to cowboys; hills are The Rockies, and Hi Ho Silver! their cry. That on which the film is explicit, however, is that they and their father are 'Indians'; a concept which is crucial to the film's overall project.

As Papa enters a travellers' camp in search of his sons he is faced with a rejection for his having become 'settled'. That evening, in a romanticized setting of campfire dancing to Uilleann pipes and bodhrans, Papa enters into the dance, his abandon suggesting both the vitality of that to which he is progressively, if unconsciously, becoming committed and the repression effected by his seven years' 'settled' state. Insulted as 'Indians' and as 'animals' by the Gardai and settled people alike, Papa and his companions finally locate the children at the grave of the mother in the west. Here, corruption is defeated, the dead mother's spirit is acknowledged and laid to rest, and Tir na Nog, the horse which is symbol of mother and authenticity, returns to the waves from which it emerged. The full significance of this westward movement towards both release and return is contained in the title of the film the boys watch while on their journey westward – *Back to the Future (III)*. While no more than the title signifies in this context, there being no narrative allusions to be drawn on, *Into the West* is explicitly concerned with the informing idea that returning to the past is a move into the future, a realized life for Papa and his sons only being possible if the old, indigenous ('Indian') way of life is embraced. The west is then revalidated as the source of a harmony abandoned within the urban east and the binary oppositions inverted once more. The fact that such a theme with its value-laden spatial dichotomies should be reintroduced within a commercial venture in 1990s Ireland says much about the current state of the nation, one in which, as Des Bell has argued, 'Ireland is witnessing a provincial flight into nostalgia'.[38] This is a response to a complex series of currents in which postmodernism's much-vaunted erasure of the metanarrative of nationalism overlaps with the more local suspicion of the impulse underpinning 'revisionist' reforms. As observed by Tom Garvin, 'The recent constitutional referenda on abortion and divorce cannot be understood except as representing the latest battles in a long, and partly symbolic, political and moral war against external secularist forces and the Anglo-American world'.[39] This struggle between, in Desmond Fennell's terms, 'nice people and rednecks', takes place on terrain dominated by the 'nice people', namely the liberal middle class of Dublin, who characterize those opposed to their various reforms as 'a horde of nasty, rough and bigoted Catholic nationalists'.[40] While in no way reducible to 'redneck' hysteria the writing of Deane provides an exemplary insight into the full complexity of the current negotiation between the previously mutually exclusive oppositions of tradition (the rural west) and modernity (the urban east).

In two seminal articles of the 1980s, 'Remembering the Irish Future' and 'Heroic Styles: The Tradition of an Idea' Deane argued for the need for Ireland to move beyond positions predicated on the mystique of authenticity and, by implication, the binary oppositions of rural and urban. 'These are worn oppositions', he declared. 'They used to be the parenthesis in which the Irish destiny was isolated. That is no longer the case'.[41] However, by the time of his 1990 introduction to *Nationalism, Colonialism and Literature*, a collection of the 1988 Field Day pamphlets by Edward Said, Terry Eagleton and Fredric Jameson, Deane could castigate the Republic for its abandonment of identity to the vagaries of the free-play of the market: '[it] has surrendered the notion of identity altogether as a monotonous and barren anachronism and rushed to embrace all of those corporate, "international" opportunities offered by the European Economic Community and the tax-free visitations of international cartels'.[42] It is impossible to comprehend this apparent volte-face without grasping the profound threat perceived in 'Revisionism', a process which, while primarily associated with the discipline of history, is above all part of a process driven by a liberal establishment committed to the 'modernization' of Ireland. As a result, argues Deane, a 'genial depthlessness' masquerading as pluralism pervades debate and the beneficiaries of such blandness 'regards the rest of Ireland as the hinterland of its benighted past'.[43] Deane is acutely aware of the paradox involved in such an argument, that in order to resist the historical thinning of consciousness which Jameson identified as the real penalty of postmodernism, he has to reaffirm a notion of identity which, in its essentialist overtones, he had struggled for a decade to deconstruct.[44] But as he noted: '[while there is] an inevitable monotony involved here [it is] inescapable in colonial conditions'.[45] That to which Deane was irrevocably moving was Gayatri Spivak's 'strategic essentialism', an appreciation of the need to mobilize identity as a site of resistance to its erasure while remaining constantly conscious of the provisional nature of that which was to be defended; above all 'the strategic use of a positivist essentialism in a scrupulously visible political interest'.[46] This achieved its fullest expression to date in a 1993 interview where, while acknowledging his previous combating of an 'essentialist version of Irish nationalism', he was equally aware of 'the need that people have to construct an historical identity [and] the viability of essentialist arguments as political strategies'.[47] Not only Deane, but also Kiberd has moved to this ground, as exemplified by his disparaging of those 'designer-Stalinists' who wish to retain the worn oppositions: 'for them, it must always be a simple choice between tradition or modernity, nationalism or social progress, soccer or Gaelic football. Those who defend tradition, nationalism or the GAA are merely jeered; but those who try to combine both elements represent an insupportable "ambivalence" and so are targeted for vicious attack'.[48] In this context the most pertinent question is asked by Benita Parry: 'Does revisiting the repositories of memory and cultural survivals in the cause of postcolonial refashioning have a fixed retrograde valency?'; a question unambiguously answered in that 'the need to renew or reactivate memories is distinct from the uncritical attempt to conserve tradition'.[49] In these terms Kiberd's 'ambivalence' becomes a means of accessing the creative possibility of a future promised in the past; a radical backward look in terms analogous to those of Jameson: 'there is no reason why a nostalgia conscious of itself, a lucid and remorseless dissatisfaction with the present on the grounds of some remembered plenitude, cannot furnish as adequate a revolutionary stimulus as any other'.[50] It is this position which is now informing critical Irish debate, whether in the literary-cultural writings of Deane and Kiberd or those of rock critic John Waters.

In his study of U2, *Race of Angels*, Waters asserts the imperative of '[going] back into the bank of knowledge which has been passed to us by the culture of which we are a part'. What is explicit, moreover, is the extent to which this is to be a creative re-appropriation of the denied, rural-based, essentialism: 'in a world being swept to its ruin by centrifugal forces, hopes of a better future may lie in a return to a view from the fringe, a view which, by virtue of its marginality is less contaminated by the forces of convergence. In other words, the extent to which Irish forms of thought remain "primitive" may be increasingly useful in the coming years'.[51] It was, however, Waters's earlier book, *Jiving at the Crossroads*, which made the simplest and clearest plea to retain that which was being too readily abandoned as anachronistic. Full of sympathy for a rural 'traditional' Ireland, while not blind to its limitations, Waters chronicles its progressively negative image as circulated by the media, above all by the mind-set known as 'Dublin 4' which 'wanted no truck with the dark, irrational, priest ridden place it called "rural Ireland". For "Dublin 4" this place was just a bad dream, a mild irritation on the periphery of its consciousness, a darkness on the edge of town'.[52] What emerged from that rejection was a situation in which 'part of the Irish public shriveled itself up into a foetal hunch' when faced with 'a new form of tyranny, at least as unpleasant as that which these voices told us they wished to remove'.[53]

The negotiation of this terrain is complex. As many critics have observed, there is the sheer irrevocability of the past within the global economy of postmodernity: 'There can be no recovery of an authentic cultural homeland. In a world that is increasingly characterized by exile, migration and diaspora, with all the consequences of unsettling and hybridization, there can be no place for such absolutism of the pure and authentic. In this world, there is no longer any place like Heimat'.[54] Such conditions affect the cultural at various levels ranging from cynical acceptance to sentimental rejection, the desolation of The Pogues' 'The Sick Bed of Cuchulain' where the ancient hero is reminded of the time 'When you pissed yourself in Frankfurt and got syph down in Cologne'[55] or Doyle's *Barrytown Trilogy* which, despite its sure grasp of the demotic, works within a sentimental construct well captured in George O'Brien's description of Barrytown as a 'version of pastoral'.[56] A less ascerbic comment, and one more indicative of the assumptions, rather than the realities, informing the emergence of Northside Realism, is that given by Ferdia MacAnna who celebrated the new Dublin it imaged as one 'beginning to stir from its literary coma and shake free of the many myths and cliches that had inhibited and prevented its literary, artistic and even social development'.[57] The idea that a shift in cultural consciousness is a prerequisite of social progress is the populist version of Friedrich Nietzsche's 'critical history' in which cultures must 'from time to time employ the strength to break up and dissolve a part of the past'.[58] While the movement from Nietzsche's 'monumental' to 'critical' history is a necessity, in that not to do so is to embrace ossification, too rapid a rush to rejection results in a cynicism towards tradition which effects a withering act of cultural deracination. What is required is what Homi Bhabha has termed the 'Third Space', the location/state which recognizes 'that [while] the meaning and symbols of culture have no primordial fixity [they] can be appropriated, translated, rehistoricized and read anew'.[59] In an argument redolent of Walter Benjamin and Jameson, Bhabha speaks of a 'projective past',[60] above all the idea that future identity is to be founded on 'the incommensurable elements',[61] those cultural remnants which combat homogenization and which, if rejected rather than accommodated, effect a profound psychic disturbance.

Tom Murphy's seminal plays of the mid-1980s, *Conversations on a Homecoming* and *Bailegangaire,* dramatize the disturbance consequent on both rejection of, and entrapment within, 'tradition', as the characters of Michael in *Conversations* and Mommo in *Bailegangaire* move to a conclusion marked by Michael's defeat and Mommo's regeneration, both predicated on their ability to grasp what Benjamin termed 'an after-life of that which is understood, whose pulse can still be felt in the present'.[62] While the prodigal Michael is paralysed by the knowledge that '[they've] probably cut down the rest of the wood by now' it is the young Anne, 'smiling her gentle hope out at the night', who articulates the possibility of redemption, above all that in the midst of despoilation '[there's] still the stream'.[63] Just as this 'backward look' is creative, so too is the movement in *Bailegangaire* in which Mommo's re-engagement with the present and projection toward the future is only possible when she finishes the narrative of the past; a movement which does not destroy connections, for the unborn baby whose arrival will provide the 'hope' for the family is also to be named Tom, a powerful connection with the dead grandson, whose unstated death has trapped Mommo until the point she can acknowledge loss and open the possibility of progress. The allusive poetic expression of these plays often belies analysis in other terms than their own but they are both powerful dramatizations of Benjamin's assertion that, properly realized, '[regression] assumes a progressive function'.[64] More recently, and more explicitly, Anne Devlin's *After Easter* expresses this theme with a fullness suggestive of an idea which has increasing currency.

In the character of Greta, Devlin also renders the breakdown of one of those people 'who leave their own country [but] stop living, in some part of themselves, in the same year in which they left'.[65] Focusing on the traumatic period of re-engagement with an Ireland not only left but rejected, Devlin articulates through the character of Greta's brother Manus, post-nationalism's reappraisal of tradition and belonging. Mocked by his sister Helen for having moved to an Irish-American sentimentalization through his concern with fiddle music, Manus rejects her characterization of this as 'Glockammora' and retorts: 'The music grows in you like a tree and I can't compose something else until I know my own tree'.[66] This evocation of the trees and music of Yeats's 'Among School Children' which addresses itself to a holistic vision of existence in which the part is inseparable from the whole signals the extent to which Devlin's theme is presaged by Yeats's concept of 'the rooted against the rootless people'.[67] Helen is rendered suspect by her adopted American accent and querying of the very basis of identity – 'What is it with you – does everything have to have a nationality?'[68] – while Manus evinces a determination to embrace that which their communist father 'robbed' from them: 'I'm talking about the music, the language, the culture. It was traditional, he said it was nationalist so we never learnt it. Now I spend all my time trying to get it back'.[69] It is this 'ignorance' based on the erroneous equation between the cultural rootedness of tradition with the political moment of nationalism that Greta too has effected. Wholeness can only be realized when that rejected can be embraced; a moment rendered as Greta adopts the traditional storytelling role of *seancha* and poetically images her embrace of the cold and hungry stag which 'leapt through hundreds of years to reach us': 'I took some berries from my bag and fed the stag from the palm of my hand. The stag's face was frozen and I had to be careful because it wanted to kiss me, and if I had let it, I would have died of cold. But gradually as it ate, its face was transformed and it began to take on human features. And then the thaw set in [. . .]. I could hear all the waters of the forest rushing and it filled my years with a tremendous sound'.[70] The 'years' which are now filled with sound are those in which she could say 'I don't want to be Irish',[71] but this is no simple and uncritical return to the source; the full implication of this closing scene which is comprised solely of Greta's fable is that 'Greta is at home, rocking a baby, telling it a story'. This return to the previously rejected new home and baby in England is the dramatization of what Kearney referred to as 'the migrant mind': 'Having taken one's distance from the "homeland", physically or mentally, you can return to it and find there something of immense and lasting value. Traditions of myth and music can be explored again with a newfound and non-fanatical freedom'. Above all, argues Kearney, 'the post-modern awareness [is] that we cannot afford to *not* know our past'.[72]

This flow across frontiers of time and space to engage with origin in a progressive rather than regressive mode has become the stuff of modern theory; in part this is the nomadism which Rosi Braidotti describes as 'an epistemological and political imperative for critical thought at the end of the millennium'.[73] While Braidotti's project is founded in modern feminism aspects of her thesis are equally applicable to all anti-essentialist movements, above all in the sense that 'nomadic identity consists in not taking any kind of identity as permanent'.[74] While Braidotti is not always clear as to how far the erasure of identity is to go, sometimes defining nomadism as 'vertiginous progression towards deconstructing identity; molecularisation of the self',[75] it is the central impulse towards a 'critical consciousness', a 'subversion of set conventions' which provides the core concept; above all the idea that it is crucially a case of 'blurring boundaries without burning bridges'.[76] 'Home' can be both accessed and redefined;

the backward look can also be a means of moving forward. While the title of the 1988 film, *Joyriders*, is the colloquial term used for car thieves, it is more pertinently taken literally; the criss-cross riding of Ireland does lead, ultimately, to the joy of a west regained.[77]

While *Into the West* essayed only one double movement – into the west and into the past so effecting an essentially conservative critique of the present – *Joyriders* is also based on a western journey, but this time the final western move being the result of human rather than mystical agency, and while it too closes on the promised harmonization of a divided family, the film is marked by an appreciation of the differing desolation of both the contemporary east and west; what is effected in the film's conclusion is a progressive reappropriation of an essentially redundant ideology and its projection into a future which is both hopeful and hesitant – the film ends as the voyagers' car enters the environs of the farm on which they are to settle.

In *Joyriders* the western journey is initially more flight than voyage as Mary, a brutalized wife, is forced to abandon her children and, in the company of Perky, a petty criminal desperate to escape from creditors, heads towards the west coast town of Killeel, the one place she remembers being happy. The west is rendered with a 'Ballroom of Romance' bleakness as ageing bachelors and a seedy proprietor variously proposition Mary who takes up a job as dance hostess. Yet it is within this west of desolate sterility that a crucial act of potential redemption occurs.

Having initially abandoned Mary, Perky returns to the dance hall and joins her in a jive of formal precision to the music of 'Carrickfergus' after which they exit and drive to the one-man farm which is to become the focus of the film's dramatic and thematic resolution. The luminosity of the moment of the dance as the couple are left alone on the dance floor, in harmony with, yet not constrained by the 'folk' song which is sung, significantly, in both Irish and English, suggests a recuperation of the culture which is both respectful and progressive as modern form is overlaid on indigenous matter; the dance then becoming the informing conceit for the film's dramatic and thematic resolution.

The farm to which they gravitate, as the whole of the west it is suggested, is home to an ageing widower who now finds 'more crack in being asleep than awake'. In a run of sequences which irresistibly evoke John Ford westerns the land is resettled as a garden is planted, a gate rehung and a tractor repaired. While there may be paradox in starting a tractor, and so allowing the machine back in to the garden, the stress here is on revitalizing that which is dying, above all in the repeopling which occurs after Mary and Perky return to Dublin to rescue her children from the orphanage and deliver them 'into the west'. The closing minutes contain all the cumulative intensity of theme and image to which the film has been pointing, as shots of the clamour of neon-lit night-time Dublin in which Mary and her children cower among the flow of traffic while street-fights occur nearby are progressively replaced by the emerging light of dawn as the 'family' enter the west to the music, once again, of 'Carrickfergus'; the echo of the dance suggesting, on the wider canvas of the west itself, that the indigenous can be rescued, as the modern is redeemed, if a creative harmony can be established between them. While the film closes with a freeze-frame as their car enters the farm, so suspending ultimate resolution, the force of the narrative to this point is clear: the modern world of youth and frustrated promise can be realized within the accommodating space of a west whose vitality has been sapped. The conclusion is more complex than that of *Into the West* in that modernity is admitted and final harmony withheld but, as with *After Easter*, what is beyond dispute is that it is the past, tradition, most literally 'the west', which must be acknowledged if a future is to be achieved.

In his article 'Of Other Spaces' Michel Foucault coined the term 'heterotopia' to describe those locations which, according to one of his definitions, are used by a culture to create a space 'as perfect, as meticulous, as well arranged as ours is messy, ill constructed and jumbled'.[78] This, says Foucault, is the heterotopia of 'compensation'. While it is clear that 'the west' can perform a consoling and compensatory role in a culture riven by uncertainty as to its relationship to the future, its more creative role is best defined in Foucault's formulation of the heterotopia of the mirror: 'From the standpoint of the mirror I discover my absence from the place where I am since I see myself over there. Starting from this gaze that is, as it were, directed toward me, from the ground of this virtual space that is on the other side of the glass, I come back toward myself; I begin again to direct my eyes towards myself and to reconstitute myself there where I am'.[79]

Notes

1. *Hear My Song*, dir. P. Chelsom, Miramax Films, 1991.
2. J.M. Synge, *The Aran Islands* in *J.M. Synge: Collected Works*, ed. A. Price (London: Oxford University Press, 1966), II, pp. 57, 116, 142, 129–30.
3. *Family* (four-part television series by R. Doyle) dir. M. Winterbottom, BBC 1, May 1994.
4. J. Derrida, *Positions* (London: Athlone, 1981), pp. 41–2.
5. Quoted in T. Brown, *Ireland: A Social and Cultural History 1922–1985* (London: Fontana, 1981), p. 93.
6. G. Moore, 'Literature and the Irish Language' in *Ideals in Ireland*, ed. Lady Gregory (London: At the Unicorn VII Cecil Court, 1901), p. 50.
7. Kearney, 'Myth and Motherland' in *Ireland's Field Day*, ed. Field Day Theatre Company (London: Hutchinson, 1985), p. 69.
8. S. Heaney, 'An Open Letter' in *Ireland's Field Day*, p. 27.
9. Quoted in F. O'Toole, 'Tourists in Our Own Land' in *Black Hole, Green Card* (Dublin: New Island Books, 1994), p. 44.
10. F. O'Toole, 'The Lie of the Land' in *Black Hole, Green Card*, p. 28.
11. Quoted in L. Gibbons, 'Romanticism, Realism and Irish Cinema' in *Cinema and Ireland*, K. Rockett, L. Gibbons, J. Hill (London: Routledge, 1988), p. 195.
12. J. Eglinton, 'National Drama and Contemporary Life' in *Literary Ideals in Ireland*, J. Eglinton et al. (London: T. Fisher Unwin, 1899, rept. New York: Lemma Publishing Corporation, 1973), p. 26.
13. J. Joyce, *Ulysses* (Harmondsworth: Penguin, 1986), p. 153.
14. L. Gibbons, 'Montage, Modernism and the City', *The Irish Review*, 10 (1991), 5.
15. F. O'Connor, 'The Future of Irish Literature', *Horizon*, 5: 25 (1942), 61.
16. S. O'Faoláin, 'Yeats and the Younger Generation', *Horizon*, 5: 25 (1942), 51.
17. S. O'Faoláin, 'This is Your Magazine' in *The Best From the Bell*, ed. S. McMahon (Dublin: The O'Brien Press, 1978), p. 13.
18. S. O'Faoláin, *The Irish* (Harmondsworth: Penguin, 1980), p. 142.
19. T. Kinsella, 'The Irish Writer' in *Davis, Mangan, Ferguson? Tradition and the Irish Writer*, W. B. Yeats and T. Kinsella (Dublin: The Dolmen Press, 1970), p. 65.
20. T. Kinsella, 'The Irish Writer', p. 65.
21. See T. Brown, 'Yeats, Joyce and Irish Critical Debate' in *Ireland's Literature* (Gigginstown: Lilliput Press, 1988), pp. 77–90.
22. S. Deane, 'Remembering the Irish Future', *The Crane Bag*, 8: 1 (1984), 82.
23. S. Deane, 'Remembering the Irish Future', 86.
24. S. Deane, 'Remembering the Irish Future', 84.
25. D. Kiberd, 'Inventing Irelands', *The Crane Bag*, 8:1 (1984), 13.
26. F. O'Toole, 'Going West: The Country Versus the City in Irish Writing', *The Crane Bag*, 9: 2 (1985), 111.

27. F. O'Toole, 'Going West: The Country Versus the City in Irish Writing', 115.
28. F. O'Toole, 'Going West: The Country Versus the City in Irish Writing', 116.
29. F. O'Toole, 'Island of Saints and Silicon: Literature and Social Change in Contemporary Ireland' in *Cultural Contexts and Literary Idioms in Contemporary Irish Literature*, ed. M. Kenneally (Gerrards Cross: Colin Smythe, 1988), p. 35.
30. D. Hyde, 'The Necessity for De-Anglicising Ireland' in *The Revival of Irish Literature: Addresses by Sir Charles Gavan Duffy, Dr George Sigerson, Dr Douglas Hyde*, Sir C.G. Duffy, Dr G. Sigerson, Dr D. Hyde (London: Fisher Unwin 1894; rept. New York: Lemma Publishing, 1973), p. 159.
31. D. Bolger, *The Woman's Daughter* (Harmondsworth: Penguin, 1991), p. 3.
32. D. Bolger, *The Lament for Arthur Cleary*, in *A Dublin Quartet* (Harmondsworth: Penguin, 1992), p. 22.
33. D. Bolger, *The Journey Home* (Harmondsworth: Penguin, 1990), p. 291.
34. M. O'Loughlin, 'Cuchulainn' in *The Inherited Boundaries: Younger Poets of the Republic of Ireland*, ed. S. Barry (Dublin: Dolmen Press, 1986), p. 122.
35. M. O'Loughlin, 'The Irish Lesson' in *The Inherited Boundaries*, p. 125.
36. M. O'Loughlin, 'On Hearing Michael Hartnett Read his Poetry in Irish' in *The Inherited Boundaries*, p. 140.
37. *Into The West*, dir. M. Newell, Majestic Films, 1992.
38. D. Bell, 'Ireland Without Frontiers? The Challenge of the Communications Revolution' in *Across the Frontiers: Ireland in the 1990s*, ed. R. Kearney (Dublin: Wolfhound, 1988), p. 229.
39. T. Garvin, 'The Politics of Denial and of Cultural Defence: The Referenda of 1983 and 1986 in Context', *The Irish Review*, 3 (1988), 5.
40. D. Fennell, 'The Nice People v. the Rednecks' in *Nice People & Rednecks: Ireland in the 1980s* (Dublin: Gill and Macmillan, 1986), pp. 87–8.
41. S. Deane, 'Heroic Styles: The Tradition of an Idea' in *Ireland's Field Day*, p. 58.
42. S. Deane, 'Introduction' in *Nationalism, Colonialism and Literature*, T. Eagleton, F. Jameson, E. Said (Minneapolis: University of Minneapolis Press, 1990), pp. 13–14.
43. S. Deane, 'Wherever Green is Read' in *Revising the Rising*, eds M. Ní Dhonnchadha and T. Dorgan (Derry: Field Day Theatre Company, 1991), p. 98.
44. See A. Stephenson, 'Regarding Postmodernism – A Conversation with Fredric Jameson' in *Universal Abandon? The Politics of Postmodernism*, ed. A. Ross (Minneapolis: University of Minnesota Press, 1988), p. 7.
45. S. Deane, 'Introduction', *Nationalism, Colonialism and Literature*, p. 11.
46. G.C. Spivak, 'Subaltern Studies: Deconstructing Historiography' in *In Other Worlds: Essays in Cultural Politics* (London: Routledge, 1988), p. 205.
47. D. Callaghan, 'An Interview with Seamus Deane', *Social Text*, 38 (1994), 40.

48. D. Kiberd, 'The Elephant of Revolutionary Forgetfulness' in *Revising the Rising*, p. 15.
49. B. Parry, 'Resistance Theory/theorizing resistance or two cheers for nativism' in *Colonial discourse/postcolonial theory*, eds F. Barker, P. Hulme and M. Iversen (Manchester: Manchester University Press, 1993), p. 174.
50. F. Jameson, *Marxism and Form* (Princeton: Princeton University Press, 1971), p. 82.
51. J. Waters, *Race of Angels: The Genesis of U2* (London: Fourth Estate, 1994), p. 282–3.
52. J. Waters, *Jiving at the Crossroads* (Belfast: Blackstaff Press, 1991), p. 109.
53. J. Waters, *Jiving at the Crossroads*, p. 86.
54. D. Morley and K. Robins, 'No Place Like Heimat: Images of Home(land) in European Culture' in *Space & Place: Theories of Identity and Location*, eds E. Carter, J. Donald and J. Squires (London: Lawrence & Wishart, 1993), p. 27.
55. S. MacGowan, 'The Sick Bed of Cuchulain', *Rum, Sodomy & the Lash*, Stiff Records, 1985.
56. G. O'Brien, 'Aspects of the Novelist', *The Irish Review*, 10 (1991), 117.
57. F. MacAnna, 'The Dublin Rennaisance: An Essay on Modern Dublin and Dublin Writers', *The Irish Review*, 10 (1991), 29.
58. F. Nietzsche, 'On the Uses and Disadvantages of History for Life' in *Untimely Meditations* (Cambridge: Cambridge University Press, 1983), p. 75.
59. H.K. Bhabha, 'The Commitment to Theory' in *The Location of Culture* (London: Routledge, 1994), p. 37.
60. H.K. Bhabha, 'Conclusion', *The Location of Culture*, p. 255.
61. H.K. Bhabha, 'How Newness Enters the World', *The Location of Culture*, p. 219.
62. W. Benjamin, 'Edward Fuchs, Collector and Historian' in *One Way Street and Other Writings* (London: Verso, 1985), p. 352.
63. T. Murphy, *Conversations on a Homecoming* (Dublin: Gallery Press, 1986), p. 74.
64. H. Marcuse, *Eros and Civilization: A Philosophical Inquiry into Freud* (London: Allen Lane, 1969), p. 19.
65. A. Devlin, *After Easter* (London: Faber, 1994), p. 58.
66. A. Devlin, *After Easter*, p. 39.
67. Quoted by R. Ellmann, *Yeats: The Man and the Mask* (New York: Thornton, 1979), p. 242.
68. A. Devlin, *After Easter*, p. 11.
69. A. Devlin, *After Easter*, p. 39.
70. A. Devlin, *After Easter*, p. 75.
71. A. Devlin, *After Easter*, p. 12.
72. R. Kearney, 'Migrant Minds' in *Across the Frontiers: Ireland in the 1990s*, p. 186.
73. R. Braidotti, *Nomadic Subjects: Embodiment and Sexual Difference in Contemporary Feminist Theory* (New York: Columbia University Press, 1994), p. 2.
74. R. Braidotti, *Nomadic Subjects*, p. 33.

75. R. Braidotti, *Nomadic Subjects*, p. 16.
76. R. Braidotti, *Nomadic Subjects*, p. 4.
77. *Joyriders*, dir. A. Walsh, Little Bird Films, 1988.
78. M. Foucault, 'Of Other Spaces', *Diacritics*, 16 (1986), 27.
79. M. Foucault, 'Of Other Spaces', 27.

7

Troubles, Terminus and *The Treaty*

Lance Pettitt

> Sinn Féin in direct talks at Downing Street with the British Prime Minister? Impossible? It actually happened 70 years ago . . . Tonight's drama brings the people and issues of that turbulent time to life.
>
> (*TV Times* preview caption for *The Treaty*, 1992)[1]

> LLOYD GEORGE: You know, you sound like you almost admire the man [Collins].
> FIELD MARSHAL WILSON: *Admire* him? I *detest* the very thought of him!
>
> (*The Treaty*)[2]

> If the implication [. . .] is that we should should sit down and talk with Mr Adams and the Provisional IRA, I can only say that that would turn my stomach and that of most honourable members. We will not do it.
>
> (John Major, House of Commons, 1 November 1993)[3]

INTRODUCTION

Historical anniversaries can present difficult moments for public service broadcasters to negotiate. When television institutions like RTÉ and ITV endorse programmes that mark significant events in national history they are duty-bound to be accurate and impartial. The RTÉ/Thames co-production of *The Treaty* was made specifically to commemorate the seventieth anniversary of the signing of the Anglo-Irish 'Treaty' in 1921 which signalled the end of the war between the IRA and the British Crown forces in

Ireland. The scheduling of twin broadcasts in December 1991 on RTÉ and January 1992 on ITV, and *The Treaty*'s impetus to 'reconstruct what had actually happened'[4] in the past, succeeded in generating some awkward questions about the politics of the present. Although it was based scrupulously on the historical 'facts', *The Treaty* nevertheless demonstrated the power of imagining the unimaginable, of foreseeing the future. Since its broadcast we have learned that while publicly refusing to 'talk with terrorists', the British government was secretly faxing with Sinn Féin.[5] *The Treaty* was one in a line of productions in the early 1990s that showed how drama-documentary can make a critical intervention by reminding us of the past and so challenge the contemporary consensus in Anglo-Irish relations.[6]

Essentially, in the figure of Michael Collins, the nature of the challenge was progressive and oppositional but, I will argue, not radically questioning. In the film Collins clearly retains his active association with and belief in the tactical use of violence, but also sees the need for a political resolution. These 'contradictions' are dramatized with a degree of sympathy and depth unusual for media representations of Irish republicans. Dramatically, Collins presents an attractive, charismatic, tragi-heroic figure in twentieth-century Irish history, particularly as he died at the age of 32. There has been a resurgence of both academic and popular interest in the Collins myth[7] during a period of secret, indirect and official negotiations between Anglo-Irish governments and republicans in what has come to be known as the 'peace process'. It is inevitable that historical parallels between 1921 and the particular conjuncture of 1991 would present themselves on the anniversary although several differences were evident too.

Nevertheless, *The Treaty* highlighted how a deeply-embedded, repulsion/fascination complex about Sinn Féin republicanism (shared in different ways by British and Irish governments) continues to exist at the expense of a convincing exploration of the logic and politics of Ulster Loyalism. If *The Treaty* is dramatically more effective for the marginalized presence of William Craig, the Ulster Unionist leader – who acted, according to Roger Bolton, 'as unseen threat'[8] in the film – there is a real political danger in contemporary peace negotiations of Loyalist feeling remaining absent. The prophetic significance of *The Treaty* can be more fully assessed if we explore the mechanics of authenticity, those complex interrelations between the film's textual matter and the different contexts (historical, cultural, televisual and generic) within which the film was planned, produced and broadcast.

TERMINUS POLITICS

The Treaty was conceived, made and shown during an eighteen-month period of rapid political change that brought about a terminus in Anglo-Irish relations. In November 1990 the Irish Republic elected Mary Robinson as its new president, signalling a change for liberal reform on social and constitutional issues. Charles Haughey faced a number of crises during 1991 and was replaced by Albert Reynolds in January 1992. This period symbolized the end of Fianna Fail's dominance of Irish party politics, giving way a year later to an era of coalition government with the Labour Party. With Haughey went one of the Southern state's craftiest politicians who espoused old-fashioned republican ideas. The questionable nature and limited extent of Haughey's republicanism had been displayed on the occasion of the 75th anniversary of the Easter Rising in April 1991 when he presided over a distinctly muted state commemoration of a founding moment in modern Irish history. This official response led some cultural critics to remark that the nationalist ideals of the 1916–23 period were being discreetly revised from the nation's official version of history and the armed rebellion simplistically compared with contemporary IRA violence.[9] Since 1988, the organization laying claim to that heritage of political violence had strategically changed the emphasis of its campaign from Northern Ireland to attacks on military, economic and symbolic targets in Britain and Europe. Bringing the war to Britain's doorstep did provoke some intellectual rationalization and popular expression for troop withdrawal from Northern Ireland (NI).[10] More to the point, Margaret Thatcher's defiance of terrorism had economic consequences: Conservative Exchequers paid out hard cash trying to contain 'terrorism'. Under John Major (Prime Minister from 1992), recession-hit Britain felt the cost of security and the threat of rising insurance payouts in the City.[11] But in Dublin, the Sinn Féin Ard Fheis of February 1991 was a subdued event. The party, having recently sustained heavy electoral losses in the Republic, was falling back on defensive positions in the North and showing signs of realigning its stance towards the military campaign of the IRA.

In the lead up to the Downing Street Declaration in 1993, it emerged that Martin McGuinness had been involved in periodic secret communications with the British government since October 1990, discussing the terms by which Sinn Féin might enter into the political process and how to achieve an IRA ceasefire. John Hume and Gerry Adams had also been engaged in a series of unofficial talks which contributed to the development of the peace process. Within NI itself, paramilitary activity became increasingly associated with Loyalist gun attacks. In 1991, between March and November, the UVF carried out five shootings in Cappagh, Moy, Markethill and Craigavon, targeting Catholics, relatives of Republican prisoners and Sinn Féin party members.[12]

It is clear that Bolton's idea for *The Treaty* was to seize the opportunity to put this contemporary violence and political change in some kind of historical context.[13] Given the co-production status of the project, it can be seen to address different but related issues for audiences in Britain and Ireland. For Bolton *The Treaty* aimed to inform an English audience largely ignorant of the complex historical connections between Ireland and Britain. For instance, the film insists on the audience recognizing that Ireland was *already* partitioned before the Treaty was negotiated. Legislation for the establishment of a NI parliament was hurriedly engineered between 1919 and 1920 in return for Craig's Ulster Unionist support to bolster Lloyd George's weak coalition government in London. The 'Treaty' of 1921 managed to end a dangerous guerrilla war in Britain's own backyard but it also confirmed the partition of Ireland and led to a civil war in the Southern state (1922–3).

From Liam Miller's (Executive Producer, RTÉ) point of view, the national broadcaster's sponsorship of the film presented a much-needed reinterpretation of 70 years of Irish history. The Irish civil war scarred the political consciousness of the new state and conditioned the pragmatism of its government. *The Treaty* offered a view that all of the main political figures involved in the negotiations acted with varying degrees of dishonesty and culpability. As one critic observed, the film 'dovetail[s] nicely with recent revisionist thinking'.[14] I do not think the film was as even-handed and neutral as some of the makers or critics of the film would like to believe. While the *RTÉ Guide*, promoting the Irish broadcast with the headline 'Truth and the Treaty', may have tended to encourage a revisionist reading of Irish history,[15] in the context of a British broadcast, *The Treaty* carried a different, potentially unsettling political charge.

TROUBLESOME ANNIVERSARIES

Mature public service broadcasting in Britain is characterized by its continual cycle of production and programming. Within this cyclical process coverage of annual state and national occasions have become part of a media invented 'tradition'. The history of relations between broadcasting and the nation shows us that television's anniversary-marking, like the recent 50th VE commemorations in Britain, forms part of a national cultural identity; television 'myths' are constructed to enable, maintain and support consensus views of national political history. The British military and financial commitment to Northern Ireland since August 1969 and the political stagnation represented by the Troubles provide ample material for 'anniversary syndrome', the troublesome demand for periodic recognition and reworking of priorities. Both major British broadcasting institutions undertook a 20-year retrospective in 1989 in the face of government restrictions on reporting Northern Ireland set in place a year earlier. Direct censorship of British broadcasting concerning Ireland was comparatively recent at the time of *The Treaty*, though Irish-related programmes have sustained considerable and varied forms of censorship in the form of professional codes, indirect legislation and self-censorship since 1971.[16] However, more recently, in the summer of 1994 the BBC and Channel Four competed for television 'Troubles' ratings.[17]

Bolton's original idea of making a programme about the 1921 Treaty negotiations was a brave and honourable attempt in a hostile climate of marginalization and the popular ignorance of Ireland in Britain. Seeking to make sense of political history for a popular audience, *The Treaty* was a standalone programme, not part of a series, which made it more difficult to finance and sell. In the event, *The Treaty* reached a creditable audience of 5.3 million viewers in the United Kingdom (BARB figures). Bolton was an experienced television producer with a proven reputation for dealing with Irish issues and had already had his fingers burned over his involvement with Thames Television's *This Week* programme 'Death on the Rock' (1988).[18] Although the programme's exposé was vindicated by the *Windlesham/Rampton Report,* it is widely accepted that its criticism of British government support for the SAS killing of IRA members in Gibraltar was responsible for the loss of Thames' licence in the ITV franchise reshuffle of 1990–1. *The Treaty* was a remarkable achievement given this wider context of change and uncertainty in television production as well as outright political hostility, but we need now to look in more detail at the specific production history of the project to examine its internal dynamics.

Bolton took his idea to Jonathan Lewis, inviting him to produce and direct a film to commemorate the anniversary. Bolton said that he 'wanted it to be a drama but was prepared to fall back on documentary',[19] whereas Lewis claims to have been approached to make a straight documentary by Bolton but that 'the idea to make it as a drama'[20] was his, largely due to the lack of archive film, surviving participants or minor eye witnesses to interview. Isobel Hinshelwood acted as associate producer and carried out valuable pre-production research. The cost of the film was split 50:50 between the main co-production companies, RTÉ and Thames but RTÉ provided resources rather than cash finance. The eventual £850,000 to £900,000 cost for the two-hour film was made up with money from John Boorman's Merlin Films and ABC television in Australia. An Irish writer living in England, Brian Phelan, was commissioned to write the screenplay once a period of intense research had been completed. The cast and crew were largely Irish and the film was shot almost entirely on location in Ireland. In sum, the production team represented a complex combination of different talents and perspectives which resulted in a highly polished television film.

David Miller has argued persuasively that the British state commands a significant proportion of informational and representational resources used in influencing public perceptions of Ireland.[21] But, as he points out, this is not an absolute form of domination because *within* and between media institutions there is professional competition to tell different stories. The media employ some individuals who wish to openly question or even oppose the political status quo. Tensions exist between programme makers, producers and senior executives when controversial programmes are planned. Senior executives anticipate ministerial intervention or pressure from boards of governors. In these ways, broadcasting institutions wrestle to facilitate but contain the dissensual views of some of its personnel by complying to statutory legislation and instituting self-imposed, professional codes of practice. *The Treaty* was different from the examples of drama-documentaries in 1990 in that instead of dealing with relatively recent events (for example, the Birmingham Pub Bombings or the Stalker Affair), it was a historical drama-documentary dealing with events beyond the contemporary period. As we shall see, historical topics are subject to censorial patrols just as much as contemporary events. *The Treaty*'s use of drama-documentary arose partly out of technical necessity but also formed part of a strategy to evade institutional and political containment.

PATROLLING THE BORDERLINES OF HISTORY?

> The drama documentary which lays claim to be a factual reconstruction of a controversial event covered by the [Television] Act is bound by the same standards of fairness and impartiality as those that apply to factual programmes in general.[22]

Television institutions seek to control the way in which their programmes are interpreted by their projected audience. As the above quotation indicates, this includes fictional programmes based on historical facts. Such control takes many forms including seemingly innocuous devices that are part of television discourse. The clearest examples are in preview publicity (listings magazines and newspaper items), continuity announcements and previews, and the less well known professional codes of practice outlined in documents like the BBC's *Producer's Guidelines* or the *ITC Programme Code.* Through such means a continual attempt is being made to shape the viewing of broadcast material but there is no guarantee that these are capable of achieving watertight control. This effort on behalf of the institution aims to produce and command a homogenous reading of material in the face of a heterogeneous *potential* for meanings. These ideas can be put in concrete terms if we examine how television treats history in the specific case of dramatized versions. In *Producer's Guidelines*, it is stressed that:

> *Difficulties do arise when a manifestly serious work of drama deals with controversial and recent history* [. . . .] *There must be strong*

> *reasons for a portrayal to be anything other than an account which is fair to the evidence* [. . .]. Programme executives should consider *how best to label and publicise the programme to ensure its nature is clear.*[23] (emphasis added)

The main objectives are clear: firstly, to stick to accepted versions of historical events, not to challenge them. Secondly, stress is placed on careful labelling of material. Individual programmes such as *The Treaty* are made within the context of institutional decision-making informed by this kind of thinking. The point is that television institutions prefer not to examine the accepted versions of national myths too closely in case it means opening them up to challenge and reinterpretation.

Television programmes do not exist in a vacuum but are surrounded by framing contexts such as TV magazine listings and previews which condition viewers' expectations. Differences do emerge between the two major listings magazines *Radio Times* and *TV Times* in the way that each promotes the other's programmes. In the *Radio Times* entry for 15 January 1992, *The Treaty* is given the caption: 'This powerful drama brings to life the people and the issues of that time',[24] whereas the *TV Times* caption is more provocative:

> Sinn Féin in direct talks at Downing Street with the British Prime Minister? Impossible? It actually happened 70 years ago' . . . Tonight's drama brings the people and issues of that turbulent time to life.[25]

This makes a direct parallel with contemporary politics and disrupts the 'no talking to terrorists' myth of British government policy. Although not directly linked, the broadcasting institutions and press do have some shared interests and exist symbiotically in Britain. Newspaper (p)reviews and post-transmission reviews also play their part in shaping the meaning of television programmes by producing critical opinion and comment. Of the newspapers that (p)reviewed *The Treaty* most felt the film brought an Anglocentric version of history into question while some felt the lesson of the film was to begin 'talking with terrorists'.[26] The scheduling of *The Treaty* is significant too. It was made for a popular audience and went out in a peak-evening slot (beginning at 9 p.m. and wrapped around the 10 p.m. news) in mid-week, reaching an audience of 5.3 million viewers. Ironically, while Churchill appeared as a character in *The Treaty*, over on the BBC a major biographical documentary series was launched at 9.25 p.m. which dealt with the English politician's early life and involvement with Ireland. Both the *Radio Times* and *TV Times* promoted *Churchill* with supporting feature articles and the programme achieved higher audience ratings which is perhaps only to be expected given the significance attributed to Churchill in modern British history.

While strategically necessary, the documentary thoroughness of *The Treaty* does not act as a guarantor of the fairness and impartiality stressed in professional codes. This much was anticipated by the ITC Code itself when it says:

> It is inevitable that the creative realisation of some elements (such as characterisation, dialogue and atmosphere) will introduce a fictional dimension, but this should not be allowed to distort the known facts.[27]

The film managed to gain maximum defensive strength from the facts but the screenplay and film text exceeded the boundaries exactly in those areas mentioned in parentheses.

FACTS LEAD TO F(R)ICTION

> Whenever programme makers, film-makers or playwrights tell True Stories, they try to persuade us to consume their product with a very particular promise – the Promise of Fact [. . .]. The power of the Fact has been leased out to drama.[28]

Derek Paget warns us to be wary about drama which purports to be based on fact. Those promoting *The Treaty*, claimed that the drama laid bare 'truths' about the historical events. The documentary evidence from the 1920s which forms the bedrock of *The Treaty* screenplay is skilfully mobilized in production and reception phases. The three main people involved in the production of *The Treaty* – Bolton, Phelan and Lewis – were all conscious of an 'audience ignorant of Irish history'[29] and Bolton in particular felt 'that side by side with contemporary current affairs reporting, of which I had done a great deal, there was a vital need for historical context'.[30]

Drama is conceived here as a necessary complement to broadcast journalism. Bolton had recently read Tim Pat Coogan's biography of Collins, Lewis had access to Robert Barton's diaries and papers, and it was decided that suitable material was available to commission Phelan to write a script, which was then checked for factual accuracy at a day-long 'seminar' attended by several leading scholars. Historical advisors to the project in the research phase included Coogan, biographer of Collins, Lord Longford and Roy Foster, thus encompassing a range of scholarly opinion. With all the 'facts' being verified, Bolton was convinced of the merit of the final product. He claimed 'the truth and authenticity of the script guarantees the success of *The Treaty*',[31] but then went further by adding that the factual accuracy extended into characterization: 'We are confident that everything said is true to the beliefs and character of those involved'.[32] If a text is factually verifiable does it follow that it is emotionally true? Bolton here claims a probity and authenticity for a film-making process that is creative and interpretative. Bolton's invocation of 'authenticity' is an ambivalent response to the material conditions in which the film was made. He anticipated the nature of the critical context within which its production and viewing would be judged. Adhering to the strictly verifiable, the film has affiliations within the kinds of dominant and popular critical discourse which lay emphasis on indisputable, empirical 'facts'. In part the film is forced, as all dissident discourses are, to play with(in) the terms of the dominant discourse. Simultaneously, however, 'authenticity' suggests that the creative representation of such historical figures carries a power that legitimates actions and beliefs which have been pushed to the margins of understanding within the dominating culture. Such legitimacy is not simply conferred on them because of a supposed, 'genuine' integrity. Rather, it is defined in relation to the unevenness and contingency of the dominating culture and is itself constructed with its own internal dissonance. Bolton, alert to this problematic, went on to explain his preferred choice of dramatizing the account of historical events because:

> *it would allow us to explore more fully the contradictions of someone like Collins,* who organised the assassinations of British Servicemen in their beds, but who saw the need to end the fighting.[33] (emphasis added)

Thus the achievement of the film is that it does not shy away from presenting Collins as a ruthless man who understood the importance of subversive intelligence and the terrorizing effect of assassination squads against the more powerful apparatus of the British state. It shows him as a shrewd military commander who understood the limitations of guerrilla warfare, and a political pragmatist, prepared to accept partial freedom in order to win further freedoms. Despite its heavy emphasis on historically verified evidence and carefully weighed factual material, the overall tendency of *The Treaty* is towards an exploratory sympathy for Collins. Seamus Keenan examined this point in a review of the film, concluding that:

> Although *The Treaty* is presented as a sober, straight recounting of historic events in the life of Ireland, one has the instinctive feeling that the author's sympathies are with Collins and Griffith.[34]

Indeed, Phelan's intention was very much to 'make a case for Collins – if that is a bias'[35] but retain Collins's close association with, and organization of, terrorizing violence, and to show him preparing for a war footing. While there was a degree of congruence in historical interpretation between Bolton, Miller, Lewis and Phelan which shaped the production, clearly Phelan in effect admits that there is some interpretative bias towards favouring Collins. Similar minor but significant differences can also be detected in views about the nature of the writing which is the basis for *The Treaty*. Phelan stresses that he is a "dramatist" and not a "documentary maker" or the hybrid, "drama-documentary maker". In these films I did not distort actual events but, rather, used them as springboards for works of the imagination'.[36]

NARRATIVE FORM AND THE TROUBLES GENRE

Despite such protestations, *The Treaty* can legitimately be termed an historical drama-documentary. While it is based on researched and documented factual events, the conventions and techniques used to portray that history are closer to dramatic realism than documentary film.[37] In terms of dramatic structure, *The Treaty* offers a readily understood confrontation between Empire and Irishmen, represented for example in the early scenes between Lloyd George and de Valera. But the British Prime Minister was a Welshman and the Irish President an American-born Irishman with Hispanic parentage. The further complications underlying the binary opposition represented by the *two* groups of negotiators are hinted at by dialogue references to the contingent parliamentary support of Craig's Ulster Unionists and political confrontations in other parts of the Empire. So, both the 'Britishness' at the centre of Empire and the 'Irishness' of the dissident Republicans is more complex that it might at first seem. In *The Treaty,* however, such complexity is hinted at but not explored since historical events are rendered through the actions of famous figures who 'come alive', are made 'ordinary' and 'human' by our privileged access into their personal and private lives. In this method of presentation, historical events occur as the outcome of personal character traits, emotional crises or flaws. These are part of television's mainstream dramatic strategies for dealing with subject matter which is notoriously 'difficult'. *The Treaty* operates on a set of assumptions about the presentation of history through dramatic verisimilitude. In script and production design, the standard of 'realism' against which such dramas are judged is how closely and accurately they imitate the visual appearance of the past. *The Treaty* is a 'period' piece *tour de force,* using props, costumes and locations to 'recreate' history. RTÉ publicity leading up to transmission stressed the use of real locations for the film in and around Dublin. Much was made of the fact that the actors playing the main historical figures bore a close resemblance to their 'characters' as if this added something to the authenticity of the drama. Phelan made a revealing comment on this point in recalling one scene in particular from his screenplay:

> I watched two actors playing Michael Collins and de Valera standing, in costume and make up, on the steps of the Mansion House. They looked like the characters, they spoke like them and they were about to play a scene in the same room, sitting in the same chairs, as the real people had seventy years before.[38]

For the Irish, the past haunts the present. Phelan's observation might seem to confirm the English view of the Irish as always being 'stuck in their history'. But the creative awakening of the past might also reveal how the English have tried to avoid any implication that history is shared uncomfortably by them too.[39]

While *The Treaty* offers a linear progression to a narrative conclusion (the signing of the Treaty), this end is linked to the credits by a coda to show the afterlives of the main characters. Still pictures of their faces are successively flipped round to reveal monochrome photographs of the real historical figures they have been ghosting, their fates summarized by explanatory caption. The use of this particular documentary device prevents closure, the imagination rebounds off the real, we are reminded of the subsequent and continuing historical crises (the Irish civil war and the current Troubles). In terms of interpreting the historical role of the main figures, the captions allow for a bias that the producer/director seems to have worked to avoid. Lewis has stated that:

> [the film] has no heroes or villains for me not because I was chasing 'balance' but because the characters in the film are duplicitous, or espouse violence or are moral cowards, or are just plain human. It is incidentally, quite possible to be accurate and investigative *and* have a hero.[40]

But saying that the actions of Collins, de Valera and Lloyd George are flawed or humanly susceptible implies that the 'truth' expressed by the film is that the assembled facts condemn *all* the major historical figures. Yet in narrative and visual terms the film operates against the grain of the 'accurately' scripted dialogue. The opening 'hook' sequence (the first five minutes into the film) establishes the main coordinates for the viewer. Collins is an attractive, romantic, likeable rogue despite his involvement with killing. Both Irish and British audiences are addressed in a way which is sympathetic to Collins in comparison to de Valera. While 'Dev' is cold and calculating, Collins has the common touch with ordinary people, he is emotional, daring and presents one of two 'love interests' in the film implied in the Lady Lavery sequences (the other is Lloyd George with his secretary). The captions reveal that while Collins died aged 32, the wily Dev who stayed at home, lived to be president and died aged 92. In considering the political impact of Collins, English audiences are in the uncomfortable position of loathing and loving the dashing terrorist rather like General Sir Henry Wilson ('Admire him? I detest the very thought of him'). In fact, English minds have been faced with this 'contradiction' for at least a century. Collins is a singularly efflorescent figure in Irish history but despite his unique qualities in photographic and filmic terms, merely one in a line of popular stereotypes.[41] What makes this Collins unusual from all the other doubting IRA men – from *Odd Man Out*, through *Cal* to *The Crying Game* – is that, instead of renouncing violence after becoming involved in it, Collins gives it up as a pragmatic military and political strategy *not* as a moral aversion to killing and, moreover, with the acute understanding of the personal consequences of this strategy. Phelan knew that he wanted the last line of the film to be Collins's own tragic premonition of his death:

> I had always known where the film should end, with the signing of the Treaty and Michael Collins' famous line, 'I have just signed my actual death warrant'.[42]

CONCLUSION

They have been many attempts to explore the role of Irish republicanism in Anglo-Irish history and *The Treaty* is one of the better productions. The insistent stress on the incontrovertible factual accuracy of the drama was, as we have seen, necessary given the hostile and censorial context of British television productions relating to Ireland in 1989–91. But such fetishist emphasis does not produce non-interpretative representation. As a result of the film an audience would be better informed and they would have been given some degree of insight into the kind of pressures on both sets of Treaty negotiators. But there still remains the need to break down both the constitutive terms and the binary opposition of Irish Republican/British (meaning English) history. In *The Treaty*, the product of a joint-venture TV project, dissonance and omissions within the production process demonstrate how complicated the mechanics of authenticity can be. Ulster Loyalist perspectives in imaginative ventures on the political actualities omitted from the film remain a subject to be tackled. This is not to criticize *The Treaty per se*, but to observe that the film reflected a percipient moment of terminus: ending an old but beginning what could be a new phase in the history of Anglo-Irish relations.

Notes

This essay is based in part on a paper titled 'Troublesome Anniversaries' delivered at the 'Imagining Irelands' Conference held at the Irish Film Institute, Dublin, in October 1993. I would like to thank my St Mary's colleague, Dr. Liam Harte, for reading an earlier draft of this essay. His critical comments were invaluable in the finishing stages.

1. *TV Times* (London), 144 (11–17 January 1992), 61.
2. All quotations from an off-air recording kindly copied by Shaun Richards. *The Treaty*, dir. J. Lewis, written by B. Phelan, Merlin Films International, 1991 is available on VHS format.
3. Quoted in *The Observer*, 21 April 1996, p. 17.
4. J. Lewis, letter to the author, 6 August 1994.
5. See E. Mallie, 'Thatcher Opened Secret Channel to IRA in 1990', *The Observer*, 21 April 1996, p. 1.
6. L. Pettitt, 'Situation Tragedy? The 'Troubles' in British Television Drama', *Irish Studies Review*, 1 (Spring 1992), 22. The productions referred to are *Who Bombed Birmingham?*, *Shoot to Kill* and *A Safe House*.
7. T.P. Coogan, *Michael Collins: A Biography* (London: Hutchinson, 1990) is cited as a source by the film's makers. Coogan himself notes the biographies of Collins by T. R. Dwyer, *Michael Collins: The Man Who Won the War* (Dublin: Mercier, 1990) and film documentary *In the Shadow of Beal na mBlath* (RTÉ, 1989). More recently, *History Ireland*, 3: 1 (1995) featured articles on Collins and Fintan O'Toole's *Under the Shadow of the Gun: The Return of Michael Collins*, a film essay dealing with the image of Collins, was broadcast in October 1995 on BBC2. At the time of writing (March, 1996) the release of Neil Jordan's long-awaited film *Michael Collins* is eagerly anticipated.
8. R. Bolton, letter to the author, 19 October 1993.
9. D. Kiberd, 'The Elephant of Revolutionary Forgetfulness' in *Revising the Rising*, eds M. Ní Dhonnchadha and T. Dorgan (Derry: Field Day, 1991), pp. 1–20.
10. See N. Ascherson, 'Troops Out, if the Nationalists Lower Their Sights', *The Independent on Sunday*, 19 January 1992, p. 28; a BBC2 'Video Nation' participant from High Wycombe articulated the argument that Britain should wash its hands of Ireland, pull out its troops and tighten immigration controls for Irish citizens!
11. O. Bowcott, 'IRA aims for the Treasury', *The Guardian*, 22 December 1992, p. 2.
12. See *Fortnight*, 299–301 (October–December 1991) and D. McKittrick, *Endgame: The Search for Peace in Northern Ireland* (Belfast: Blackstaff, 1994), pp. 131 and 263.
13. R. Bolton, 'The Truth Behind the Treaty', *The Guardian*, 13 January 1992, p. 23.
14. S. Keenan, 'The Treaty', *Film Ireland*, 27 (1992), 7.
15. A preview inside claimed that the agreement known as the Treaty was 'the document that *split the nation* in two', *RTÉ Guide*, 49 (30

November – 6 December, 1991), p. 1 (emphasis added). Ireland had effectively been geo-politically divided by partition in 1920 and the sub-editor's phrase, while referring to the Civil War in the 26 counties 1922–3, unconsciously uses 'nation' in a loose sense.
16. L. Curtis, *Ireland: The Propaganda War* (London: Pluto Press, 1984); L. Curtis and M. Jempson, *Interference on the Airwaves: Ireland, the Media and the Broadcasting Ban* (London: Campaign for Press and Broadcasting Freedom, 1993), and D. Butler, *The Trouble with Reporting Northern Ireland* (Aldershot: Avebury, 1995).
17. L. Pettitt, 'A Camera-Woven Tapestry of Troubles', *Irish Studies Review*, 8 (1994), 54–6.
18. R. Bolton, *Death on the Rock and Other Stories* (London: Optomen/ W.H. Allen, 1990).
19. R. Bolton, letter to the author, 19 October 1993.
20. J. Lewis, letter to the author.
21. D. Miller, *Don't Mention the War: Northern Ireland, Propaganda and the Media* (London: Pluto Press, 1994), pp. 273–83.
22. *The ITC Programme Code* (London: ITC, 1993), 3.7. This code of practice governs ITV/C4 programmes and is similar to the BBC's *Producer's Guidelines* (London: BBC, 1989).
23. *Producer's Guidelines*, 'History in Drama', n.p.
24. *Radio Times*, 3550 (11–17 January 1992).
25. *TV Times*, 44 (11–17 January 1992), p. 61.
26. See reviews in microfiche collection of British Film Institute. In particular: P. Corry, *The Morning Star*, 15 January 1992, p. 4; A. Penmen, *Today*, 16 January 1992, p. 30; J. Rayner, 'In at the Birth of a Nation', *The Times*, 11 January 1992, p. 3; and R. Last, *The Daily Telegraph*, 16 January 1992, p. 15.
27. *ITC Programme Code*, 3.7.
28. D. Paget, *True Stories? Documentary-Drama on Radio, Screen and Stage* (Manchester: Manchester University Press, 1990), p. 3.
29. B. Phelan, 'Writing The Treaty' in *The Treaty*, eds M. Lennon and R. Diski (London: Thames TV Screen Guide, 1991), p. 20.
30. R. Bolton, letter to the author.
31. R. Bolton, quoted in *The Times*, 11 January 1992, p. 3.
32. R. Bolton, 'The Truth Behind the Treaty', p. 23.
33 R. Bolton, 'The Truth Behind the Treaty', p. 23.
34. S. Keenan, 'The Treaty', 7.
35. B. Phelan, telephone interview with author, 26 October 1993.
36. B. Phelan, 'Writing the Treaty', 10.
37. P. Kerr, 'F is for Fake: Friction Over Faction' in *Understanding Television*, eds. A. Goodwin and G. Whannel (London: Routledge, 1990), p. 83.
38. B. Phelan, 'Writing The Treaty' (1991), p. 22.
39. M. Ní Dhonnchadha and T. Dorgan, *Revising the Rising* (1991). In his 'Elephant of Revolutionary Forgetfulness' essay, Declan Kiberd notes that dwelling on history is an Irish ploy to avoid the deficiencies of the present, a way of forgetting those aspects of the past which remain uncomfortable to the current ruling class in Ireland.

40. J. Lewis, letter to the author.
41. John Hill has written extensively on this topic as it relates to cinematic images in *Cinema and Ireland* (London: Routledge, 1988), pp. 147–93 and there is certainly a crossover into television drama, for example Ronan Bennett's recent *Love Lies Bleeding* (BBC, 1993). Fintan O'Toole's film essay *Under the Shadow of the Gun* on the visual media's image of Collins is pertinent here (see note 7).
42. B. Phelan, 'Writing The Treaty', p. 21.

8

Reading Responsibility in *Castle Rackrent*

Claire Connolly

Readers of Maria Edgeworth's *Castle Rackrent* find themselves returning to two central and related sets of questions. Firstly, does Edgeworth represent Ireland accurately? Are we offered the condescending viewpoint of an Anglo-Irish woman whose vision is unavoidably skewed by her own class loyalties? Or an authentic portrayal of family dynamics and shifting class structures in pre-Union Ireland? These questions might be easier to address if critics agreed on the political implications of the tale *Castle Rackrent* tells, and yet the second problem – just who is to blame for the demise of the house of Rackrent? – reveals the depth of uncertainty on that score. Did the Rackrents fall or were they pushed? The question dissolves into the layers of irony, ambiguity and allusion that constitute *Castle Rackrent*. This essay considers the vexed questions of Maria Edgeworth's own allegiances, *Castle Rackrent*'s textual politics and the economic meanings of Union, as they relate to the politics of authenticity in Ireland.

INTIMACY

J.C. Beckett contrasts Maria Edgeworth with the Catholic novelists of the 1820s, who 'described the life of rural society from the inside and with an intimacy that Maria Edgeworth, shrewd observer as she was, could not attain'.[1] Poised on this peculiarly Anglo-Irish threshold between writing and belonging, Edgeworth has proved a source of much critical anxiety. Do her writings indict or exculpate her own class? Thomas Flanagan waxes eloquent on this subject: he describes *Castle Rackrent* as 'the brilliant requiem of the Protestant Nation', a 'unique record' of life in the

noticed how Thady is always strategically placed when his son's plots are afoot. Although such a reading of the novel goes against the grain of Thady's narrative, which continually reminds the reader of the devoted loyalty of the servant and his ancestors to 'the family', it is these very protestations of loyalty which have themselves caused readers to question his fealty to the family. Recent critics have tended to agree that the servant probably protests his loyalty to the family too much, and to suspect his proclaimed ignorance of his son's machinations.

GENRE

But readings which aim to uncover Thady Quirk's real or authentic motivations neglect the generic commitments of the text. In the first place, the diverse cast of *Castle Rackrent* does not respond well to a character-based analysis. Although the reader 'knows' Thady to some extent, his is not a narrative designed to yield the history of a single personality. It is Thady's narrative function in particular, which exists alongside his role in the action, that makes it difficult to read him as a character. This is in part a function of the first-person narrated text, and is as true of *Castle Rackrent*, as it is say, of *Heart of Darkness*. The narrator is paradoxically absent, at most functioning as an empty presence. This structural difficulty makes it almost impossible to distinguish the teller from the tale. As a participant in the history of the Rackrent family, however, Thady does display certain characteristics, which make it possible for the reader to turn him into a character, filled with desires, motivations and symptoms. However, the narrative itself impedes this response by embedding Thady's characteristics within his own linguistic world. This may well derive from Edgeworth's philosophy of fiction, as even in the later, more novelistic writings, where the characters have more of a psychological profile, there is a strong tendency towards representative or exemplary types.

Even the notes and Glossary offer comments on Thady's language and clothes, never on his personality. If anything, his symptoms are national rather than personal, and the Glossary insistently broadens the textual focus to offer a wider and more authoritative understanding of Ireland. The first note, on the narrator's use of *'Monday morning'*, is typical in this respect:

> *Monday morning*. – Thady begins his memoirs of the Rackrent Family by dating *Monday morning*, because no great undertaking can be auspiciously commenced in Ireland on any morning but *Monday morning*. [. . .] All the intermediate days, between the making of such speeches and the ensuing Monday, are wasted: and when Monday morning comes, it is ten to one that the business is deferred to *the next* Monday. The editor knew a gentleman, who, to counteract this prejudice, made his workmen and labourers begin all new pieces of work upon a Saturday.[16]

Thady's narrative only exists in relation to this density of other information. Thus, when Anthony Mortimer elaborates on 'the absence of Jason as a fully-realised character', he makes the mistake of assuming that this is a text crammed with fully-realized characters.[17] The case of Jason Quirk is not unusual, for, as with Thady, *Castle Rackrent*'s 'characters' all consist of an elaborate layering of Edgeworth's political and economic concerns.

Feminist readings also tend to assume that *Castle Rackrent* is peopled with coherent bundles of drives and desires, rather than with ciphers, markers of class and economic boundaries. Ann Owens Weekes's overly optimistic feminist reading, for example, founders on the problem of character. Weekes interrogates *Castle Rackrent* for symptoms of the author's suppressed feminist concerns. She does this by isolating the figures of the Rackrent wives, and considering how they relate to 'the complicating, ironic foil of the domestic plot' which she sets out to uncover.[18] The narrative makes it difficult to even name the Rackrent wives, yet Weekes obscures this problem in a manner typical of her approach. In her account, Sir Murtagh's wife, whom Thady refers to as 'my lady', is referred to as 'Skinflint', probably because the only information we have is that 'she was of the family of Skinflints, and a widow'. Her first name, or her previous married name do not concern Thady. Sir Kit's wife is variously described as 'the grandest heiress in England', 'little better than a blackamoor' and 'a *Jewish*', but is just 'my lady' when Thady refers to her actions. Weekes, however, anxious to get to grips with the Rackrent wives as characters, refers to her as Jessica, presumably because Sir Kit is once reported as referring to her as 'my pretty Jessica' (shortly after calling her 'his stiff-necked Israelite'). The text gives us no grounds, however, for turning this Shakespearean allusion into the proper name of Sir Kit's wife. The next wife does, perhaps for the reasons I suggest below, have a name; and thus Weekes is more comfortable with the last wife, Isabella, whom she can describe as the 'fashionable, lovely, and wealthy' victim of romantic love.[19]

Castle Rackrent does not resemble nineteenth-century realist fiction, where the social meanings of masculinity and femininity exist in dynamic relation to the novel genre itself. *Castle Rackrent* does of course draw on existing cultural understandings of gender – how could it not? – but does not make them pivotal to its plot. Gender does not make a difference in the way it does in, for example, Sydney Owenson's *The Wild Irish Girl* (1806), which made the plotting of national politics in terms of sexual relations part of the nineteenth- and twentieth-century cultural vocabulary. Perhaps this is why there have been so few successful feminist readings of the text. To adopt the mode of Anglo-American feminist literary criticism, and to seek out oppressed victims or angry rebels, is to misread *Castle Rackrent*, and to ignore its literary-historical moment.

A more immediate problem in assigning any generic stability to *Castle Rackrent* is that it is not one text, but many. *Castle Rackrent*'s origins are of a hybrid nature: it combines elements of several previous traditions and creates something quite new. In this the text resembles nothing so much as the genealogy of the Rackrent family itself: when the estate passes into the hands of the O'Shaughlins, they assume the identity of Rackrent and become, as Thady puts it, '*the* family'.[20] This giddy play with the notion of origins is characteristic of Edgeworth's early writings. In the *Essay on Irish Bulls*, for example, the Edgeworths mischievously criticize 'certain spurious alien blunders, pretending to be native, original Irish bulls'.[21] Applying antiquarian notions of nativism to material that was more commonly disowned than disputed serves to ridicule the very notion of pure national origins. A later novel, *Ennui* (1809), carries this project across into the field of personal origins, and its plot consists of a sustained investigation of notions of innate versus acquired identity. Its uses of devices such as the change at nurse plot suggest that education might prove more significant than birth, in political as well as personal history. The plot of *Castle Rackrent* only tentatively considers such a possibility, whereas its form presents a more radical challenge to the laws of genre.

Furthermore, the history of its composition is such that it defies any account which reduces it to a single narrative. According to the chronology Marilyn Butler presents in her biography of Edgeworth, there were 'three distinct stages in the evolution of *Castle Rackrent*'.[22] The dates she suggests illuminate much of the layering of different histories within the text itself. The first half of the text was completed by 1796 at the very latest; two years after completing this first part Edgeworth was able to add Sir Condy's story to the manuscript; and by October of 1798 she was preparing the text for her publisher. The Glossary was not compiled until 1799, and was added last of all.[23] The Edgeworth family circle read the text in several of its stages, and it was circulated for comment to friends and relations.[24] In its earliest incarnation, then, it is the product of a kind of composite voice, representing a liberal group of midlands gentry. These fissures remain to some extent visible in the text: Sir Condy's history, for example, precipitates a break in the text and is presented as the 'CONTINUATION OF THE MEMOIRS OF THE RACKRENT FAMILY'.[25] Much as this text is a composite of other texts, however, its voices are arranged in a meticulously orchestrated play of language and idioms. *Castle Rackrent* thus demands a reading attentive to the operations of language within specific cultural constraints and conditions.

FOREIGN FORMS

Nowhere is the need for such a reading clearer than in the feminist reception of Edgeworth's work. Irish feminism, historically inseparable from the politics of the nation, is traditionally uncomfortable with the traditions of Anglo-Irish women's writing. MacCarthy's comments on Edgeworth, quoted above, are a case in point. During her time as professor of English in University College Cork, MacCarthy produced an exemplary two volume history of seventeenth- and eighteenth-century British women's fiction. Published in 1946 and 1947, MacCarthy's generously inclusive study pre-empted many of the 'discoveries' of second-wave feminist literary criticism, and yet her discussion of Edgeworth sounds a harsh and disapproving note.

Allied to these Irish debates, there are important issues at stake within Western feminist cultural politics. Kowaleski-Wallace has recently characterized Edgeworth as an uninvited guest at the feminist table. A political conservative and a colonist to boot, Kowaleski-Wallace informs us that Edgeworth makes 'the process of celebrating our heritage as women more difficult'.[26] What Kowaleski-Wallace implicitly acknowledges here is the desire within Anglo-American feminist criticism to find historical subjects with which it can identify. On those terms, Edgeworth is indeed an unsettling figure: rather than providing contemporary feminist theory with a comfortable companion, her writings serve to point up some of the difficulties in addressing the past in terms of any single set of questions. When Sandra M. Gilbert and Susan Gubar read the plot of Edgeworth's life alongside the plots of her fiction, they find a coded cry for help. Edgeworth is only intelligible to them as a Dorothea Brooke figure, presumably with her father cast as Mr Casaubon and the Chevalier Edelcrantz – apparently Edgeworth's only suitor – as Will Ladislaw.[27] A more recent discussion of Edgeworth's life and writings echoes this same judgement: the novelist John Banville comments that '[i]f Maria Edgeworth had not existed, George Eliot would have had to invent her'.[28] Gilbert and Gubar argue that, like Christina Rossetti and Jane Austen, Edgeworth 'concealed' her truths 'behind a decorous and ladylike façade', dispersing her 'real wishes or translating them into incomprehensible hieroglyphics'.[29] Such a reading shuts down the formal difficulties of these writings, all of which deploy their 'façades' to great effect. In the case of Edgeworth especially, to say that she concealed her 'real wishes' is to evade, once more, the didacticism of her writings.

Gilbert and Gubar's reading of *Castle Rackrent* focuses contentedly on its imprisoned wife. Sir Kit, one of the more financially reckless of the Rackrents, marries 'a lady with I don't know how many tens of thousand pounds to her fortune', as Thady tells us. Thady's lack of knowledge is only intensified by her arrival on the estate, for despite her being 'a stranger in a foreign country', she does not respond to his attempts to communicate with her: 'never a word she answered, so I concluded she could not speak a word of English and was from foreign parts'.[30] When Thady discovers she 'was a *Jewish*', he is better able to decipher his new lady, and can conclude that she is rich, foreign, 'could not abide pork or sausages, and went neither to church or mass'.[31] Her husband, in what is thought to be one of the strangest aspects of the plot of *Castle Rackrent*, punishes her for refusing to share her fortune with him by locking her in her room and feeding her on a strict diet of pork.

Gilbert and Gubar find Sir Kit's wife touching in her 'pathetic ignorance and vulnerability'.[32] They are particularly concerned with her fast, which they read as 'an act of revolt': '[s]ince eating maintains the self, in a discredited world it is a compromise implying acquiescence'.[33] Gilbert and Gubar argue that just as hunger for Caroline Helstone in *Shirley* signifies rebellion against the men who dominate her life, so the repressed story of Lady Rackrent opens up a 'critique of patriarchy' within the text.[34] For Gilbert and Gubar, Sir Kit's Jewish wife retains something of her selfhood by refusing to 'feed on foreign foods'. Yet, as I have been arguing, the Rackrent wives do not have selves to defend in this text: rather, they each represent a nexus of cultural and economic concerns. In any case, Sir Kit's wife's hunger is only partly a matter of choice: she does refuse to eat, but this is because the only food her husband will offer her is 'sausages, or bacon, or pig meat in some shape or other', food that is 'foreign' in culturally specific terms.[35] She is not, contrary to Gilbert and Gubar's claim, like 'so many later heroines' in her 'refusing to eat forbidden, foreign foods': in fact, she is quite unlike any woman in nineteenth-century literature in being force-fed food prohibited to her by her religion.

This aspect of Sir Kit's treatment of his wife passes without comment in the narrative, but when Thady explains how his master locked his wife up for seven years, we are provided with a footnote to authenticate the detail:

> This part of the history of the Rackrent family can scarcely be thought credible; but in justice to honest Thady, it is hoped the reader will recollect the history of the celebrated Lady Cathcart's conjugal imprisonment. – The Editor was acquainted with Colonel McGuire, Lady Cathcart's husband; he has lately seen and questioned the maidservant who lived with Colonel McGuire during the time of Lady Cathcart's imprisonment.[36]

Although this footnote is intended to verify the truth of Thady's tale, the note suggests that Lady Cathcart's story has also been gleaned from a servant. This sets up a rather circular narrative, leaving the reader is some doubt as to who or what to believe. Thus, the status of Thady's tale is even more questionable than usual here. Most significantly, however, Gilbert and Gubar ignore the economic details which underpin the representation of Sir Kit's wife. The narrative itself makes no attempt to cover up these details, and has Thady assuring the reader that '[h]er diamond cross', which serves in the text to signify her fortune, 'was, they say, at the bottom of it all'.[37] In Thady's account, then, we find the cultural and economic factors ignored by Gilbert and Gubar brought to our attention. In the strange image of a diamond cross owned by a Jewish woman, however, we encounter the difficulties of reading this set of concerns.

Further evidence of these competing narratives of class, gender and culture is found in the relationship between Thady and his various mistresses. Owens Weekes reads *Castle Rackrent*'s politics in terms of mutually reinforcing instances of gender, class and national oppression. She finds buried connections between Thady and his mistresses, reading the narrator 'as a colonized Gaelic-Irish servant' who 'can be seen as a surrogate woman, one prevented from supporting her natural allies by the need to remain in the good grace of the powerful'.[38] Uneasy with the lack of textual evidence for this support and Thady's apparent neglect of his 'natural' allies, Weekes uncovers a secret solidarity between the missing women's stories and Thady's disrupted and incomplete syntax. Following Joanne Alteiri's reading of Thady's style as paratactic and therefore subversive, Weekes suggests that 'the persistent jettisoning of the women's, or domestic, plot into the lacunae created by Thady's parataxis calls attention to the discarded plot'.[39] In proposing this continuity, Weekes ignores the differences of language, class and culture that divide the Gaelic retainer from the Anglo-Irish, English and Jewish ladies he serves.

Rather than proposing an alliance of the weak, I would suggest that *Castle Rackrent* allows antagonistic voices to inhabit the same discursive space. The narrative does show, for example, how Thady and Isabella, Sir Condy's wife, share some verbal excesses, but in the text this serves to signify conflict rather than unity. This conflict is not so much personal as textual: what we witness is not a clash of personalities or even character types but the meeting of two narrative modes. Thady's voice represents the articulation of regional difference, a narrative experiment unique to Edgeworth at this point. Isabella's speech, on the other hand, derives from the existing vocabulary of sentiment and sensibility. That these voices are placed side by side in *Castle Rackrent* is evidence of the competing frames within which Edgeworth inscribed Ireland. Describing their relationship, Edgeworth adopts some of the clichés of sentimental fiction, which she then turns to ludicrous effect, partly by allowing the narrative to point up the disjunctions between sentimental discourse and Thady's local style.

However, the narrative also reveals some intriguing similarities between these modes of speech. Miss Isabella Moneygawl is an alien presence in the world of *Castle Rackrent*, and Thady registers her oddness by recounting her linguistic peculiarities. On arriving at the gates of the house, the new Lady Rackrent wonders if she is meant to walk through the back entrance, which is surrounded by servants:

> 'My dear,' said Sir Condy, 'there's nothing for it but to walk, or let me carry you as far as the house, for you see that back road is too narrow for a carriage, and the great piers have tumbled down across the front approach; so there's no driving the right way, by reason of the ruins.' 'Plato, thou reasonest well!' said she, or words to that effect, which I could no ways understand; and again, when her foot stumbled against a broken bit of a car-wheel, she cried out 'Angels and ministers of grace defend us!'[40]

Isabella's imprecations are strange to Thady's ears because he is not familiar with the exaggerated vocabulary of sentiment. What is striking in this passage is the way in which Isabella's excesses of sentiment are prompted by the crumbling house and its surrounds. The apparent distance between Thady's and Isabella's vocabulary is somewhat diminished, however, when we hear Lady Rackrent admonishing her husband with the words: 'Oh, say no more, say no more; every word you say kills me'.[41] This everyday hyperbole is not glossed when it issues from Isabella's lips, although when Thady espouses a similarly broad understanding of death we are provided with a note. In fact, the Irish use of 'kilt' is finally explained in the editorial apparatus surrounding the scene of Isabella's near-fatal accident, when she is found 'all kilt and smashed'. The note preserves a careful distinction between 'kilt' and 'killed', implying that cultural difference resides in language, specifically pronunciation and orthography. The Glossary, however, in its effort to provide further etymological evidence, opens up the range of reference:

> *Kilt.* – This word frequently occurs in the preceding pages, where it means not *killed*, but much *hurt*. In Ireland, not only cowards, but the brave 'die many times before their death'. – There *killing is no murder*.[42]

Thus, Thady and Isabella can be seen to trade in the same linguistic currency, albeit to very different ends. What is striking here is the skill with which *Castle Rackrent* assembles these different voices. The narrative neither attempts an impossible dialogue, nor reaches for linguistic or political reconciliation. Rather, it places rival linguistic regimes side by side, and generates much of its fictional effect from the discordance. Nowhere is *Castle Rackrent*'s staging of differing textual registers more evident than in the relationship between the editorial preface and glossary and Thady's own tale.

TRANSLATION

The narrative design of *Castle Rackrent* brings enlightened paternalism to bear on the vicissitudes of Irish history. The competing narrative frames testify to the complexity of Edgeworth's literary and political affiliations; and they also serve to remind the reader that there is no question of an unmediated access to Irish reality. The sense that Ireland requires at least two viewpoints or modes of vision pervades *Castle Rackrent*. Thady is described as 'an illiterate old steward', who 'tells the history of the Rackrent family in his vernacular idiom'.[43] His idiom is comprehensible to the reader in so far as he speaks English, although Thady's is a distinctly Irish version of the metropolitan tongue. Butler has commented on the 'virtual absence of reference to the Irish language in the Irish tales', which she describes as Edgeworth's 'equivalent of Wordsworth's decision to steer clear of dialect' in the interests of rational cultural and political communication.[44] *Castle Rackrent* does not ask its readers to confront the difference of the Irish language, then, but registers instead its inflections on spoken English in Ireland.

Yet *Castle Rackrent* is not quite like the Edgeworths' *Essay on Irish Bulls* (1802) either, which is a far more sustained attempt to flatten out the peculiarities of Irish speech. The *Essay* takes a strict philosophical approach to Irish use of language, and sets out to show that 'the vulgar herd of Irish bulls' belong, in fact, to the world. Furthermore, the Edgeworths show that much of the amusement to be gleaned from Irish bulls derives merely from English expectations rather than Irish mistakes, so that

> The blunders of men of all countries, except Ireland, do not affix an indelible stigma upon individual or national character. A free pardon is, and ought to be, granted by every Englishman to the vernacular and literary errors of those who have the happiness to be born subjects of Great Britain. What enviable privileges are annexed to the birth of an Englishman! and what a misfortune it is to be a native of Ireland.[45]

The desire to present a scientifically accurate view of Hiberno-English seems to require this curious screening out of the history of linguistic colonialism. In *Castle Rackrent*, on the other hand, this history is never far from the surface of the story: we know from the outset that the name of Edgeworth's protagonists has been changed from the Irish O'Shaughlin to the English-sounding Rackrent, to facilitate a transferral of property. Exotic traces of the original family name do remain, as with the bog of Allyballycarricko'shaughlin, the name of which inspires such hilarity in one of the Rackrent wives. Thady's own idioms are equally likely to cause amusement, and they, too, impede a clear understanding of the world he inhabits. *Castle Rackrent* thus differs from the *Essay* in foregrounding, almost in spite of itself, some elements of the strange linguistic habits of the native Irish.

Castle Rackrent's model of cultural exchange is perhaps best exemplified in its infamous closing lines which inquire in well-ordered prose: '[d]id the Warwickshire militia, who were chiefly artisans, teach the Irish to drink beer? or did they learn from the Irish to drink whiskey?'.[46] The glib question is not even answered, suggesting perhaps that under the Union such trifling differences will cease to matter. Yet the inquiry itself suggests another understanding of the differences between Ireland and Britain, one marked by the violence of recent history: the Warwickshire militia consisted of some 80,000 extra troops sent to Ireland in the 1790s, when rebellion seemed likely.[47] *Castle Rackrent* concludes on an ambivalent note, at once seeking to level the differences between Ireland and Britain and invoking a necessary memory of conflict.

The possibilities of cultural exchange are further disrupted by the text's return to the question of translation. It is in fact this issue which makes *Castle Rackrent*'s narrative power play critically different from eighteenth-century texts which deploy an authoritative editorial voice to introduce intimate narratives. Unlike Daniel Defoe's *Moll Flanders* (1752) or Samuel Richardson's *Pamela* (1740), *Castle Rackrent*'s narrative voice is that of an uneducated Irish peasant, whose levels of literacy are in doubt. Thady's comments on his masters are at once more nugatory and more incisive than those of Moll or Pamela, and it could be argued that the gap between Thady's tale and the editorial interventions is the site of *Castle Rackrent*'s politics. In the space of translation we confront not only what Jacques Derrida calls 'the multiplicity of idioms' but also, and simultaneously, the multiplicity of cultures and beliefs.[48] Recent accounts of translation have theorized the intimate relationship between language, culture and power: according to Tejaswini Niranjana, '[w]hat is at stake here is the representation of the colonised'.[49] Translation, in its concern with authenticity and fidelity, is described by Niranjana as 'a significant technology of colonial domination'.[50] Gayatri Spivak states the post-colonial case against translation vehemently: '[w]hen [. . .] the violence of imperialism straddles a subject-language, translation can become a species of violation'. Spivak locates 'translation *as* violation' in the work of Rudyard Kipling, where the authority of empire pervades the representation of native speech, marking the lines of colonial power everywhere in his work.[51] Her analysis will not do for Edgeworth, however, who renders Thady far more comprehensible than one of Kipling's natives. Furthermore, even as the purveyor of an untranslatable and unproductive narrative, Thady possesses a certain legitimacy: the editor tells us that 'the authenticity of his story would have been more exposed to doubt if it were not told in his own characteristic manner'.[52]

Here, the questions of authenticity and allegiance posed earlier manifest themselves as problems of translation. The authority of Thady's utterances are underpinned by their strangeness. This is in sharp contrast to the view of translation expressed by late eighteenth-century colonialists. Sir William Jones' essay on Mahomedan law undertakes a 'line for line, and word for word' translation, which stresses the need for a lucid, clear and faithful rendition of native culture. For Jones, the unreliability of native interpreters made translations of Muslim law essential to imperial government, so that in effect translation is necessary to secure British rule in India.[53] Faced with such evidence of the contemporary political implications of 'line for line, word for word' translations, Edgeworth's editorial decision demands closer consideration. By allowing Thady's speech to retain traces of another language and culture, Edgeworth refuses to eradicate a potential threat. Yet hers is not necessarily a radical stance: Thady's narrative is only available within the authoritative if magnanimous frame established by the editor figure. In fact, one might adapt Spivak's earlier phrase and argue that in the place of Jones's tyrannical fidelity, *Castle Rackrent* offers a model of 'translation-as-benevolence'. In this, it resembles the principles of good government as set out in 'The Grateful Negro', one of Edgeworth's moral tales. In it, a good slave master manages his estate according to principles of justice 'confined [. . .] within the bounds of reason'.[54] The slave owner's reward is the unstinting loyalty of his slave, who prefers his master above his community and averts a rebellion on the estate. The linguistic benevolence of *Castle Rackrent* would appear to operate on similar lines, tolerating Thady's linguistic differences in the name of reasonable rule. More than ever, however, this leaves us with the perplexing question of Thady's loyalties. In order to come to terms with these, we need to interrogate the textual politics of Thady's narrative.

The editor, assuming a lofty third-person stance, 'had it once in contemplation to translate the language of Thady into plain English', but decides against it. Significantly, this untranslatability is not presented as a measure of the translator's inadequacies, or even of the opacity of culture, but rather as a function of the language itself: 'Thady's idiom', the reader is informed 'is incapable of translation'.[55] The notion that some idioms are more capable of translation than others is a curious one. It might be understood in terms of the dynamics of cultural exchange discussed above. Eric Cheyfitz, for example, considers the possibilities of cross-cultural communications under colonial conditions, and recommends 'practising the difficult politics of translation, rather than the politics of translation that repress this difficult politics'.[56] The notion of difficulty is a positive one for Cheyfitz, who argues that any easy understanding of another language or culture is illusory, deceptive and dangerous. Walter Benjamin approaches the question of translatability in philosophical terms:

> The question of whether a work is translatable has a dual meaning. Either: Will an adequate translator ever be found among the totality of its readers? Or, more pertinently: Does its nature lend itself to translation and, therefore, in view of the significance of the mode, call for it?[57]

Benjamin concludes that 'translatability' is 'an essential quality of certain works' where 'a specific significance inherent in the original manifests itself in its translatability'.[58] The 'original' in this account is not betrayed by the act of translation; if anything it is enhanced by being brought into dialogue with another idiom. The notion of translatability thus allows Benjamin to renegotiate the rights and wrongs of translation, and propose instead a theory which considers the 'reverberation' between the original and the translation: the translator must allow 'his language to be powerfully affected by the foreign tongue'.[59] In bringing Thady's idiom into such close contact with the Enlightenment prose of the Preface, notes and Glossary, *Castle Rackrent*'s narrative does suggest the 'reverberation' described by Benjamin. To declare that Thady's idiom is untranslatable however, is to acknowledge the possibility of such an effect but to refuse its implications.

In Benjamin's other work, the notion of allegory comes to describe this shuttling back and forth between modes of understanding. The doubled structure of signification characteristic of allegory is closely related to issues of language and mutual comprehension. All of Edgeworth's Irish tales are, as Butler has suggested, importantly indebted to allegorical narrative, and all foreground issues of cultural communication.[60] It is tempting to extend this observation and to consider the linguistic operations of allegory in more detail. Recent theoretical re-evaluations of rhetorical strategies suggest that whereas symbol strives to conceal the operations of the signifying process, allegory exploits the difference between the signifier and the signified. Doris Sommer provides an incisive summary of these discussions when she writes of how post-structuralist theory, in sharp contrast to the Romantic tradition we have inherited, seeks to privilege 'allegory's pause over symbol's rush'. Much of this thinking is derived from Benjamin, for whom, as Sommer says, 'allegory is the trajectory of a philosophically felicitous failure, the recurrent waking from an endless dream of absolute presence'.[61] This notion of a 'felicitous failure', of a productive rift in understanding, might well serve as a description of the politics of cross-cultural communication in *Castle Rackrent.*

It may be helpful here to turn to Richard Lovell Edgeworth's definition of allegory in *Poetry Explained for the Use of Young People* (1802), which he derives from Blackwell:

> There is a general analogy and relation between all *tropes,* and that in all of them, a man uses a foreign or strange word instead of a proper one, and therefore says one thing and means something different. [. . .] When he says one thing and means another like it, it is a metaphor. A metaphor continued and often repeated, becomes an *allegory.*[62]

The definition cited by Richard Lovell Edgeworth foregrounds the connection between language and home, here understood as the 'proper' site of meanings. He points to how the use of foreign words or tropes produces a disparity between what is said and what is intended. This is not an unbridgeable gulf, however, as the impact of a trope depends on a necessary connection between 'foreign' and 'proper' meanings. In particular, metaphor and allegory rely on a relationship of 'likeness' or similarity between the 'foreign or strange' and the 'proper'.

The definition of allegory which Richard Lovell Edgeworth cites relies on Aristotle's theory of metaphor, which, according to Cheyfitz, 'is inseparable from an idea of place that draws frontiers between the "domestic" and the foreign'.[63] Cheyfitz's own discussion of the politics of metaphor rests on the assumption that 'the very idea of metaphor seems to find its ground in a kind of territorial imperative, in a division, that is, between the domestic and the foreign'.[64] This relationship is central to *Castle Rackrent,* which refuses to reconcile the foreign and the familiar: Thady's narrative is marked by outlandish rhetorical flourishes which are glossed and interpreted by the editor. Its narrative structure represents a sustained attempt to establish two incongruous viewpoints. Yet the text as a whole does exploit Thady's strange verbal ways, and *Castle Rackrent* is largely remembered for its articulation of linguistic difference. Cheyfitz's discussion may be helpful here, as he notes how the foreignness of metaphor invades 'proper' language:

> From its theoretical beginnings, then, metaphor comes under suspicion as the foreign, that which is opposed to the 'proper',

> defined inescapably, as we have noted, as the *national*, the *domestic*, the *familiar*, the *authoritative*, the *legitimate*. And yet just as the foreign is never simply that which is outside the national, but is also that by which the national constitutes, or defines, its own identity [. . .] so our theories [. . .] have not understood metaphor simply as displacement of proper language but simultaneously as the place of proper language itself [. . .] as the heart, the very motor, of eloquence.[65]

Thus, much as *Castle Rackrent* attempts to hold Thady's 'foreign' speech patterns at arm's length, his metaphors form the heart of the text, invading 'the place of proper language'. In this account, the notes and Glossary form part of 'the Western rhetorical tradition [which] has attempted to master or domesticate metaphor'.[66] *Castle Rackrent* participates in this attempt, and in it we can see a clear contest between foreign and domestic modes of speech.

An early example of this struggle occurs in a note to one of Thady's phrases. The narrative presents us with the following image:

> On coming into the estate, he gave the finest entertainment ever was heard of in the country: not a man could stand after supper but Sir Patrick himself, who could sit out the best man in Ireland, let alone the three kingdoms itself.[67]

The glossary note to the phrase '*Let alone the three kingdoms itself*' reads as follows:

> *Let alone,* in this sentence, means *put out of consideration*. The phrase, *let alone,* which is now used as the imperative of a verb, may in time become a conjunction, and may exercise the ingenuity of some future etymologist. The celebrated Horne Tooke has proved most satisfactorily, that the conjunction *but* comes from the imperative of the Anglo-Saxon verb (*bouant*) *to be out;* also that *if* comes from *gift*, the imperative of the Anglo-Saxon verb which signifies *to give*, &c.[68]

Butler suspects that for Edgeworth to champion John Horne Tooke's linguistic theories as she does here was probably 'risky'. Tooke, whom Butler describes as a 'notorious democrat', argued that the prime operators on the growth of the English language were natural and organic factors, not the classical authorities.[69]

His version of English looked to local circumstances not polite society for the development of the language, and thus constituted a populist, democratic gesture. Edgeworth's citing of Tooke thus lends radical authority to Thady's defiantly regional language. The text affirms the importance of the local, however, by reference to the three kingdoms – understood since the early eighteenth century as England, Scotland and Ireland – with their certain associations remaining the horizon of any such exploration of the local.

All this further complicates the readings of *Castle Rackrent* cited earlier, which suggest that Thady's narrative is driven by rebellion, indicating just how difficult it is to analyse a turn of phrase in terms of motivation or intention. Such a moment reveals how the narrative dynamism of *Castle Rackrent* derives from contending linguistic and political impulses, not from any deep desire for revenge.

THE DIVISION OF NARRATIVE LABOUR

Butler has persuasively argued that Adam Smith's *Wealth of Nations* (1778) is 'the most suggestive text for a *political* reading of the Irish tales' (emphasis added).[70] I wish to suggest here that Edgeworth's interest in political economy also provides a key to important *textual* dimensions of *Castle Rackrent*. In particular, the narrative structure of the text is indebted to Smith's theory of the division of labour. A reading of *Castle Rackrent* attentive to questions of economy *and* textuality allows us to pose what has become the key question – who is responsible for the downfall of the Rackrent family? – in a new and productive way.

Kathryn Sutherland's detailed discussion of Walter Scott's novels in terms of Adam Smith's theory of the division of labour is helpful here. Smith contended that the division of labour allowed a commercial society to progress and prosper. This arrangement has implications for the whole society, as Sutherland suggests:

> [W]hen each individual concentrates on one skill or function to the exclusion of others, not only does he make improvements to it, he also reduces his own self-sufficiency and renders himself dependent on other specialised workers for those wants which his independent labour can no longer supply.[71]

Sutherland argues that 'the surrender of narrative initiative to the peculiar dynamism of individual characters' was 'an essential creative policy' for Scott, and indeed for the emerging genre of the nineteenth-century novel.[72] Thus, according to Sutherland,

> the presentational masks – antiquaries, schoolmasters and retired soldiers – who introduce Scott's novels are socializing agents, restoring to reader and writer, somewhat tediously for modern taste, that sense of community through story-telling which is endangered in the privatization consequent upon a literate culture.[73]

In the case of *Castle Rackrent*, it would appear to be this 'sense of community through story-telling' that motivates the text, but it is worth noting that this is a community that must define itself within the pressures of a new commercial culture.

The Preface to *Castle Rackrent* goes to some length to stress the fragile nature of Thady's reminiscences, informing the reader of Thady's reluctance to have his story rendered in a permanent form:

> Several years ago he related to the editor the history of the Rackrent family, and it was with some difficulty that he was persuaded to have it committed to writing; however, his feelings for *'the honour of the family'*, as he expressed himself, prevailed over his habitual laziness, and he at length completed the narrative which is now laid before the public.[74]

There is a marked division of labour implicit in this account: Thady's tale is separate from the written narrative, and we are given to understand that he recounted the story while the editor wrote it down.

Smith further investigates the idea of dependency, particularly in the feudal economy:

> The labour of the menial servant [. . .] does not fix or realise itself in any particular subject or vendible commodity. His services generally perish in the very instant of their performance, and seldom leave any trace or value behind them.[75]

Thady Quirk might be a textbook example of the 'unproductive labourer' described by Smith, whose 'maintenance [. . .] never is restored', and whose work 'perishes in the very instant of its production'.[76] Thady nonetheless has a place in the economic cycle. According to Smith, '[b]oth productive and unproductive labourers and those who do not labour at all, are all equally maintained by the annual produce of the land and labour of the country'.[77] Not only does 'maintaining a multitude of menial servants' make the individual employer poor, as in the earlier argument, but maintaining unproductive labourers (and 'those who do not labour at all') also saps the strength of the whole economic system. The implications of this for revenue and resources are far-reaching, and Smith elaborates them fully. On these terms, Smith's theory would implicate Thady in his masters' downfall.

Smith, however, makes it abundantly clear that owners 'have some predilection' for employing unproductive hands, and thus are also themselves to blame for this drain on '[t]he rent of land and the profits of stock [which] are everywhere [. . .] the principal sources from which unproductive hands derive their subsistence'.[78] Smith also notes the abdication of responsibility towards feudal retainers occasioned by the advent of commerce:

> But what all the violence of the feudal institutions could never have effected, the silent and insensible operation of foreign commerce and manufactures gradually brought about. These gradually furnished the great proprietors with something for which they could exchange the whole surplus produce of their lands, and which they could consume themselves without sharing it either with tenants and retainers. All for ourselves, and nothing for other people, seems, in every age of the world, to have been the vile maxim of the masters of mankind. [. . .] For a pair of diamond buckles perhaps, or for something as frivolous and useless, they exchanged the maintenance, or what is the same thing, the price of the maintenance of a thousand men for a year. [. . . Thus], for the gratification of the most sordid of all vanities, they gradually bartered their whole power and authority.[79]

A complex distribution of guilt and blame thus emerges, where allegiance and dependence are qualities of both master and servant, and where responsibility is as difficult to attribute as narrative authority.

Following Smith's theory of labour, Thady's narrative is an elaborate gesture of linguistic servitude, which perishes even as it is performed. Thady's unproductivity is as much a function of the narrative as it is the plot. He undertakes to tell his story 'out of friendship for the family, upon whose estate, praised be Heaven! I and mine have lived rent-free time out of mind' and in whose service he has 'voluntarily undertaken to publish the MEMOIRS of the RACKRENT FAMILY'.[80] This act of friendship is further illuminated by Smith's other examples of unproductive labour, which include the endeavours of monarchs, military men, opera-singers and dancers. This emphasis on unproductivity as performance, indeed as entertainment, points to Thady's role as story-teller. When this menial servant holds up his master's looking glass, it is to aesthetic as well as practical ends. Rather than simply pouring forth anecdotes, then, Thady is involved in a kind of artistic production, significantly one from which he himself will not reap any commercial benefit.

The closing lines of Thady's narrative implicitly raise this question of gain. Ending on a characteristically dubious claim to veracity, Thady summarizes his labours thus:

> As for all I have here set down from memory and hearsay of the family, there's nothing but truth in it from beginning to end: that you may depend upon; for where's the use of telling lies about the things which every body knows as well as I do?[81]

Alert to the same tension between performance and profit, the editorial voice also concludes by invoking a notion of 'use', wondering of what value the Union will be to Ireland:

> It is a problem of difficult solution to determine, whether an Union will hasten or retard the melioration of this country. The few gentlemen of education, who now reside in this country, will resort to England: they are few, but they are in nothing inferior to men of the same rank in Great Britain. The best that can happen will be the introduction of British manufacturers in their places.[82]

Castle Rackrent's world is a feudal one, yet the text was published in the immediate context of the Act of Union and 'the introduction of British manufacturers'. Both its critique of feudal authority and its more optimistic prescription for progress are informed by this temporal tension.

By disinheriting the Rackrent family, *Castle Rackrent* leaves the reader with alienation and estrangement to contemplate. The mention of the Act of Union invokes unity but also suggests the economic disparities that will continue to divide Ireland from Britain. Edgeworth's formulation of the problem marks an important moment in the history of political economy in Ireland: for her editor, Union, moral improvement, education and business all form part of the same continuum, helping to secure Ireland's place in an enlightened future. The tale Thady Quirk tells is a reminder that this narrative did not emerge uncontested, that it encountered – and perhaps even engendered – key instances of linguistic, cultural and political incomprehension. That Thady Quirk's own notoriously dubious loyalties are manifestly a problem of their untranslatability is a measure of *Castle Rackrent*'s desire to perform the process of communication, its commitment to 'practising', in Cheyfitz's terms 'the difficult politics of translation'.[83]

Notes

1. J.C. Beckett, 'The Irish Writer and his Public in the Nineteenth Century', *Yearbook of English Studies*, 11 (1981), 108.
2. T. Flanagan, *The Irish Novelists 1800–1850* (New York: Columbia University Press, 1959), pp. 23, 33.
3. T. Flanagan, *The Irish Novelists*, pp. 42–3.
4. S. Deane, 'Fiction and Politics: The Nineteenth-Century National Character', *Gaeliana*, 6 (1984), 99.
5. B. Sloan, *The Pioneers of Anglo-Irish Fiction 1800–1850* (Totowa, New Jersey: Barnes and Noble, 1986), p. 6.
6. E. Kowaleski-Wallace, *Their Father's Daughters: Hannah More, Maria Edgeworth and Patriarchal Complicity* (New York and Oxford: Oxford University Press, 1991), p. 98.
7. W.J. McCormack, 'Maria Edgeworth' in *The Field Day Anthology of Irish Writing*, ed. S. Deane, 3 vols (Derry: Field Day, 1991) I, p. 1013. The quote is from W.B. Yeats, 'A Commentary on "Parnell's Funeral"'.
8. B.G. MacCarthy, *The Later Women Novelists 1744–1818* (Cork and Oxford: Cork University Press, 1947), p. 219.
9. S. Deane, 'Fiction and Politics: The Nineteenth-Century National Character', p. 90.
10. Tom Dunne is a notable exception. See his '"A gentleman's estate should be a moral school": Edgeworthstown in Fact and Fiction' in *Longford: Essays in County History*, eds R. Gillespie and G. Moran (Dublin: Lilliput, 1991), pp. 89–114.
11. B.G. MacCarthy, *The Later Women Novelists*, p. 221.
12. B.G. MacCarthy, *The Later Women Novelists*, p. 222.

13. T. Flanagan, *The Year of the French* (New York: Holt, Rhinehart and Winston, 1979), p. 398.
14. D. Corkery, *Synge and Anglo-Irish Literature: A Study* (Cork: Cork University Press, 1931), p. 7.
15. P.F. Sheeran, 'Colonists and Colonized: Some Aspects of Anglo-Irish Literature from Swift to Joyce', *Yearbook of English Studies*, 13 (1983), 104–6.
16. M. Edgeworth, *'Castle Rackrent' and 'Ennui'*, ed. M. Butler (Harmondsworth: Penguin, 1992), p. 123.
17. A. Mortimer, '*Castle Rackrent* and its Historical Contexts', *Etudes Irlandaises*, 9 (1984), 118.
18. A.O. Weekes, *Irish Women Writers: An Uncharted Tradition* (Lexington, Kentucky: University of Kentucky Press, 1990), p. 41.
19. A.O. Weekes, *Irish Women Writers*, p. 57.
20. M. Edgeworth, *Castle Rackrent*, p. 66.
21. R. L. Edgeworth and M. Edgeworth, *Essay on Irish Bulls* in *Maria Edgeworth: Tales and Novels*, 10 vols (Hildesheim: Georg Olms, [1893] 1969), IV, p. 92.
22. M. Butler, *Maria Edgeworth: A Literary Biography* (Oxford: Clarendon Press, 1972), p. 353.
23. M. Butler, *Maria Edgeworth*, pp. 353–4.
24. Butler points out, for example, that D.A. Beaufort had read the manuscript by October 1798. Butler, 'Introduction' to *'Castle Rackrent' and 'Ennui'*, p. 5.
25. M. Edgeworth, *Castle Rackrent*, p. 85.
26. E. Kowaleski-Wallace, *Their Father's Daughters*, p. 5. I do agree with Kowaleski-Wallace that it is necessary to confront the difficulties of Edgeworth's political position. However, she locates Edgeworth's relationship with her father as the single site of these difficulties, as if those troublesome aspects of the daughter's politics can simply be assigned to the malign influence of her father. Kowaleski-Wallace is, to this extent, part of the Victorian tradition of Edgeworth criticism which uses the figure of Richard Lovell Edgeworth to explain away unpalatable aspects of Maria Edgeworth's writing. Kowaleski-Wallace only differs from late nineteenth-century critics of Edgeworth like Helen Zimmern, Anne Thackeray Ritchie and Grace A. Oliver in having Richard Lovell Edgeworth stand in for patriarchy in general. See M. Butler, *Maria Edgeworth*, pp. 271–304 on this 'question of authorship', especially pp. 273, 282–5.
27. S. Gilbert and S. Gubar, *The Madwoman in the Attic: The Woman Writer and the Nineteenth-Century Literary Imagination* (New Haven and London: Yale University Press, 1979), p. 152.
28. J. Banville, 'Introduction' to M. Edgeworth, *Ormond* (Belfast: Appletree Press, [1817] 1992), p. v.
29. S. Gilbert and S. Gubar, *The Madwoman in the Attic*, p. 101.
30. M. Edgeworth, *Castle Rackrent*, pp. 75, 76.
31. M. Edgeworth, *Castle Rackrent*, p. 76.
32. S. Gilbert and S. Gubar, *The Madwoman in the Attic*, p. 149
33. S. Gilbert and S. Gubar, *The Madwoman in the Attic*, p. 391.

34. S. Gilbert and S. Gubar, *The Madwoman in the Attic*, p. 152.
35. M. Edgeworth, *Castle Rackrent*, p. 79.
36. M. Edgeworth, *Castle Rackrent*, p. 79.
37. M. Edgeworth, *Castle Rackrent*, p. 83.
38. A.O. Weekes, *Irish Women Writers*, p. 43.
39. A.O. Weekes, *Irish Women Writers*, p. 43. Weekes here is referring to J. Altieri, 'Style and Purpose in Maria Edgeworth's Fiction', *Nineteenth-Century Fiction*, 23 (1968), 265–78.
40. M. Edgeworth, *Castle Rackrent*, p. 90.
41. M. Edgeworth, *Castle Rackrent*, p. 92.
42. This phrase may have a further resonance. In his *History of Ireland in the Eighteenth Century*, W.E.H. Lecky considers 'the legal maxim that killing an Irishman is no felony', in other words that 'killing is no murder'. Attempting to counter the charges of 'partisan writers' against English law, Lecky points out that the phrase 'means merely that the bulk of the Irish remained under their own Brehon jurisdiction, according to which the punishment for murder was not death, but a fine'. W.E.H. Lecky, *History of Ireland in the Eighteenth Century*, 5 vols (London, 1892), I, pp. 3–4.
43. M. Edgeworth, *Castle Rackrent*, p. 62.
44. M. Butler, 'Introduction', p. 20.
45. R. L. Edgeworth and M. Edgeworth, *Essay on Irish Bulls*, p. 104.
46. M. Edgeworth, *Castle Rackrent*, p. 122.
47. See Butler's note to this effect in M. Edgeworth, *Castle Rackrent*, p. 351.
48. J. Derrida, 'Des Tours de Babel' in *Difference in Translation*, ed. and trans. J.F. Graham (Ithaca and London: Cornell University Press, 1985), p. 165.
49. T. Niranjana, *Siting Translation: History, Post-Structuralism and the Colonial Context* (Berkeley and Oxford: University of California Press, 1992), p. 2.
50. T. Niranjana, *Siting Translation*, p. 21.
51. G.C. Spivak, 'Imperialism and Sexual Difference', *Oxford Literary Review*, 8 (1986), 234.
52. M. Edgeworth, *Castle Rackrent*, p. 63.
53. Sir W. Jones, 'The Mahomedan Law of Succession to the Property of Intestates' in *The Works of Sir William Jones* (London, 1749), III, p. 471.
54. M. Edgeworth, 'The Grateful Negro' in *Maria Edgeworth: Tales and Novels*, II, p. 400.
55. M. Edgeworth, *Castle Rackrent*, p. 63.
56. E. Cheyfitz, *The Poetics of Imperialism: Translation and Colonization from 'The Tempest' to 'Tarzan'* (New York and Oxford: Oxford University Press, 1991), p. xix.
57. W. Benjamin, 'The Task of The Translator' in *Illuminations: Essays and Reflections*, ed. H. Arendt and trans. H. Zohn (New York: Shocken Books, 1968), p. 70.
58. W. Benjamin, 'The Task of The Translator', p. 71.
59. W. Benjamin, 'The Task of The Translator', p. 81.

60. M. Butler, 'Introduction', p. 26.
61. D. Sommer, *Foundational Fictions: The National Romances of Latin America* (Berkeley, Los Angeles and London: University of California Press, 1991), pp. 44, 45.
62. R. L. Edgeworth, *Poetry Explained for the Use of Young People* (London, 1802), pp. xiii–xiv. B.G. MacCarthy describes this as 'a monstrous little book' (*The Later Women Novelists*, p. 219).
63. E. Cheyfitz, *The Poetics of Imperialism*, p. 88.
64. E. Cheyfitz, *The Poetics of Imperialism*, p. 36.
65. E. Cheyfitz, *The Poetics of Imperialism*, p. 90.
66. E. Cheyfitz, *The Poetics of Imperialism*, p. 90.
67. M. Edgeworth, *Castle Rackrent*, p. 66.
68. M. Edgeworth, *Castle Rackrent*, p. 123.
69. M. Butler, 'Introduction', p. 19.
70. M. Butler, 'Introduction', p. 28.
71. K. Sutherland, 'Fictional Economies: Adam Smith, Walter Scott and the Nineteenth-Century Novel', *NLH*, 54 (1987), 103.
72. K. Sutherland, 'Fictional Economies', 104.
73. K. Sutherland, 'Fictional Economies', 104.
74. M. Edgeworth, *Castle Rackrent*, p. 63.
75. A. Smith, *An Inquiry into the Nature and Causes of The Wealth of Nations*, ed. R.H. Campbell, A.S. Skinner and W.B. Todd, 2 vols (Oxford: Clarendon, 1976) I, Book II. iii. p.1.
76. A. Smith, *An Inquiry into the Nature and Causes of The Wealth of Nations*, Book II. iii. pp. 1, 2.
77. A. Smith, *An Inquiry into the Nature and Causes of The Wealth of Nations*, Book III. iii. p. 3.
78. A. Smith, *An Inquiry into the Nature and Causes of The Wealth of Nations*, Book III. iii. p. 7.
79. A. Smith, *An Inquiry into the Nature and Causes of The Wealth of Nations*, Book III. iv. p. 10.
80. M. Edgeworth, *Castle Rackrent*, p. 65.
81. M. Edgeworth, *Castle Rackrent*, p. 121.
82. M. Edgeworth, *Castle Rackrent*, p. 122.
83. E. Cheyfitz, *The Poetics of Imperialism*, p. xix.

9

'Could anyone write it?': Place in Tom Paulin's Poetry[1]

Eamonn Hughes

The centrality of place in Irish writing has long been recognized. But 'place' does not occupy this role in Irish writing only and analysts from a variety of disciplines are currently undertaking its reconsideration as:

> [t]he presumed certainties of cultural identity, firmly located in particular places which house [. . .] stable cohesive communities of shared tradition and perspective, though never a reality for some, [are] increasingly disrupted and displaced for all.[2]

Because 'places' are lived and we need to make sense of and in them they are never merely geographical spaces; they are points of origin, sources of values, territories of lived experience constructed according to determinate needs. Place is therefore always full, always ideologically fraught: 'the chosen ground is always packed / with skulls'.[3]

The conceptualization of place in Ireland is habitually made within the terms of custom, convention and community rather than in terms of law, polity and society. We can see this clearly in, for example, Seamus Heaney's 'The Toome Road':

> How long were they approaching down *my* roads
> As if *they owned* them? The whole country was sleeping.
> I had rights-of-way, fields, cattle in *my* keeping [. . .][4]

The insistence on the speaker's ownership of place is an assertion of his prior rights as a member of the community over the politico-legal rights of the army. It can be argued, however, that the army, as the state's legitimate force, have at least equal claim to assert ownership. This struggle is resolved, typically in Heaney, at the level of gender with the male power of the army opposed by an emphatically phallic 'omphalos' ('vibrant', 'untoppled'), in contrast to 'Mossbawn' where, despite its phallic potential, the omphalos is associated more with the navel and (female) nurture.[5] Unspoken then, though evident, in the poem is a conflict between national (customary, conventional, communal) rights and state (legal, political, social) rights, as each party asserts ownership on behalf either of a community which is ultimately the nation, or of the state. The linkage of place conceptualized in these terms – standing metonymically for 'nation' – with other concepts such as identity, history and language necessarily sets a limit to the interrogation of those other concepts, which, insofar as place is accepted on its own terms, seems to be a natural limit.

Place is assumed to be the one stable element within the Irish matrix, and thus to supply unproblematically the epistemological frame within which experience is to be understood:

> We are dwellers, we are namers, we are lovers, we make homes and search for our histories. And when we look for the history of our sensibilities I am convinced, as Professor J. C. Beckett was convinced about the history of Ireland generally, that it is to what he called the stable element, the land itself, that we must look for continuity.[6]

This is the process David Lloyd calls 'grounding' 'by which "a people separated from their forefathers" are [. . .] given back an alternative but equally arbitrary and fictive paternity'[7] but Lloyd's assertion of a British Romantic[8] context suggests too easily that the issue of place and its meaning has been resolved within that framework, and leaves his own work haunted by the sense of an Irish nation as still somehow natural and authentic. The Irish nation, like Beckett's land, derives a stability by apparently pre-existing all that happens on or within it. Kenneth Olwig has remarked on the 'subtle way, in the definition of nature [. . .] in which the meaning shifts from that of a people defining an area to that of an area defining a people'.[9] Place, therefore, is not merely where one lives, nor even just a metonym for a set of communal relations; it is understood to stand for an authentic identity, beside which issues such as legal title, citizenship and social relations are mere contingencies. This is what Edna Longley refers to as 'Heaney's religious sense of landscape as the primal source' and she notes that '[h]is recurrent landscaped female figure represents origins: the eternal mythic presence of the past, as opposed to the father who participates in historical process'.[10] For Heaney, as for others, place and identity are in quasi-mystical conjunction (to be expressed through a natural language) outside history. It is the sense of place as constant, as apart from history, that enables it to authenticate identity.

This understanding of place, and the context within which writing about place is most often considered, derives from Romantic ideas about place, or more accurately from received opinion about those ideas. When Heaney and others, in their treatment of place, are seen as Romantic insofar as they respond to that which endures it is because of an acceptance of Victorian and New Critical constructions of Romanticism as a poetry of authenticity-in-nature. Kelvin Everest has written about this construction of Romanticism as:

> [. . .] a lyric subjectivity and a love of nature which, taken out of their context in the fuller Romantic representation of social experience, constitute a body of Romantic verse which appeared remote from social concerns, and indeed positively to recoil from such concerns.[11]

English Romantic poetry is rather a response to the ways in which place changed materially as a consequence of new financial, agricultural and industrial practices and conceptually in response to the ideological ferment embodied in the French Revolution.[12] Rather than thinking of English Romantic poets as evading social and ideological issues through a retreat into an enduring nature, critics now see their work as an anxious engagement with changing places:

> In a Romantic poem the realm of the ideal is always observed as precarious. [. . .] Romantic poems take up transcendent and ideal subjects because these subjects occupy areas of critical uncertainty. The aim of the Romantic poem [. . .] is to rediscover the ground of stability in these situations.[13]

The reconceptualization of place arising from such anxieties is best known through M.H. Abrams's discussion of the shift from the mimetic to the expressive.[14] However, it is a mistake to think of Romanticism as having resolved this issue. Marilyn Butler, for example, comments on William Wordsworth's neo-classicism in *Lyrical Ballads* and how it privileged 'social utility [. . .] above the claims of self-expression'.[15] There is then within Romantic writing a conflict between the mimetic representation of place and the appropriation of place to the expressive needs of an individual subject. This gives rise, in Jerome McGann's phrase, to the 'landscape of contradiction'.[16] If the Romantic context has a value then it is as a signal that place and the relationship to it can change radically, just as it did in the Romantic period. In the Irish context such changes arise often (though not exclusively) from the relationship between Irish place and the British state. However, in a cultural refusal to recognize the state, 'grounding' always happens in relation to the nation.

Though the Romantic context remains undeniable it is not a clearly understood set of practices and ideologies within whose terms Irish writers are trapped. It is therefore worth thinking of it not only as a context for but also as a useful but inexact parallel to the present situation in Northern Irish writing. One example of the inexact fit between Romantic and current Irish senses of place is the difference between the predominant modes of representation of place in the two writings. Where the common term in English writing – 'landscape' – stresses the visual and pictorial,[17] Irish writing habitually figures place as linguistic and literary. This distinction carries with it a distinction also between space, in the immediate apprehension of the pictorial, and time, in the sequence of narrative,[18] and the shift within Romanticism from the mimetic to the expressive is a move from defined space to place in process.

In a poem such as 'Requiem for the Croppies', place defines the people who live in it to the extent that place and people coexist in mutual nurture.[19] There is little in it expressive of Heaney's subjective history – though it may be read as expressive of his desire to step out of history – as the poem is doing something else. The anxiously social expressivity of Romantic writing displaced a conventional iconography of landscape which still operates in Northern Irish poetry, though not in a straightforward manner. In 'Requiem for the Croppies' there is a move from the visual ('blushed, soaked in our broken wave') but the final image of resurrection defies temporality as Heaney characteristically compresses history into a simultaneity in place. The argument that Northern Irish poetry functions solely within a Romantic context cannot be sustained in the face of this strong tendency towards a sense of landscape as there to be (iconographically) read rather than (expressively) inscribed. Heaney has quoted approvingly John Montague's lines:

> The whole landscape a manuscript
> We had lost the skill to read[20]

Such an approach to place is, in its iconography, pre- rather than post-Romantic, as is the organic(ized) community of a poem such as 'Requiem for the Croppies'. The supposed constancy of place similarly informs, even sanctifies, language in poems such as 'Anahorish' and 'Broagh',[21] refusing both arbitrariness and history by locating language in a communal, essentialist and ahistoric dimension. In such poems Heaney is reading rather than writing place, trying to make the iconography of place constant. This is evident in a poem such as 'The Strand At Lough Beg'.[22] Heaney has famously excoriated himself for this poem and the way it 'saccharined' death[23] but what concerns us here is the presence of the two approaches to place that he details in 'The Sense of Place': 'lived, illiterate and unconscious [. . .] learned, literate and conscious'.[24] We will look in vain in 'The Strand at Lough Beg' for an expressive significance to the landscape in which Colum McCartney dies. The problem is rather that he is unable to read place satisfactorily. The speaking voice stresses the literary iconography of place in its reference to the Sweeney myth and by implication the poet's ability to read it as against McCartney's ignorance of it. In these terms, death is caused by ignorance; McCartney, illiterate, is trapped in the visual domain ('red lamp [. . .] driving mirror, tailing headlights') and dies because he does not know his place, or rather knows only his own place ('far from what you knew'). He is remarkably similar to John Clare, his homeplace being 'at once the place he knew and everything he knew' while Heaney, like Wordsworth, has a knowledge which extends beyond a particular place – a knowledge of as well as in place.[25] What both Wordsworth and Heaney are responding to is a change in the relationship between experience and place, as described by Fredric Jameson:

> [W]hile in older societies and perhaps even in the early stages of market capital, the immediate and limited experience is still able to encompass and coincide with the true economic and social form that governs that experience, in the next moment these two levels drift ever further apart. [. . .] At this point the phenomenological experience of the individual subject [. . .] becomes limited to a tiny corner of London or the countryside or whatever. But the truth of that experience no longer coincides with the place in which it takes place. The truth of that limited daily experience of London lies, rather, in India or Jamaica or Hong Kong.[26]

Heaney's response to the dilemma occasioned by the clash between his knowledge that he has changed and his wish that place has not is to make of place a palimpsest in which all history is simultaneously present, rather than to acknowledge simultaneity across space. Thus he constantly invokes an iconography in order to assert the constancy of place as if trying to reach back to a point at which experience and place coincide;[27] in this regard he may be said to be operating within a residual structure of feeling in relation to place. Heaney's work, however, also constantly acknowledges that place too has changed and that such iconography is no longer shared with a community. This is also the dilemma to which Romanticism responds: the widening gap between personal experience and communal place as history alters both, forcing an uneasy straddling of iconographic and expressive modes of response to place. In the Irish context the need to repress the sense that place has changed is best exemplified by Heaney's response to a famous passage in Wordsworth's *The Prelude* in which during prayers for English victories against revolutionary France:

> [. . .] 'mid the simple worshippers perchance
> I only, like an uninvited guest
> Whom no one owned, sate silent [. . .][28]

Heaney comments that '[i]n this passage we can see how the good place where Wordsworth's nurture happened, and to which his habitual feelings are most naturally attuned, has become, for the revolutionary poet, the wrong place. [. . .] He is displaced from his own affections by a vision of the good that is located elsewhere'.[29] Heaney parlays this dilemma into a discussion of how Northern Irish writers '[l]ike the disaffected Wordsworth [. . .] take the strain of being in *two* places at once'.[30] That Wordsworth's dilemma arises from two actual places – England and France – is ignored by Heaney so that one place with two conflicting histories can be treated as two places which protects the integrity of Heaney's place by treating potentially conflicting meanings as different places. Resolution of the dilemma, then, must happen at the level of individual subjectivity (Heaney uses a Jungian framework in 'Place and Displacement') rather in the public sphere since that would involve acknowledging the ultimate inconstancy and instability of place. The balance between iconography and inscription is thus sustained.

The engagement with place in contemporary Irish poetry is therefore at best problematically Romantic in its effort to maintain the stability and integrity of place in the face of historical change. The relationship to place, 'a dig for finds that end up being plants'[31] in Heaney's phrase, balances iconography and inscription. Heaney's career is founded on his ability to voice a once-shared iconographical sense of place. Place is represented as authenticating rather than determining; it is the landscape which possesses the identity and the poet's role is to inhabit and give voice to that identity, to speak of how the land defines the people, even when that requires that the poet represses the knowledge of change in place and the material ways in which people (the poet included) perennially define and redefine place.

It is against this background that three younger poets reconsider the nature of place. Paul Muldoon's poetry dissolves the fixity of place in the cosmopolitan while Ciaran Carson's explorations of Belfast as paradigmatic city will not allow place to have integrity. Their iconoclasm is shared by Tom Paulin, on whose work I want to concentrate for the rest of this essay. Paulin significantly alters the ideas of stability and constancy when he states that the Irish sense of place is 'exacting and intransigent'[32] thereby replacing an authenticating constancy with a sense of claustrophobic stasis. Furthermore, his Enlightenment-derived civic republicanism leads to a critique of Romanticism founded on a suspicion of the nation and associated concepts:

> How easily Romantic ideas of authenticity, rootedness, traditional crafts, folklore, take on the stink of power politics and genocide.[33]

For Paulin, it is the Heidegger of 'Building Dwelling Thinking' with its 'farmhouse in the Black Forest [. . .] built some two hundred years ago by the dwelling of peasants'[34] who stands for this concept of authenticity. In his most ambitious poem to date, 'The Caravans on Lüneberg Heath',[35] Paulin contrasts two moments and their attitudes to place. The first is symbolized by the 'cultured place' to which 'every stranger was made welcome'[36] in which Heidegger's two meanings of building – cultivation and construction[37] – are innocently combined in the cucumber lodge, the 'grow[n] house', of the Dach circle at the end of the Thirty Years War. The second moment and its attitude is symbolized by the eponymous caravans in which the German surrender at the end of the Second World War was accepted. What separates the two moments and gives rise to suspicion about authenticity in place is indicated in the lines: 'could you feel could you really feel any joy/ watching the nation states rising up like maggots?'[38] The emergence of modern nations marks the point at which a combination of cultivation and construction can no longer be innocent, hence the grotesque parody of the organic claims of nations in the image of maggots. Heidegger's appeal to continuity is countered by the poem's stress on the discontinuity between the mid-seventeenth century of Simon Dach and the Thirty Years War and the mid-twentieth century of Martin Heidegger and the Second World War. Between comes the moment at which a nascent Romanticism began to turn to uncultivated, 'authentic' landscapes in protest against Enlightenment utilitarian and progressivist attitudes to place and landscape which had followed on from the financial revolution of the 1690s[39] and that had enabled the founding of estates such as that in 'Mount Stewart'.[40]

The question then is the one Paulin poses in his essay on Elizabeth Bishop – how in the face of 'the inauthenticity of transient habitation in modern buildings' 'can writers come to terms with this tainted cultural inheritance?' since '[to] rip up all those deep-laid roots [. . .] is to place oneself in a minority and erect a makeshift building nowhere'[41] – and to answer it we need to consider the centrality of place in his work. Paulin's places are not the typical sites of Irish poetry, being often urban and explicitly politicized landscapes. Despite the absence of piety of place from his poetry, it is just such pietism which leads critics to see Paulin as endlessly analogizing Northern Ireland in his references to other places. It is true that analogies are frequently drawn, but the sheer range of places invoked – the North (as Northern Ireland and as a generalized hyperborean landscape), the city (often Belfast but also the urban in general), Audenesque borderlands, Presbyterian America, Eastern Europe, and an exoticized India among them – signals movement beyond Northern Ireland as well as reflection on it. A move beyond piety of place is necessary to see that Holyhead can be a destination as well as a staging post on the road to Tara. This is most obvious in *Liberty Tree*[42] and *Fivemiletown* in which Northern Irish Protestantism, in particular, is referred outwards to a history which extends across Northern Europe and America, in poems which in their stress on Enlightenment and civic republican ideas and values privilege universality over particularity of place. The range of place also, again anti-analogically, produces culture clashes, demonstrating how particularity of place is counteracted in the modern world by geographical miscegenation. Although evident in the earlier work[43] this becomes central in *Fivemiletown*:

> [. . .] the new wallpaper they'd bought in Wellworths –
> tequila sunsets
> on the Costa Brava –
> [. . .] the Bluestacks
> and the Glen River[44]

Not only has the opposition between culture and nature broken down here, but both the wallpaper and the scenery are part of the same place, not to draw an analogy between Northern Ireland and the Costa Brava (though the thought has its appeal) but to demonstrate the impossibility of integrity of place in the contemporary world.

This range of places also emphasizes the absence of a homeplace in Paulin's work, which sets him apart from most Irish poets who are more readily associated with a place than with a style. Even Derek Mahon or Paul Muldoon whose politico-religious background or commitment to cosmopolitanism make them comparable to Paulin diverge from him on the issue of home; it is always the Moy that Muldoon is a far cry from.[45] Paulin's statements about 'home' are always qualified (and in this case Joycean):

> this disappointed bridge
> is home – home of a kind[46]

Similarly, a poem set in his parents' new flat[47] refers to a non-existent address, while 'Peacetime'[48] is about making a bonfire of the past as one leaves a home. The temptation to explain Paulin's lack of piety of place by his politico-religious background is undercut by reference to Mahon or Michael Longley who are not poetically homeless.[49]

Paulin's account of his beginnings as a poet is useful here. Having moved to Nottingham's bedsitter-land with its Larkinesque 'decay and seediness' he finds that 'that disintegrating neighbourhood had a curious freshness for me'.[50] In response to this neighbourhood, its transient mode of habitation, and Douglas Dunn's poetry about such places, Paulin begins to write. He connects the 'extreme and terrible' situation in the North of Ireland in 1972 with this impulse as well – 'It was like watching two crumbling societies' – though importantly Northern Ireland is observed from a distance. This arises not from a potentially glamorous 'exile' (the mainstay of the 'homeless' Irish writer) but from the more mundane fact of migration. The defining experience of migration, the realization that one can never return home, is thus inscribed in Paulin's genesis as a poet in the link between distance from Northern Ireland and transience; the primary place of the poetry is thus 'der Fremde'.[51] His poetry, particularly the earlier work, is as a result, multivocal and this wrongfoots critics who assume a unifying voice speaking in tones of disenchantment and disgust.[52] Some of this confusion also arises from the assumption that his criticism, which speaks to 'the dramatic intensity of the polemical Now'[53] with clarity and polemic certainty, is immediately continuous with the poetry. As a result Paulin is frequently treated as if he matched his own description of V.S. Naipaul,[54] whose 'audience is pleased to notice his disdain, because that disdain feeds its self-esteem. [. . . He] writes for nothing and nowhere. He is simply against certain ghastly elsewheres'.[55] All of which is to overlook the poetry's dislocated and uncertain voices which alongside the range of places in his writing confirms that Paulin's judgement about place does not conform to the Irish paradigm that place should be authenticating and permanent. The transient rather than the rooted is attractive to Paulin, and elsewhere is as close to home as he gets.

This poetic 'homelessness' has two important consequences. First, place in his poetry is nearly always public and in turn the lyric, traditionally reliant on the private, is necessarily reformed. Central to an understanding of Paulin's poetry is the radical disaffection with lyric privacy in one of his most formally achieved and personal poems. 'A Lyric Afterwards' is Paulin's farewell to lyric tradition. In a traditionally cast poem in exact iambic pentameters set initially in a domestic garden, a lyric voice meditates on personal considerations. Retreating into a 'square room' the poet appears to be following a path into the lyric space of the self. At the centre of the poem, however, the phrase 'musical // snuff-boxes', William Hazlitt's description of Tom Moore's lyric poetry,[56] is broken across a stanza break indicating that even as Paulin constructs an elaborate trinket suitable to the private spaces of the poem, he rejects the lyric sweetness derived from the cultivation of a poetic garden. The poem thus registers a suspicion of its enterprise and setting. Never again will Paulin's poetry be so confined by a private space, nor by 'neat metre and full rhymes'.[57] This is not to say that this problematic has been resolved. When 'The Other Voice' asks 'What does a poem serve?' the answer acknowledges both private, aesthetic space ('the pure circle of itself') and the public, ideological domain of the 'servants of the state'.[58] This conflict between an 'untrammelled art' and the 'effort at responsibility'[59] is also played out in 'A Lyric Afterwards' in its simultaneous expression and suspicion of lyric experientiality.

In consequence Paulin's use of vernacular and dialectal language, rather than being a failed attempt to establish a Heaneyesque homely tongue as some critics have suggested[60] has to be understood instead as part of the effort to place the dislocated voices of the poetry. Throughout Paulin's writing there is, despite an ambivalence towards them, a sense of the importance of institutions. *A New Look at the Language Question* argues for a dictionary that will institutionalize Hiberno-English while the statement of affiliation[61] in the 'Introduction' to *Ireland and the English Crisis* rejects the nationalist and the authentic in favour of the state and the institutional. Paulin writes of how he used to identify 'with a form of [. . .] Lawrentian provincialism [. . .] hostile to the idea of institutions' but it now:

> [. . .] seems wrong to hug too closely that 'provincialism of feeling' which [is] opposed to Arnold's metropolitan ideal of cultivation and [. . .] anticipates Lawrence's ethic of authenticity. [. . .] My own critical position is eclectic and is founded on an idea of identity which has as yet no formal or institutional existence. It assumes the existence of a non-sectarian, republi-

> can state which comprises the whole island of Ireland. It also holds to the idea of sanctuary and to the concept of 'the fifth province'. This other, invisible province offers a platonic challenge to the nationalistic image of the four green fields.[62]

It is in institutions that Paulin places such wary trust as can be mustered in 'a bust-up, dirty time to be alive'.[63] Language cannot be a return to an originary, authenticating place but it can be used both to destabilize aesthetic and ideological rigidity and in the hope that its full range will be institutionalized.[64] Paulin's linguistic range therefore matches the range of place in his writing and includes Hiberno-English dialect ('stramash', 'jeuk', 'wick', 'jap'), dialect words which are not confined to Northern Ireland ('screggy', 'biffy', 'clachan', 'quop'), and foreign borrowings ('fremd', 'bistre', 'crise', 'pissoir'), as well as slang, jargon and nonsense or onomatopoeic terms. What a number of critics take as dialect is more often than not words which are not institutionalized in Standard English, and while this category may contain Northern Irish dialect, it is by no means confined to it; such critics confirm Paulin's arguments about language by assuming that any strange (to them) term must be dialect. Paulin is not, however, writing dialect verse but avoiding 'the full fake cadence'[65] of Standard English in favour of a more richly flavoured and inclusive language which is not tied to a place.

The attempt to inscribe language on the world can only result in a separation from that language: 'we cut our girls' names on pumpkins and melons – *Arsille Rosita Emilie/* the letters grew distorted as they grew/ and our writing stopped being ours'.[66] Equally, Paulin's places actively resist iconographic readings as the available signs blur[67] or mislead, '*I keep telling my husband to take that silly sign down*'.[68] There is no longer any consensus to sponsor such iconography:

> from now on in
> I'll be writing in a vacuum about a vacuum
> – there's no such thing as society
> only men and women living together
> on the great open site of human freedom
> so in the East Midlands of England
> you'll find the first and last frontier
> and then face the question – could anyone write it?[69]

Central to this aspect of Paulin's work is the pairing of 'Mount Stewart' and 'Fivemiletown' (partly parodies of Heaney's place-language poems) in which Neil Corcoran has identified the importance of post-structuralist theory.[70] In 'Mount Stewart' there is an appalled response to the certainty with which the place has been named, though it is evident that the place resists naming: 'floating letters' placed on 'sloping fields' are 'rubbed out / by the local demotic'.[71] The change from 'Mount Stewart' to 'Fivemiletown' is not just from eponymity to anonymity but from possession to displacement as it is now named only by means of its distance from other places.[72] Places cannot be named authentically.

'The Book of Juniper'[73] meditates on the relationship of place to a potential new language in its central allusion to the Northern European but culturally variable Brothers Grimm tale 'The Juniper Tree'. Clustered around this are images of the intersection between historical change, religion and language in references to the Austro-Hungarian empire, the 1798 Rising, St Patrick, puritanism (associated with Holland and Geneva through the wittily unlikely medium of gin), and Osip Mandelstam's vision of writer as hierarch. Throughout the shrubby persistence of juniper is preferred to a Burkean arboreal magnificence: 'its green / springy resistance / ducks its head down and skirts / the warped polities of other trees'.[74] The poem attempts to produce a new 'natural' language, most evidently in its last lines, but its invocation of John Clare's 'green language' acknowledges that social transformation,[75] can lead to a 'vanished integrity'[76] as well as to utopia. The poem's utopianism is similarly offset by its kinship to Thomas Hardy's 'In A Wood'[77] in which strife predominates: 'Great growths and small / Show them to men akin – / Combatants all!'. The utopianism of 'The Book of Juniper's last lines transforms the trees from combatants to companions just as a Pentecostal wind and fire engulfs the juniper tree in the Grimm tale and thus engenders the language symbolized by its regenerative sweet-singing bird[78] which, like Amphion, will have:

> [. . .] a voice
> that imagines what it describes
> and draws from the earth and the air
> the new-strung form
> that betters what we are[79]

Paulin's concern with a new utopian and public language is also evident in poems such as 'Where Art is a Midwife'[80] and 'A Written Answer'[81] where poetry's actual implication in the constitution of the state is offset against its potential subversion.[82] In each a desperate comedy is generated by the dislocation between a formalistic critical language, inadequate to the brutality of states which use the aesthetic for their own ends, and the promises held out by the aesthetic.

Paulin's uncertainty about home, and consequent need for the security of institutionalized structures, leads to the contradictions in his work.[83] However, those contradictions signal one of its principle features: the absence of an integrated identity. Paulin has remarked on the contrast between the empirical 'cult of experience, of the past, of memory that is so dominant in English writing' and the more 'theological cast of mind people growing up in Ireland are given by whatever culture or community they're thrown into'.[84] This opposition lies at the heart of his rejection of the conventional lyric and its associated voice. Experience in Paulin's poetry is more often negative or absent than positive and present, and rarely can a reader rely on the autobiographical basis that often underpins lyric writing. Paulin sees this 'autobiographical tendency', this 'passionate self-regard' as 'one of the strongest features of puritanism'[85] though it cannot be wholly approved since it is driven by '[that] enduring presbyterian preference for the direct testimony of consciousness over formal argument [which] creates a solipsistic universe gnawed at its edges by anger and incoherence'.[86] Given this, the absence of an expressive subjectivity writing from an accommodated position is to be expected; neither is there any iconographic ease since the consensus upon which iconography depends no longer exists. The very category of the individual – notably in lyric poetry the individual in love – is suspect: love is associated with retreat, with '[the] release of putting off / who and where we've come from'.[87] Such retreat is impossible to achieve since it requires a move into placelessness.

The keynote of the poems' subjectivity is therefore guilt '[. . .] for no reason, or cause, I could think of'.[88] This echoes Heaney's 'A Constable Calls'[89] – both poems share the 'heavy ledger' or 'stained register' of the state apparatus, and take an 'innocent' occasion productive of guilt. Heaney's is recognizably a voice out of a community defined, as in 'The Other Side',[90] by difference;

his guilt arises from that difference and the imbalance of power on which it rests. 'The Other Side' acknowledges that two sets of meanings may be in play – the landscape as pun – but that the landscape can be read is never in doubt, as there is still a community for which Heaney can at least aspire to speak and it is from that subject position that he can in turn speak to 'the other side'. Paulin's guilt has more to do with Protestant angst than with experience. In his work difference is internalized; 'The Other Voice' speaks from within about subjective integrity rather than, as in Heaney, from without about territory. 'The Other Voice' is the prompting of a questing Protestant conscience. However, this dislocated subjectivity cannot find inward integrity since such inwardness leads to solipsism. Celebrations of the 'I' are correspondingly rare in Paulin's poetry. 'I Am Nature'[91] celebrates the 'expressionist' Jackson Pollock who has the confidence of his own subjectivity which Paulin links back to Presbyterianism's

> volatile consciousness [which] expands moment by moment and pushes far beyond conventional and restraining notions of decorum, propriety and 'gentlemanly civility'. Such an ethic is hostile to hierarchical codes of manners and expresses itself in a free unpolished vernacular. Its equivalent in the visual arts is action painting, and it is no accident that Jackson Pollock was of Scotch-Irish descent.[92]

The emphasis here is on the idea of painting, and the self it represents, as process, but the poem is also suspicious of the ways in which this testifying expressionist relation to place can become essentialist and uncontrolled ('Cruthin', 'Hurricane Higgin'); it can also become queasily narcissistic and forget that 'After extremity / art turns social / and it's more than fashion / to voice the word *we*'.[93] The shift from 'To the Linen Hall' to 'I Am Nature' is the crux of the contradiction in Paulin's work. The former rejects 'philosophies of blood' in its 'demand / for arts and skills / to be understood' and celebration of 'that eighteenth-century, / reasoned library'[94] while the latter celebrates nature and self-expression. This is a shift from Enlightenment, civic republicanism to irrational subjectivism. Significantly, however, Paulin represents both in visual, rather than verbal, terms: the geometric and civic sculpture of the mason versus the irrational and personal process of Pollock. It is in the city that such contradictions are most forcefully present.

Paulin's favouring of cities, until recently not a significant locale in Irish writing, is another distinctive feature of his work. The city's marginal position in Irish culture[95] arises not least because in a Catholic-dominated culture it is an obvious instance of what Seán Lysaght refers to, in a different context, as the 'socialised landscape' of the Protestant imagination.[96] Despite this, the Protestant imagination shares with its Catholic counterpart a theologically-sponsored, puritanical distrust of the city which is often reflected in Paulin's work: cities are unnatural ('The Book of Juniper', 'I am Nature'[97]), dangerous ('Under the Eyes'[98]), places of distrust ('An Ulster Unionist . . .'[99]), and massacre ('The Defenestration . . .'[100]). Paulin's work, despite its reservations, follows that of John Hewitt and, particularly, Louis MacNeice in making use of the city as a significant place: 'Those city states [. . .] / Are the theoretical locations/ Most of us inhabit'.[101] It is because of this habitation that the poet must consider cities and find an aesthetic within which to represent them:

> I pop the question again: can this nissen plain,
> this fifties boredom by a dual carriageway,
> *really* be a poetic? Must every civic
> eye unpeel
>
> identical versions of the same damned spot?[102]

This is a version of the question which Paulin poses in regard to Bishop. The city in his writing is not just established as a secular location in opposition to the allegedly enduring qualities of pastoral, it is also, in a MacNeicean echo, a place of instability 'built on mud and wrath'[103] for which Paulin supplies an imagined topography derived from W.H. Auden's *The Enchafèd Flood*.

Auden uses *The Prelude* (V, 56–139) to establish oppositions between the desert and the sea, and the stone of abstract geometry and the (Yeatsian) shell of imagination and instinct.[104] He also identifies a new attitude to the sea arising in the Romantic period when 'the voyage' becomes the 'true condition of man'[105] as an Enlightenment concern with equality gives way to a Romantic concern with individuality.[106] Paulin's city is located between desert and sea. The mutability of the city is threatened on the one side by the negative pastoral of the desert where a 'plain / Presbyterian grace sour[s], then harden[s]' into 'Egyptian sand dunes and geometry'.[107] As Auden puts it:

> [. . .] the desert may not be barren by nature but as the consequence of a historical catastrophe. The once-fertile city has become, through the malevolence of others or its own sin, the waste land.[108]

Through this desiccation the city's free association becomes restrictive orthodoxy as the 'Word [. . .] wither[s] to a few / Parched certainties'.[109] Paulin's 'factual idealism' therefore also requires 'a visible water'[110] as part of his 'maritime pastoral'.[111] Waters which 'might be kind' are required to counteract the potential desiccation of the 'angry polity'[112] not least through associations of fluidity. However, the sea itself, another distinctive feature of Paulin's poetry,[113] can become a temptation to be avoided, as it represents a blandishment to privilege the individual conscience above the social imperative of association, as in 'Inishkeel Parish Church' in which 'the recognitions and the talk' are opposed by 'an enormous sight of the sea, / A silent water beyond society'.[114]

The sea and the desert are both wildernesses: in the one community becomes absolutist orthodoxy; in the other the individual, while free of the evils and responsibilities of community, is also alienated.[115] The 'maritime pastoral' epigraph to *Walking a Line* from *Moby Dick*, arguably a Presbyterian novel,[116] seems also to owe a debt to *The Enchafèd Flood* which is largely about the novel. In 'Basta' Paulin achieves an image of place which, combining the maritime and the pastoral with the association of 'we', rewrites that epigraph:

> what we found was simply
> a green field site
> its grass almost liquid
> like duckweed or cress
> – so we waded right into
> that watery plain
> that blue blue ocean
> and started diving and lepping
> like true whales in clover[117]

Despite the merging of land and sea in this utopian image, Paulin's work does not allow Heaney's elision of nature into nation. This is because the primary place in Paulin's poetry is not the nation (nor its attenuated analogues: home, parish, townland, region) but that ultimate institution the state. Where Heaney reads *The Prelude* for Wordsworth's dilemma as his place becomes inauthentic, Paulin reads it as discussing the Lockean and Rousseauesque social contract.[118] From his earliest writing onwards the state and its dialectic – Hegelian '"affirmative factor"' or Nietzschean '"coldest of all cold monsters"'[119] – is central. Paulin argues that both Hegel's contractarian optimism and Nietzsche's disillusion, rooted as it is in the supremacy of the individual conscience, arise from Protestant culture. The poetry oscillates between seeing the state as a Lockean contract and as a Hobbesian absolute. Either way, the state is set against the nation towards which Paulin's work is consistently hostile in its distrust of the autochthonous: 'the *chthon-chthon* / that spells *must*'.[120] This also comes across in his rejection of the North as a chosen ground for a chosen people, 'a paradisal garden occupied solely by hardworking Bible-reading protestants'.[121]

The providential landscape takes on the absolutism that Paulin rejects. Paulin therefore praises Ian Adamson's *The Identity of Ulster* because 'it denies an absolute territorial claim to either community in Northern Ireland and this allows him to argue for a concept of "our homeland" which includes both communities'.[122] Elsewhere, however, references to the Cruthin, Adamson's foundation myth,[123] display an uneasiness that intransigence and authenticity are not far away as in 'Cadmus and the Dragon' with its Loyalist claim that:

> we're no Piltdown Planters
> but the real autochthonous thing
> – we're the Cruthin aye [. . .][124]

The poem deconstructs its opposed attitudes to place ('*Cadmus is himself the dragon*') but the 'parish dragon' is 'forever trying to snuff / a cosmopolitan enlightenment' and a Unionism which turns its back on Enlightenment rationalism in favour of a mystificatory and authenticating relationship to place is therefore also seen to be giving up on the possibility of transformation offered by transience.

Paulin's poetry, having rejected the nation and its chthonic intransigence – the 'blood and soil' nationalism underpinning Heidegger's philosophy of 'dwelling' – returns constantly to the state as place. It may well be that the state is 'infinitely rigid in preservation of the coercion on which it ultimately relies' but 'the supple and durable structures of the bourgeois state [are] endlessly elastic in adjustment of the consent on which it immediately rests'.[125] In this latter regard it is preferable to 'exacting and intransigent' place as it can be seen (in Lockean terms) as a rational organization of space, with the potential for a 'factual idealism'.[126] Paulin's work rejects the organicist (veering always towards essentialist) organization of space in its awareness that:

> the earth is bent
> by blades and machines [. . .]
> – but what nature is
> and what's natural,
> I can never tell just now[127]

His is a poetry which 'know[s] the natural order / for the vigilant fake it is'.[128] It is because appeals to the chthonic are always suspect in Paulin's poetry that I would want to take issue with Peter McDonald's reading of 'The Red Handshake'.[129] McDonald asks 'how ironic is the alignment of the Third Force with the *Táin*?' and goes on to argue that '[w]hatever its ironies, the poem seems to collaborate with the cliché of the Protestant Ulsterman as both tenuously rooted and somehow cheap and nasty, vulgarised, wilfully blinded to realities'.[130] Such a reading fails to take into account what seems to be the companion poem in the volume, 'The House of Jacob from a People of Strange Language':

> Slips from me like a tongue
> I don't want to know
> – cattle-raid,
> book of the tribe[131]

In both poems there is reference to the *Táin* as a founding myth, the central figure of which – Cuchulain – is now claimed by both sides in Ulster as a means precisely of showing that their position is grounded – a chosen people in a chosen land – and thus in no need of rational statement.[132] The rejection of the 'tribal' book and language of the one indicates that the irony of 'The Red Handshake' is real and is at the expense of a Protestantism which casts its relationship to place in chthonic terms.

Paulin's own position is to be found in 'States'[133] which opens his first collection and which it is tempting to read programmatically as a statement of intent for a career. The poem's location – shipbound between Britain and Ireland – echoes the opening of MacNeice's autobiography[134] and like it invokes the sea as a symbol of the individual Protestant conscience. 'That stretch of water' is 'always / There for you to cross over', always, that is, available for the individual to take refuge in the contemplative, conscience-examining mode of the poem. However, the poem cannot be read as an examination of an individual conscience due to its sense of the ship as a symbol of the state[135] and the poem confronts the nature of the state and its contracts. The central figure is dressed in a leaking 'army jacket' indicative of the implicit contract of the individual with the legitimate violence of the state, while commenting on its inadequate protection against an unyielding nature. The state is 'a metal convenience' whose cost is 'the price of lives / Spent in a public service' and in the end it can offer no clarity to those, like the central figure, engaged in 'vigils', seeking an always ambiguous enlightenment. Here a word needs to said about the ambiguity of the poem's speaker. While the second person indicates an omniscient narrator, it is more probably a colloquial version of the first person used to avoid the lyric 'I', because the poem moves to the first person plural acknowledging the shift from the subjective conscience-ridden mode of the early stanzas into a complicity (already signalled by the 'army jacket') with others. However, the ambivalence as to whether the speaker and central figure are one and the same again disallows that autobiographical reading which Paulin finds disabling within the Irish and specifically Protestant traditions. Paulin's characters carry within themselves both the self and other just as the state carries within itself both security and threat. The state is a necessary evil carrying one across the sea of individual subjectivity but at the same time being a burden: 'freighting us'. It is the state which, for all its threats and violence allows for the move from a tempting but disabling individuality to a collectivity in which security is bought at the expense of others and ultimately of one's own complicity. Peter McDonald has written on this aspect of Paulin in discussing his reading of MacNeice's 'House on a Cliff' and its confusion of 'outside/inside' which:

> [. . .] raises notions which trouble and stimulate his own poetry: extremity, loneliness [. . .] an impossible imperative of 'belonging' to something which, under scrutiny, ceases to exist.[136]

Paulin's homeless position is like that of the community from which he comes; they are 'a people that is not a nation'[137] though they are in a state.

Paulin's apparent negativity towards Unionist culture is undercut not least by his sense that Protestant traditions are progressive as well as hidebound as in 'Paisley's Progress'[138] which combines condemnation of Paisley's reactionary ideology with admiration for his energy and his writing's taproots in popular culture. Paulin has also written about Protestantism's 'proenergetic iconoclasm' as well as its 'single-minded driven violence and ferocity'.[139] These apparently inseparable characteristics are reminiscent of the gusto and intensity which Paulin follows Hazlitt in valuing.[140]

The central figure of 'An Ulster Unionist Walks the Streets of London'[141] faces a similar dilemma of definition, finding no comfort among the 'London Irish' nor in his apparently authentic dwelling, the House of Commons. The result is a series of inversions:

> But I went underground
> to the Strangers' House
> *We vouch*, they swore,
> *We deem*, they cried

The House of Commons is seen as chthonic ('underground') and its language is turned back on it in the use of 'stranger', by a Unionist, in the Irish nationalist sense of English invader to undercut its parliamentary meaning ('One who is not a member or official of the House and is present at its debates only on sufferance': *OED*), just as the archaisms ('vouch', 'deem') normally associated with Northern Irish usage are now the hallmark of 'the house of speech'.[142] The Ulster Unionist walking the streets 'searching my own people' to find himself is by contrast a curiously modern figure. Transit and transience, reminiscent of 'States', are also central to 'The Caravans on Lüneberg Heath'. The caravans, unlike the House of Commons, are transient buildings which Heidegger would not allow the name of dwelling:

– bridge and hangar
stadium and factory
are buildings
but they're not dwellings[143]

Such transient buildings and their 'throwaway permanence'[144] are celebrated in *Walking a Line*, most particularly in 'History of the Tin Tent',[145] though this has been an aspect of Paulin's work from the beginning:

here where some people live for some reason [. . .]
when someone is building
it looks like a joke, as though they're having us on.[146]

The 'steel tent', the Nissan hut, is a version of the 'metal convenience' in 'States':

so complete societies
could be knocked and bent
into sudden being
by a squad of soldiers with a truck[147]

Without losing sight of the violence of the state Paulin celebrates the makeshift and transient aspect of it which his poetry must try to catch: 'texts prefabs caves / a whole aesthetic in reverse'.[148] In 'The Caravans on Lüneberg Heath' the caravans are linked to four figures who represent an antithesis to Heidegger: 'Dill Alexander / Montgomery Alanbrooke'.[149] They represent the military traditions of Northern Ireland and those who fought the Nazis and accepted their surrender on Lüneberg Heath. It is for these figures that the school blocks are named and the school itself is significantly described as a building not a dwelling: 'onestorey partitioned / tacked out of hardboard / and scrap fuselage / this aluminum school / is split in four sections'.[150] Bernard O'Donoghue has commented that:

> Paulin is here [in *Fivemiletown*] dramatizing what he sees as a rather desperate attempt to supply the lack of a local historical mythology (of which Irish republicanism is full – perhaps to a fault) by drawing on the whole history of Protestantism in Europe.[151]

More than merely counterbalancing Irish nationalism, this process is consonant with the range of place in Paulin's poetry and shows that values and ideas need no grounding to authenticate them. This international aspect of Protestantism, imaged through transient buildings, appeals to Paulin. The admirable energy of Protestantism is seen in its fissile nature; as against the 'negative pastoral' of desert places where the letter has hardened into a spirit-killing law, there is what could be called a critical Protestantism, one which constantly re-invents itself and the letter. This aspect of Protestantism is found in the tin tabernacle (as it is called in Belfast), the often makeshift meeting hall in which small breakaway sects hold their services. This critical Protestantism is, however, not without its faults for its atom-splitting can be equated with the dry academicism into which Enlightenment empiricism is seen to have degenerated in poems such as 'In the Meat Safe', 'Anonymous Biography' and 'An English Writer on the French Revolution'.[152] The last acknowledges the seductions of academic empiricism and is echoed in 'Sure I'm a Cheat Aren't we All?'[153] in which the speaker's unease 'in my own church' is not to be allayed by the amassing of file cards.

Paulin's aesthetic as represented through place is founded not on authenticity and integrity of place as in Heaney's case but rather on an awareness of the relativity and interconnectedness of places. In this his poetry bears striking similarities to Fredric Jameson's description of that writing which breaks beyond the confines of the supposed organic community:

> [. . .] forms that inscribe a new sense of the absent global colonial system on the very syntax of poetic language itself, a new play of absence and presence that at its most simplified will be haunted by the erotic and be tattooed with foreign place names, and at its most intense will involve the invention of remarkable new languages and forms.[154]

Paul Klee, the artist of an irrational geometry, displaces both the mason and Jackson Pollock to become the sponsoring (and again visual) representative of this necessarily makeshift aesthetic in *Walking a Line*. His presence rebuts the Heidegger of 'The Caravans on Lüneberg Heath'; while the Nazis endorsed Heidegger, they dismissed Klee from Dusseldorf Academy for his 'degenerate' art.[155] 'Klee/Clover' (the title connects with the 'whales in clover' of 'Basta') is based on Klee's First World War service in an air-force depot and how, by making art out of the offcuts of the violence of the state, he brings statist ambitions down to earth:

> each time a plane crashed [. . .]
> he cut squares of canvas
> from the wings and fuselage [. . .]
> [the pilots] never knew they were flying
> primed blank canvases
> into his beautiful airfield[156]

Klee is thus associated with the 'hardboard / and scrap fuselage' of the school in 'The Caravans on Lüneberg Heath' and becomes an image of the artist who, no longer able to rely on the organicism of the Dach circle, must forge his art from, and in opposition to, the ideology of the state when that ideology ceases to acknowledge its own transience; this is the artist as complicit subversive.

In all of Paulin's places there is a rejection of absolutism; the 'negative pastoral' of desert places and the 'permafrost' of his Eastern European poems[157] both reveal an abhorrence of regimes in which the state has changed – and with it its landscapes – from rational mutability to absolutist stasis. In 'Line on the Grass'[158] Paulin equates such fixity of landscape with the denial rather than the embodiment of history. 'This looks so fixed, it could / be anytime [. . .]'. The 'Shadow in the mind' that is the apparently immutable border relies on both the violence of the state ('A tank engine rusting') and a particular form of culture (the Yeatsian 'man / with a fly rod') for its existence, but what that amounts to is the 'burnt-out customs' of an archaic ideology of place which sees it as authenticating because stable. Hence Paulin's approving quotation from Hegel about *Antigone*: 'As Hegel shows, in the play "neither the right of family [which in our context can stand for custom and community], nor that of the state is denied; what is denied is the absoluteness of the claim of each"'.[159] Paulin is aware that in Northern Ireland, in particular, both 'family' and 'state' continue to make absolute claims and in his best poems he strives for a way beyond such absolutes. Of those poems we can say, adapting his own judgement on another writer firmly tied to a place: 'They are true visions [. . . but unfortunately . . .] they are somewhere else'.[160]

Notes

1. T. Paulin, 'The Firhouse' *Walking a Line* (London: Faber, 1994), p. 18. In writing this essay I have benefited enormously from discussions with Patricia Horton based on her research and writing on the intersections between Romanticism and Northern Irish poetry.
2. E. Carter, J. Donald and J. Squires, eds, 'Introduction' in *Space and Place: Theories of Identities and Location* (London: Lawrence and Wishart, 1993), p. vii. See also B. Bender, ed., *Landscape, Politics and Perspectives* (Providence and Oxford: Berg, 1993).
3. T. Paulin, 'The Caravans on Lüneberg Heath' *Fivemiletown* (London: Faber, 1987), p. 58. See N. Corcoran, ed., *The Chosen Ground: Essays on the Contemporary Poetry of Northern Ireland* (Bridgend: Seren Books, 1992), p. 11.
4. S. Heaney, *Field Work* (London: Faber, 1979), p. 15. Emphasis added.
5. S. Heaney, 'Mossbawn' in *Preoccupations: Selected Prose 1968–1978* (London: Faber, 1980), p. 17.
6. S. Heaney, 'The Sense of Place' in *Preoccupations*, p. 149.
7. D. Lloyd, '"Pap for the Dispossessed": Seamus Heaney and the Poetics of Identity' in *Anomalous States: Irish Writing and the Post-Colonial Moment* (Dublin: Lilliput, 1993), p. 16 and see R. Kirkland, *Literature and Culture in Northern Ireland since 1965: Moments of Danger* (London: Longman, 1996), p. 24 and E. Longley 'The Aesthetic and the Territorial' in *Contemporary Irish Poetry: A Collection of Critical Essays*, ed. E. Andrews (London: Macmillan, 1992), pp. 63–85.
8. D. Lloyd, '"Pap for the Dispossessed"' in *Anomalous States*, p. 14. This unusual phrase prompts the question: why not the more usual 'English Romanticism' or 'European Romanticism'? 'British Romanticism' blurs the more focused English version by bringing in figures such as Burns and Scott (on whom see R. Crawford, *Devolving English Literature* [Oxford: Clarendon Press, 1992], pp. 88–144) while still denying the full intellectual framework of European Romanticism as discussed by Jerome McGann in *The Romantic Ideology: A Critical Investigation* (London & Chicago: University of Chicago Press, 1983).
9. K.R. Olwig, 'Sexual Cosmology: Nation and Landscape at the Conceptual Interstices of Nature and Culture; or What Does Landscape Really Mean?' in *Landscape, Politics and Perspectives*, p. 310, n. 2.
10. E. Longley, '"When did you last see your father?": Perceptions of the Past in Northern Irish Writing, 1965–1985' in *Cultural Contexts and Literary Idioms in Contemporary Irish Literature*, ed. M. Kenneally (Gerrards Cross: Colin Smythe, 1988), p. 104.
11. K. Everest, *English Romantic Poetry: An Introduction to the Historical Context and the Literary Scene* (Milton Keynes: Open University Press, 1990), pp. 86–7.
12. See J. Barrell, *The Idea of Landscape and the Sense of Place 1730–1840*, (Cambridge: Cambridge University Press, 1972); J. McGann, *The Romantic Ideology*; and R. Williams, *The Country and the City* (London: The Hogarth Press, 1985) especially chapters 12 and 13.
13. J. McGann, *The Romantic Ideology*, pp. 72–3.

14. M.H. Abrams, *The Mirror and the Lamp: Romantic Theory and the Critical Tradition* (Oxford: Oxford University Press, 1953).
15. M. Butler, *Romantics, Rebels and Reactionaries: English Literature and Its Background 1760–1830* (Oxford: Oxford University Press, 1981), pp. 58–60.
16. J. McGann, *The Romantic Ideology*, p. 86.
17. See J. Barrell, *The Idea of Landscape* especially Chapter 1.
18. See L. Gibbons, '"A Shadowy Narrator": History, Art and Romantic Nationalism in Ireland 1750–1850' in *Ideology and the Historians*, Historical Studies XVII, ed. C. Brady (Dublin: Lilliput, 1991), pp. 99–127, especially pp. 102–3; and E. Longley, 'No More Poems about Paintings' in *The Living Stream: Literature and Revisionism in Ireland* (Newcastle upon Tyne: Bloodaxe, 1994), pp. 227–52.
19. S. Heaney, *Door into the Dark* (London: Faber, 1969), p. 24 and see *Preoccupations*, p. 56.
20. S. Heaney, *Preoccupations*, p. 132, quoting J. Montague, 'A Severed Head' in *The Rough Field* (Dublin: Dolmen, 1979), p. 35.
21. S. Heaney, *Wintering Out* (London: Faber, 1972), pp. 16, 27.
22. S. Heaney, *Field Work*, pp. 17–18.
23. S. Heaney, 'Station Island VIII', *Station Island* (London: Faber, 1984), p. 83.
24. S. Heaney, *Preoccupations*, p. 131.
25. See J. Barrell, *The Idea of Landscape*, p. 182 for this distinction between Wordsworth and Clare.
26. F. Jameson, 'Cognitive Mapping' in *Marxism and the Interpretation of Culture*, ed. C. Nelson and L. Greenberg (Urbana and Chicago: University of Illinois Press, 1988), p. 349.
27. See R. Williams, *The Country and the City*, pp. 9–12 on the endless regression necessitated by the search for organic community.
28. W. Wordsworth, *The Prelude* 1805, X, 272–4 in *The Prelude: A Parallel Text*, ed. J. C. Maxwell (Harmondsworth: Penguin, 1971), p. 414.
29. S. Heaney, 'Place and Displacement: Reflections on Some Recent Poetry from Northern Ireland' in *Contemporary Irish Poetry: A Collection of Critical Essays*, pp. 125–6.
30. S. Heaney, 'Place and Displacement', p. 127. Emphasis added.
31. S. Heaney, *Preoccupations*, p. 41.
32. T. Paulin, 'The Man from no Part: Louis MacNeice' in *Ireland and the English Crisis* (Newcastle upon Tyne: Bloodaxe, 1984), p. 75.
33. T. Paulin, 'Dwelling without Roots: Elizabeth Bishop' in *Minotaur: Poetry and the Nation State* (London: Faber, 1992), p. 190.
34. M. Heidegger, 'Building Dwelling Thinking' in *Basic Writings*, ed. D.F. Krell (London: Routledge and Kegan Paul, 1978), p. 338 and see T. Paulin, *Minotaur*, p. 190.
35. For an interesting and informative discussion of this poem see C. Wills, *Improprieties: Politics and Sexuality in Northern Irish Poetry* (Oxford: Oxford University Press, 1993), pp. 148–55.
36. T. Paulin, *Fivemiletown*, p. 56.
37. M. Heidegger, 'Building Dwelling Thinking', pp. 325–6.
38. T. Paulin, *Fivemiletown*, p. 59.

39. See A.M. Duckworth, 'Literature and Landscape' in *Encyclopaedia of Literature and Criticism*, eds M. Coyle, P. Garside, M. Kelsall and J. Peck (London: Routledge, 1990), pp. 1018–19.
40. T. Paulin, *Fivemiletown*, pp. 38–9.
41. T. Paulin, *Minotaur*, pp. 190–1.
42. T. Paulin, *Liberty Tree* (London: Faber, 1983).
43. See 'Thinking of Iceland', 'A Traveller' in *A State of Justice* (London: Faber, 1977), pp. 11, 30; and 'Traces', 'Hidden Face', 'In the Egyptian Gardens' in *The Strange Museum* (London: Faber, 1980), pp. 7, 13, 24.
44. T. Paulin, 'The Bungalow on the Unapproved Road', *Fivemiletown*, p. 1.
45. P. Muldoon, 'Paris', *Mules* (London: Faber, 1977), p. 40.
46. T. Paulin, 'Portnoo Pier', *Walking a Line*, p. 65.
47. T. Paulin, '51 Sans Souci Park', *Walking a Line*, pp. 33–4.
48. T. Paulin, *Fivemiletown*, p. 9.
49. P. McDonald, 'Michael Longley's Homes' in *The Chosen Ground*, pp. 65–83.
50. T. Paulin, 'Living out of London – VII', *London Magazine* (April/May 1979), 86. I am grateful to Richard Kirkland for this reference.
51. T. Paulin, 'Chucking it Away', *Fivemiletown*, p. 52.
52. See G. Dawe, 'A Gritty Prod Baroque: Tom Paulin and the Northern Politik' in *A Real Life Elsewhere* (Belfast: Lagan Press, 1993), pp. 71–87; E. Longley, *Poetry in the Wars* (Newcastle upon Tyne: Bloodaxe, 1986), pp. 190–9; A. Robinson, *Instabilities in Contemporary British Poetry* (London: Macmillan, 1988), p. 104.
53. T. Paulin, *Minotaur*, p. 23.
54. Given the games with naming – Linda Nicklin ('Linda Nicklin'), Jacklin ('Painting the Carport'), Neilson ('Kinship Ties'), Tommy Pallin ('Portnoo Pier') – in *Walking a Line*, pp. 5, 13, 35, 65, it is tempting to think of a Paulin poem on his near-anagram Naipaul. These near-anagrams, like the lines 'as to being Irish I'd like to believe / it's only the difference / between calling yourself James instead of Philip / if your name happens to be Larkin' ('Chucking it Away', *Fivemiletown*, p. 53) suggest an arbitrary rather than an authentic quality in naming, and in the relation between names and places.
55. T. Paulin, *Ireland and the English Crisis*, p. 18.
56. T. Paulin, *Ireland and the English Crisis*, p. 39.
57. T. Paulin, 'The Caravans on Lüneberg Heath', *Fivemiletown*, p. 55.
58. T. Paulin, *The Strange Museum*, p. 45.
59. N. Corcoran, *English Poetry Since 1940* (London: Longman, 1993), pp. 213–14.
60. For different views of Paulin's language see E. Andrews, 'Tom Paulin: Underground Resistance Fighter' in *Poetry in Contemporary Irish Literature*, ed. M. Kenneally (Gerrards Cross: Colin Smythe, 1995), pp. 338–41; N. Corcoran, *English Poetry Since 1940*, p. 214; E. Longley, 'Poetry and Politics in Northern Ireland' in *Poetry in the Wars*, p. 197; A. Robinson, *Instabilities*, p. 112; C. Wills, *Improprieties*, pp. 89–94, 151–2.

61. I use the term 'affiliation' in Edward Said's sense that since filiation (roughly Heaney's 'lived, illiterate and unconscious') is no longer possible, affiliation (roughly Heaney's 'learned, literate and conscious') must take its place; see E.W. Said, 'Secular Criticism' in *The World, the Text, and the Critic* (London: Faber, 1984), pp. 16–17.
62. T. Paulin, *Ireland and the English Crisis*, pp. 16–17.
63. T. Paulin, *Fivemiletown*, p. 55.
64. C. Wills, *Improprieties*, p. 132.
65. T. Paulin, 'Those Gamey Locutions', *Fivemiletown*, p. 21.
66. T. Paulin, 'The Caravans on Lüneberg Heath', *Fivemiletown*, p. 58.
67. T. Paulin, 'Going in the Rain', *The Strange Museum*, p. 21.
68. T. Paulin, 'The Firhouse', *Walking a Line*, p. 18.
69. T. Paulin, 'The Firhouse', *Walking a Line*, p. 18.
70. N. Corcoran, 'Strange Letters: Reading and Writing in Recent Irish Poetry' in *Irish Writing: Exile and Subversion*, eds P. Hyland and N. Sammells (London: Macmillan, 1991), pp. 234–47.
71. T. Paulin, 'Mount Stewart', *Fivemiletown*, p. 38.
72. See the folk rhyme: 'Augher, Clogher, Fivemiletown/ Sixmilecross is seven mile round'.
73. T. Paulin, *Liberty Tree*, pp. 21–8.
74. T. Paulin, *Liberty Tree*, p. 26.
75. R. Williams, *The Country and the City*, p. 132.
76. T. Paulin, *Ireland and the English Crisis*, p. 61.
77. T. Hardy, *Selected Poems*, ed. and intro. D. Wright (Harmondsworth: Penguin, 1978), pp. 196–7.
78. *The Complete Grimm's Fairy Tales*, intro. P. Colum (London: Routledge and Kegan Paul, 1975 [1943]), pp. 220–9. A. Ussher and C. van Metzgradt interpret the tale as one of Pentecostal rebirth; 'An Interpretation of Grimm's Fairy Tales: 2, The Greatest Fairy Tale', *The Dublin Magazine* (April-June 1950), 11–15.
79. T. Paulin, 'Amphion', *Liberty Tree*, p. 66.
80. T. Paulin, *The Strange Museum*, p. 35.
81. T. Paulin, *Liberty Tree*, p. 40.
82. See T. Paulin, 'Milton – One of Us' in *Power and the Throne*, ed. and intro. A. Barnett, (London: Vintage in association with Charter 88, 1994), pp. 178–81 in which he quotes William Hazlitt on how '[the] language of poetry naturally falls in with the language of power'.
83. See A. Robinson *Instabilities*, pp. 105–8 and C. Wills, *Improprieties*, pp. 121–3.
84. E. Hughes, 'Question and Answer with Tom Paulin', *Irish Literary Supplement* (Fall 1988), 32. See also A. Robinson, *Instabilities*, pp. 119–20 on 'Mandelstam's late-Symbolist reminder that poetry is composed in response to absence [. . .]'.
85. T. Paulin, *Ireland and the English Crisis*, p. 158.
86. T. Paulin, 'Introduction: Northern Protestant Oratory and Writing 1791–1985' in *The Field Day Anthology of Irish Writing*, 3 vols, ed. S. Deane (Derry: Field Day, 1991), Vol. 3, p. 315.
87. T. Paulin, 'Fivemiletown', *Fivemiletown*, p. 15.
88. T. Paulin, 'Martello', *Liberty Tree*, p. 56.

89. S. Heaney, *North* (London: Faber, 1975), pp. 66–7.
90. S. Heaney, *Wintering Out*, pp. 34–6.
91. T. Paulin, *Fivemiletown*, p. 32–4.
92. T. Paulin, 'Northern Protestant Oratory and Writing' in *The Field Day Anthology*, p. 316. For an account of how Pollock, far from being spontaneous, negotiated with art theory see T. Wolfe, *The Painted Word* (New York: Bantam, 1976), pp. 52–64.
93. T. Paulin, 'To the Linen Hall', *Liberty Tree*, p. 77.
94. T. Paulin, *Liberty Tree*, p. 77.
95. See F. O'Toole, 'Going West: the Country versus the City in Irish Writing', *The Crane Bag*, 9: 2 (1985), 111–16; L. Gibbons, 'Montage, Modernism and the City', *The Irish Review*, 10 (Spring 1991), 1–6; L. O'Dowd, 'Town and Country in Irish Ideology', *Canadian Journal of Irish Studies*, 12: 2 (1987), 43–53.
96. S. Lysaght, 'Heaney versus Praeger: Contrasting Natures', *The Irish* Review, 7 (1989), 71.
97. T. Paulin, *Liberty Tree*, p. 21; *Fivemiletown*, p. 32.
98. T. Paulin, *A State of Justice*, p. 9.
99. T. Paulin, *Fivemiletown*, p. 42.
100. T. Paulin, *Fivemiletown*, p. 54.
101. T. Paulin, 'The Hyperboreans', *A State of Justice*, p. 22. See 'Under a Roof', 'Free Colour', 'Newness' and 'Young Funerals' in the same volume as other examples of poems obviously written in response to the environment described in 'Living out of London' and note how this 'sequence' culminates in 'The College Newsletter' which refuses the alternative community offered by education.
102. T. Paulin, 'Yes, the Maternity Unit', *Liberty Tree*, pp. 36–7.
103. T. Paulin, 'Under the Eyes', *A State of Justice*, p. 9. See L. MacNeice, 'Autumn Journal XVI', *The Collected Poems*, ed. E.R. Dodds (London: Faber, 1979), p. 133.
104. W.H. Auden, *The Enchafèd Flood, or, The Romantic Iconography of the Sea* (London: Faber, 1951), p. 18.
105. W.H. Auden, *The Enchafèd Flood*, p. 23.
106. W.H. Auden, *The Enchafèd Flood*, p. 55.
107. T. Paulin, 'Desertmartin', *Liberty Tree*, pp. 16–17.
108. W.H. Auden, *The Enchafèd Flood*, p. 25. See also K.R. Olwig, 'Sexual Cosmology: Nation and Landscape at the Conceptual Interstices of Nature and Culture', p. 318.
109. T. Paulin, *Liberty Tree*, p. 16.
110. T. Paulin, 'A New Society', *A State of Justice*, p. 19.
111. T. Paulin, 'Purity', *The Strange Museum*, p. 5.
112. T. Paulin, 'A Just State', *A State of Justice*, p. 24.
113. See E. Hughes, 'Sent to Coventry: Emigrations and Autobiography' in *Returning to Ourselves: Papers from the John Hewitt International Summer School*, ed. E. Patten (Belfast: Lagan, 1995), pp. 99–113.
114. T. Paulin, *A State of Justice*, p. 15.
115. W.H. Auden, *The Enchafèd Flood*, p. 25–6.
116. See 'I was a good Christian; born and bred in the bosom of the infallible Presbyterian Church', H. Melville, *Moby Dick* (Harmonds-

worth: Penguin, 1972 [1851]), p. 147.
117. T. Paulin, 'Basta', *Walking a Line*, p. 103.
118. *Minotaur*, pp. 1–2. See S. Seth, 'Nationalism in/and Modernity' in *The State in Transition: Reimagining Political Space*, eds J.A. Camilleri, A.P. Jarvis, A.J. Paolini (Boulder and London: Lynne Rienner, 1995), pp. 41–59.
119. T. Paulin, *Minotaur*, p. 1.
120. T. Paulin, 'At Maas', *Liberty Tree*, p. 63. See N. Corcoran, *English Poetry Since 1940*, p. 207.
121. T. Paulin, 'Northern Protestant Oratory and Writing' in *The Field Day Anthology*, p. 318. See also T. Brown, 'Poetry in a Colony' in *Northern Voices: Poets from Ulster* (Dublin: Gill and Macmillan, 1975) and M. Elliott, *Watchmen in Sion: The Protestant Idea of Liberty* (Derry: Field Day, 1985).
122. T. Paulin, *Ireland and the English Crisis*, p. 189.
123. I. Adamson, *The Cruthin: The Ancient Kindred* (Belfast: Pretani, 1974).
124. T. Paulin, 'Cadmus and the Dragon', *Walking a Line*, p. 95.
125. P. Anderson, *In the Tracks of Historical Materialism* (London: Verso, 1983), p. 80.
126. T. Paulin, 'A New Society', *A State of Justice*, p. 19.
127. T. Paulin, 'Now for the Orange Card', *Fivemiletown*, p. 11.
128. T. Paulin, 'The Caravans on Lüneberg Heath', *Fivemiletown*, p. 55.
129. T. Paulin, *Fivemiletown*, p. 4.
130. P. McDonald, 'History and Poetry: Derek Mahon and Tom Paulin' in *Contemporary Irish Poetry*, p. 102.
131. T. Paulin, *Fivemiletown*, p. 14.
132. See *Ireland and the English Crisis*, p. 156. As I write Northern Ireland is recovering from just such assertions of groundedness, arising from what can only, in this context, be called the dwelling at Drumcree.
133. T. Paulin, *A State of Justice*, p. 7.
134. L. MacNeice, *The Strings Are False*, ed. E. R. Dodds (London: Faber, 1982).
135. See W.H. Auden, *The Enchafèd Flood*, p. 61.
136. P. McDonald, 'History and Poetry: Derek Mahon and Tom Paulin' in *Contemporary Irish Poetry*, p. 91, and T. Paulin, 'The Man from God Knows Where', *Ireland and the English Crisis*, pp. 75, 79.
137. T. Paulin, *Minotaur*, p. 15.
138. T. Paulin, *Ireland and the English Crisis*, pp. 155–73.
139. T. Paulin, *Minotaur*, p. 12.
140. M.H. Abrams, *The Mirror and the Lamp*, p. 134.
141. T. Paulin, *Fivemiletown*, pp. 42–3.
142. T. Paulin, *Fivemiletown*, p. 41.
143. T. Paulin, 'The Caravans on Lüneberg Heath', *Fivemiletown*, pp. 59–60. These and the following lines in German are taken directly from M. Heidegger, 'Building Dwelling Thinking', p. 323.
144. T. Paulin, *Walking a Line*, p. 4.
145. T. Paulin, *Walking a Line*, pp. 3–4.
146. T. Paulin, 'Thinking of Iceland', *A State of Justice*, pp. 11–12.

147. T. Paulin, 'History of the Tin Tent', *Walking a Line*, p. 3.
148. T. Paulin, 'History of the Tin Tent', *Walking a Line*, p. 4.
149. T. Paulin, *Fivemiletown*, p. 65.
150. T. Paulin, 'The Caravans on Lüneberg Heath', *Fivemiletown*, p. 65.
151. B. O'Donoghue, 'Involved Imaginings: Tom Paulin' in *The Chosen Ground*, p. 184.
152. Respectively *The Strange Museum*, pp. 9, 11; *Fivemiletown*, p. 3.
153. T. Paulin, *Fivemiletown*, pp. 40–1.
154. F. Jameson, 'Cognitive Mapping' in *Marxism and the Interpretation of Culture*, pp. 349–50.
155. G. Di San Lazzaro, *Klee: His Life and Work*, trans. S. Hood (London: Thames and Hudson, 1964), p. 254.
156. T. Paulin, 'Klee/Clover', *Walking a Line*, p. 2.
157. For instance 'Voronezh', *Fivemiletown*, p. 25.
158. T. Paulin, *The Strange Museum*, p. 20.
159. T. Paulin, *Ireland and the English Crisis*, p. 28.
160. T. Paulin, *Thomas Hardy: The Poetry of Perception* (London: Macmillan, 1975), p. 210.

10

The Body's in the Post: Contemporary Irish Poetry and the Dispersed Body

Tom Herron

I

The body in Irish poetry has traditionally been that of woman. In poetry written by male poets, woman has been metaphorized as land, as nation, as nature, as degraded place, as colonized, ravished Other of imperially male Britain, as desirous territorial unity, as rallying call for the national struggle, as Mother Ireland, as *Shean Bhean Bhoct*, the Old Woman, as Kathleen Ní Houlihan, as Sheela Na Gig, as sky woman, dream woman, *spéirbhean*, or *aisling*, as Mise Eire, as Dark Rosaleen, as muse, as earth goddess, as kitchen dweller. Recent work carried out by feminist critics has interrogated the use of the female body within poetry written by men. Women poets themselves have, of course, begun to revisit these feminine figures, to ironize them, to revitalize the possibilities of metaphor, to warn against the appropriation of the feminine by male poets.[1] It is perhaps surprising, therefore, that so little attention has been paid to the other side of bodily things: the male body in Irish poetry. This is my focus here. The poems I want to discuss are concerned with the violence done to the male body in political assassination perpetrated in Northern Ireland. I am interested in how the damaged male body operates in these poems of atrocity, and in how a range of anxieties are at play in the poets' use of the body image. While my focus is on how these poems stage types of negotiation with the body as a dispersed object of political power, it is impossible to ignore questions of masculinity, of desire, of the erotically charged activity of gazing at the violated body. The question of how the male body is mobilized in different ways and with different effects from the use of the female body in Irish poetry is not my concern here and now. Because all the poems I discuss are interested in power, in the body as the site of punishment and as a site of political communication, I think it is useful to consider very briefly at the beginning of the essay an exemplary anatomization of power enacted on the body. While there are clear differences between the power exerted on the body in Michel Foucault's 'The Body of the Condemned'[2] and the poems – in that the first documents state power, while the poems are to do with counter-state formations – I want nevertheless to situate Foucault's text as exemplary and paradigmatic, as providing access to the poems' anxious avoidances and insights concerning how the sign system of violence is written on the damaged and dispersed human body.

'The Body of the Condemned' which opens Foucault's *Discipline and Punish* is the unforgettable account of the interminable torture, dismemberment and final execution (by being torn apart by four horses and the assistance of the executioner's knife) of Damiens the would-be regicide, who on 5 January 1757 tried to stab Louis XV. The torture which Damiens endures is known as the *amende honorable*. The chapter produces a wide range of effects: a sense of voyeurism, of horror, of fascination, of pathos, of honour, of resilience, of brutality operating hand in hand with technological ambition, if not expertise. Foucault's text provokes numerous questions: at what point does the human subject die or end? At what point does the body cease to be corporeal? At what point does it become a non-body? What does the body turn into in such a total dispersal of its constituent elements? Is the proper name Damiens appropriate for what is left after the execution? What about the question of desire? Violent desire is undoubtedly at work. There is the state's political desire to obliterate absolutely; the executioner's professional and technical desire to achieve the same; the crowd's desire for spectacle and enjoyable entertainment; the guilt-laden, fascinated desire of the reader to engage in this text of horror and pleasure.

For Foucault, the body is always, of course, political. It is a contested site of numerous power plays, which range from the sexual and the epistemological, through to the disciplinary and the carceral. The extremity of the punishment carried out on Damiens is an enactment and an anatomy of regal power: this is what the state can do to the body; it can reduce the subject to nothingness. The King, as Head of State, takes the place of God, and is capable of reducing the human to ashes. The last signs of the unfortunate Damiens in Foucault's text are the smouldering embers of his bodily remains; otherwise, '[i]n accordance with the decree, the whole was reduced to ashes'.[3] Indeed, it is impossible to distinguish with any certainty where the remains of Damiens are, as his embers and ashes have merged with the cinders of the execution pyre. Most of 'him' has been scattered by the wind. Hence we enter into an undecidability to do with dispersion and the infinite trajectory of the trace (which Jacques Derrida has preferred to replace with the terms cinders and ashes).[4] Damiens, as a temporal and spatial arrangement of traces/ashes, enters into a certain universalism. The destruction of his boundaries opens him into overt relationship (which has always been there, only hidden) with the outside. Such a revelation of the material relationship between body and human subject and the world produces, for Kristeva, the experience of abjection,[5] and when I turn to the poems, it will be clear that much of the horror generated in the encounter between viewer/poet and the body is bound up precisely in the abjected nature of dispersal. Much of the anxiety will be concerned with the uncertain status of the trace and the even more unstable nature of its, forever absent, signified.

Foucault's recounting of the various narratives of Damien's torture is remarkable for several reasons: its responsibility in *staying* with the victim, or at least staying with minimal comment or elaboration with the narratives that construct the ordeal of the victim; its attempt to politicize and anatomize what is at stake in such terrible actions; and its clear-eyed detailing of just how the human subject – a relatively recent invention as far as Foucault is concerned of course – can suffer, persist and then become annihilated in an exercise of awesome power. In this form of public torture – which has a range of functions and effects – the self is dismantled, exploded, publicized, invaginated, its interiority reversed: the inside becomes the outside, the outside enters in. The boundaries of the subject are destroyed. And the human body is in the post – posthumous, post-human, and liable to publication and circulation. The *amende honorable* (like all public punishments) has a postal effect; its significances would be reduced to nothing if it did not produce publicity, if its signs did not circulate, if the victim was not the *courier* of the dreadful message: 'this could also happen to you'.

It is important to remember that this is image (in all its banality and shallowness): there is no access to this 'event' apart from textual production. Damiens is nothing more than a scattering of traces, ashes, cinders of signification; a simulacrum carrying a particularly vivid reality effect, which is revivified every time Foucault's text is reopened, reread, and remembered. And the huge irony of textual death should be borne in mind: textual death is a production of absence, of nothingness, of something beyond the limits of the sayable or the writable, of an affront to signification. But Foucault's text, which itself is nothing more than an arrangement of other already written texts, has the remarkable power to create the effect of presence, the effect of state power condensed in all its violence and extremity into this single act of retribution and obliteration, the effect of Damiens' suffering terribly, the effect of Damiens' presence (through the trajectory of the trace) even in his remaindered, absented state.

Foucault's text is for me exemplary in its persistence that every laceration, every drop of molten lead poured into the wounds, is linked somehow to regal power. Each terrible moment is a calculated and predictable component of the *amende honorable*. Even the use of the knife to sever his arms and legs when the horses are not able to pull him to pieces mimics Damien's 'original' crime: his attempt to stab the king. In this context, it is easy to agree with Regina James in her article 'Beheading' that the adoption of the guillotine by the French revolutionary authorities (acting in the name of the people) in 1792 was, in important ways, a truly democratic innovation.[6] Foucault's text raises so many issues of what it means to represent not only death, but also violent atrocity that I offer it here as a kind of paradigmatic text; one that I place beside the poems to which I now turn in order to analyse their anatomization of political and poetical power through the 'mediated encounter' of poet/speaker and dispersed human body.

II

The poems I want to discuss stage a confrontation with death in a mediated encounter between subject/poet and the post-human object. This object, in most cases, is itself an effect of simulacra, a trace in distribution in the chains of media signifiers, a media image. I will return to this later on, as this aspect of the *production of the image* is largely elided in the poems. These deaths are imposed by extreme force generated within a conflictual political structure, and they articulate the violence implicit within that structure. The poems enact particular ways of regarding atrocity, a fascinated gazing at the violated body, or perhaps more accurately a fascinated and repelled glimpsing of the body-image as it makes it way into infinite reproduction.

Michael Longley's 'The Linen Workers'[7] is part of a triptych of poems entitled 'Wreathes', all of which stage political murder and enact several of the meanings of dispersal: dispersal of forces within a military manoeuvre (these deaths are perpetrated in a variety of locations, such as the kitchen, the grocery store, a road near the border), and dispersal of the human subject into separate elements. The business man murdered in his house is dispersed at the moment of death into 'the books he had read, the music he could play'. From its Daliesque opening, through the recollections of the poet's father, through the brief attention to the scene of murder, back to the positioning of poet in relation to the father the poem adopts a curious stance towards its own apparent foundation or centre: the murder of the linen workers. The scene of murder, though announced as the centre or starting point of the poem, in fact seems to operate in a secondary manner, by providing the materials (the objects separated from the workers) by which the poet can achieve a positioning with the figure of the father, who himself comes to emulate the figure of Christ at the top of the poem. The poem displays an anxiety to do with the dispersal of the body, and a concomitant concern to reformulate the father's body in order to lay it/him to rest. There is an overriding will towards intactness, towards reformulating the body of the father. The dispersed objects (spectacles, wallets, small change, dentures, and so forth) are gathered up to provide the poet the opportunity to recover, to replace, to reach *into* the father's body and restore its parts, its dignity. This gesture is an inversion of that of the killers' actions: they have undone the men, undone the protection of body and clothes; they have publicized their privacies, and have sent these body images into the postal system of infinite media reproduction. They are the post-men.

Three unsettling features of the poem need to be examined in relation to the speaker's use of the displaced personal effects.

First, in gathering the objects, the poet simultaneously continues their scattering, removes further from the men on the road the objects that will facilitate his negotiation with the f/Father. Second, the sacrificial transformation of the scene, effected through the (insertion of?) the incongruities of the bread, the wine, should be inspected: this is not merely a personal attempt to reformulate, to reshape the image of the father: it appeals to and depends upon a higher agency. Third, the dispersed elements are still in circulation, still scattered beyond the grasp of the poet, and therefore still disseminating other significances other than that insisted upon by the poet. It is significant that the outcome of the poem for at least the poet/speaker is the acceptance of death in its dignity. However, in order to achieve a perfected, beautiful, transcendent death, the chaotic non-meaning of the roadside atrocity must be supplemented by the poet's personal drama; it must be passed over quickly and yet transformed into a sacrificial opportunity. So, the question is this: why, when its focus would appear to be one thing (the murder of the linen workers), is that focus relegated to a secondary position vis-à-vis the central drama of the piece – that is, the poet's relationship to the F/father? What is at stake in such elision? To begin to answer these questions we should be aware of the poem's act of violence (announced in the title of the sequence) against its own production of political atrocity; the fact that the text touches upon and then steers swiftly away from a politically produced death and dispersal of the subject that fundamentally assaults the idea of the lyric poem.

The poem can not admit both the absoluteness and the disseminating capacity of death; so the murders are neutralized through recuperation. In the movements away from the dispersal of elements the poem enters into a blindness to do with the politics and sectarianism that are the motivation of this attack. I want to argue that the dispersal of elements is the scandal upon which the poet happens (that is, comes across in his reading, or viewing of a news 'event'), but which the poem (the product, the present to the reader, the wreath) cannot confront. The trajectory of the poet towards the father is motivated by a demand for presence, and the blindness is a narrative of origin and telos which avoids that which does not fit into its self-generated schema. The scandal which is only just registered by this lyric poem is bodily dispersion and non-meaning. The disaster of death, and the obscenity of atrocity are the excess which cannot be accommodated within or by a poem that insists on presence, on integrity, even if the signifiers of integrity are shaky indeed. The demand of the poem, it seems to me, is that we confront the text's concealed extremity, that we attend to the irrecuperable body, to the terrible site/sight of violence, without recourse to metaphor. What appears as centre is supplemented by the text's dynamic progression, its movement from Father to father to Father, via the religious sacrifice of the men on the road. However, reading it iconoclastically, and sceptical of both its virtuoso hieratic performance and the dangerous attractions of metaphor, we see what has been supplemented return to centre stage in order to reveal the aesthetic violence that has attempted to put it in its place.

I want now to move on to two poems by Seamus Heaney, in which atrocity is first of all metaphorized by the poet/priest, and then re-produced in a new version which constitutes an autocritique of the desire to allegorize violent political murder/death into anything other than that which it is: personal and communal catastrophe.[8] The first poem is one of a series of elegies for victims of violence in Heaney's 1979 volume *Field Work*. While each of these elegies testifies to violent death (notably 'Casualty' and 'A Post-Card from North Antrim'), they at the same time attempt to re-vivify the victims. The old man blown up by a pub bomb in 'Casualty' becomes a revenant, and Sean Armstrong, whose 'forehead stopped' a 'teatime bullet', is told by the speaker of 'A Post-Card' to get up out of the blood on the floor. Something even more extraordinary occurs in the poem that I want to concentrate on now, in that the attention is focused firmly on the poet's *hieratic* powers at the expense of the degradation of the victim himself.

'The Strand at Lough Beg'[9] constructs an audacious conceit, in that while it is clear, from details in the first half of the text, that the victim is on his own at the moment of attack, and that the poet is uncertain of the exact circumstances immediately preceding the attack, the cousin's death is nonetheless transformed into a phantasmagoria in which the poet is present at the scene, is *there* in front of the victim as he falls to his knees. Things become anachronic and transpatial: the poet has inserted himself into the scene. This is a crucial manoeuvre for the achievement of the poem's metaphorical *coup de force*. What occurs in the final lines is an extraordinary play of aesthetization and the sacral as the poet cleans, lays to rest, and finally solemnizes over the body of the cousin. The doubled green within the final two lines implies the possibility of regrowth and rebirth, not just for the victim but for the poet/priest as well. The growth is the poem, the poem is the fully achieved thing, the thing that presents itself as sacred object (as in the 'Green scapulars'), the ultimate compensation for horror and loss. The poem survives and transcends the horror it produces itself by transcending the horror in that not all is lost. Poetry and the poetic canon are fortified: the return to Dante signifies their victory, their completeness. The problem with this is that the wider significations and in fact non-significations of the politically motivated murder are ignored at the dramatic centre of the poem. The circumstances offered in the first half of the poem are elided, until eight years later, when their significance resurfaces (as a return of the repressed) in a poem which fascinatingly takes to task the earlier text.

This second poem is part of the 'Station Island' sequence.[10] Here, as the poet is on a penitential vigil at St Patrick's purgatory in Co. Donegal, a series of figures appear to him in a sequence of hazy encounters in which the distinctions between prosopopoeia, dream, and ghosting are blurred. The 'spectres' include William Carleton, Patrick Kavanagh, an old school friend murdered by off-duty policemen in his grocery shop, a dead hunger striker, and finally the ghost of James Joyce who advises the poet to write for himself, and for pleasure. One of the ghosts is the cousin from 'The Strand at Lough Beg'. In place of ceremony, of the ritualized appropriation of the beautified dead body in the earlier poem, the poet is now interrupted in his difficult devotions (indeed the whole poem-sequence is in the form of interruption) by the ghost of the murdered cousin who this time presents a narrative that disrupts virtually every premise on which the earlier drama depended. The cousin was, he states, murdered. The passivity of 'The Strand at Lough Beg' and the 22-line spacing between initial threat and moment of death is replaced with the cousin's assertion: 'The Protestant who shot me through the head'. The ghost emphasizes distance. Whereas in the earlier poem the poet presents himself at the scene of the crime (it *was* a crime the ghost insists), he is now seen to have been distanced from the event, with the poets at Jerpoint. And the crucial difference is to do with the pleasures and the dangers of poetry. The formalized solemnity and beauty of 'The Strand' are replaced by accusation, condemnation, a sense of the poem simply slipping away rather than culminating in an arresting or transformative symbolism. The poet is arraigned (a favourite strategy of Heaney's) and the cousin (the family ties are themselves distanced here) becomes the *second* cousin. In setting the two poems side by side, the intention is not to valorize one over the other, but to ask what is at stake in their differing productions of the deathly body, what is produced in the dispersal of the body between the two texts? Assuagement of poetic guilt, it seems to me, is the least interesting element at work here. I want rather to foreground the oscillation between the two texts, to argue for the creation of a dialectical consideration of poetry's relationship to violent death and the dispersed body, a deathly dialogue between the violently inscribed body and the poet. Whereas 'The Strand' attempts to undo time, space and event, the second poem recognizes the irremediable belatedness of representation: it is always too late. 'Station Island' also attests to the inevitable and irrecoverable movement of the trace, in that the ghost, the spectre represents a potentially endless textual repetition. Ghostliness signifies the never-ending and futile movements of desire and the impossibility of capturing the real. The containment of the body (which, of course, only occurred in imagination and desire) of the first poem is replaced by repetition, by difference (this ghost cannot be situated within any notion of the cousin's selfhood). Finally, the urge to feminize, and to eroticize the dead body is absent in the second poem. In its place there is the hard insertion of recrimination, an insistence on the inescapable fact of sectarian murder.

In Ciaran Carson's poetry the categories of the subject, of consciousness, and of the body are always already dispersed, always already in circulation, and indeed, often in danger of disappearance. Much has been written about Carson's postmodernism, or post-structuralism, but suffice to say that such neat definitions raise more problems than satisfactory answers, in that the poetry is more a play of modern and postmodern, traditional and innovative, oral and semiotic. But in asserting the post-humanism of the poetry this is not to erase the traces of the human subject in all its integrity or of a sense of community or civility: Carson's poetry is full of nostalgia of some plenitude, some moment of origin which is always desired, always out of reach, but continually and unstoppably at play. 'Campaign'[11] would appear to exemplify Carson's stated lack of interest in explaining violence, of offering an answer. His poetry is sometimes characterized as possessing a photographic clarity and distance; a view promoted by Carson himself. On the face of it 'Campaign' might seem to simply offer itself in these terms: nobody is named, the perpetrators of the violence remain unclear, the reasons for the violence remain untouched. Similarly, the poem seems not to be interested in a *post-mortem* recuperative ritual. But I am going to argue that the poem does, in fact, construct a political critique, or more accurately an anatomization, and therefore remains close to my paradigm in the shape of Foucault's 'Body of the Condemned'.

Like Foucault, Carson's poem stays with the victim: the poem *is* the damage done. As in the *amende honorable*, the violence to the body is an anatomy of political power. In order to explain, I have to say a few words about the title.[12] As a noun 'campaign' can be described as 'a connected series of military operations that forms a distinct phase of a war or takes place in a particular geographical area', 'military life in the field', and as 'a connected series of operations designed to bring about a particular result'. So at one level the poem would seem to be operating ironically: tracing the disparities between military-political respectability of the term, and the vicious psycho-sexual drama acted out on the wastetip. This is a valid reading, but it only takes us so far. If we look further at the word campaign, we will see that it derives from 'campus', the Latin for 'field', and that the field has a certain iconic status and function with both Irish nationalism and loyalism. The field for nationalists is the island, it has its metonymies in the idea of the green, it is associated both with integrity, wholeness, unity and at the same time with loss, with the loss of the best lands in the Ulster Plantations. The island is referred to in terms of four green fields, de Valera's speeches often referred to Ulster after partition as the lost field. The island as field also implies its secondariness and superiority to England: the island is exploited for imperial gain whilst at the same time retaining its Edenic resonances in contrast to crowded, industrialized England. For loyalists the field is the alpha and the omega of the 12 July parades. It is the place of tenure, the place in which the Orange Order presents itself as community to itself, it is associated with the Garden of Eden, and with the agriculturation of wild territory, it is associated also with the fields of battle in which Ulster Protestant identity was forged or fortified: most notably, the Boyne (1690) and the Somme (1916). The field is therefore both an originary and a carceral icon; strangely shared and contested within nationalism and loyalism and enforcing notions such as enclosure, boundaries, threat, community and homeotopia. I want to argue that the poem works within the contradictions of this playful signifier 'campaign'. The poem hinges on contradictory suggestions: first, that the event (again the word is in fact inappropriate for this activity) is a fall away from principled action (the ironic reading), second, that on the contrary the dystopic, detrital space of the waste-ground (the urban field) in which the boundaries between human and non-human are dissolved is, in fact, the underside of those mythological spaces of both loyalism and nationalism; in other words, those exclusive notions of nation and identity that I suggested were imagined in terms of the field, and which find expression in the military and political campaign. The waste-ground is the ground upon which zero-sum politics play: the way that the purity of the political idea of the field will be won will be to obliterate, to disperse the 'enemy' into the post-human, to do away with the idea of the human, to invaginate the boundaries of interior and exterior, to transform the subject into dust, detritus. And through this process any productive resonances of the field itself will be lost, as it too is transformed into its opposite.

I want finally to consider a dispersed figure and how his dispersal operates within two texts: the figure is Robert Nairac, the poems, 'On Slieve Gullion'[13] by Michael Longley, and 'Mink'[14] by Paul Muldoon. I choose Nairac, the British Army's Special Air Services (SAS) soldier captured, tortured and executed by Provisional Irish Republican Army (PIRA) in the borderlands of South Armagh in 1977, and these poems out of several examples of victims of atrocity reappearing in various poems because of their particularly extreme enactment of dispersal. Both operate under the aegis of synecdoche, a figure which produces tremendously powerful effects of pathos, loss and, in the case of 'Mink', macabre humour. In Longley's poem Nairac is passed over swiftly (in a tantalizing line break) as if he were a minuscule feature of landscape or botany:

> To the south the Border and Ravensdale
> Where the torturers of Nairac left
> Not even an eyelash under the leaves
> Or a tooth for Maccecht the cupbearer
> To rinse, then wonder where the water went.

Such microscopic detail forces the point that the body is missing, that not even these minute traces – an eyelash under the leaves, a tooth – are available to reconstruct the man, his story and his fate. There is a terrible incompletion to Nairac's history; even in death he may be scattered around the landscape; he is still in circulation. The territory in which Nairac, or at least traces of Nairac, may be concealed is a territory which once again threatens to disembody the British paratrooper on reconnaissance from the garrison at Dromintee. The soldier is imagined as moving through the landscape far below the safety of the helicopter; he is a 'wine-red spot / Swallowed by heathery patches and ling'. He is first encountered by the poet/speaker 'through a gap in the hazels' as 'A blackened face, the disembodied head / Of a mummer who has lost his bearings'. He is sweating up the slopes of Slieve Gullion towards 'The lake of Cailleach Beara at the top / That slaked the severed head of Conor Mor'. The entire poem constructs a narrative of disconnections and dismemberments, but in the form of a local history.

Muldoon's 'Mink' imagines the most aleatory and unconfirmable sort of meeting, a connection of sorts between the mink escaped from the mink farm in South Armagh and Nairac in his grave. Much could be made of the implied cruelty at work here; the simultaneously gnomic and over-interpretable resonances of South Armagh; the terrible sense of inconsequentiality and irrecoverableness in the meeting between unknowing animal and lost soul; the playful and painful Muldoonian word play: Nairac is found because of his relation to the fur-lined hood of his anorak. The mink finds the fur-lined hood in, presumably, a futile attempt to find partnership, to establish connections. The mink is led to a no-where, an undefinable place in which the body is no doubt on the way to total decomposition; its traces existing in its exterior and now ironic covering. Nairac is once again uncovered; the first time he was uncovered by his captors (he was operating in South Armagh in a bizarre way – both incognito, but also possibly already known as a British agent)[15] and now by the burrowing mink. Nairac is reduced to secondary status in comparison to his anorak. It is the anorak which has attracted the mink, and Nairac's only significance lies in the fact that his name rhymes with the object of the mink's desire. And, in fact, even this tenuous connection will be lost on the mink. Whereas in Longley's poem there is still a slight possibility of connection with

Nairac's body, Muldoon's 'Mink' disperses the elements of Nairac even further. He is even further away from himself. This is a crucial element, of course, of his myth. The lack of a body signifies the most inhumane of actions; not even in death is dignity restored to the abused and damaged body. Longley's and Muldoon's poems recognize the simultaneous desire for *habeas corpus* and the fascinated realization that the body is still not there. Nairac is not there; the mink will pass on unconcerned, his eyelash or tooth will not be noticed, and will be swallowed by the landscape. There is no body there, Nairac is still in the postal system of myth, of story, of political manoeuvring. He exists now only in the form of question: was he indeed a member of the SAS? Was he involved in the killings of members of the Miami Showband? Will his grave be revealed once there is a proper settlement? Is there a grave at all? A footnote to my discussion of both poems proves the point that the dispersal of the body is indeed well within the realms of political strategy. Following the announcement by PIRA of Nairac's execution on 17 May 1977, this opinion appeared in *Republican News*: 'SAS morale must now be shattered as one of their most high-ranking officers has been arrested, interrogated, executed, and has disappeared without a trace'.[16]

III

In this discussion I have signalled my caution with the notion of 'event' (by placing the term within quotation marks) because it seems to mark out a uniqueness and a singularity to the idea of atrocity. In fact atrocity is always already textual in that it is predictable and understandable, and is always part of, and constitutive of, a series of repetitions ('tit-for-tat' is the most obvious expression of the already written nature of political violence). The body in atrocity is textual and spectral in that the violence marks the body in particular ways that have to transfer through space and time and mark out the 'event' of the execution or assassination in question. A certain globalized play of presence and absence is already there: film footage, video clips, long-shot photography are already there, at what is not a primal scene. 'Events' take their place in a long and desperate history of images of violence, in which the language is conventional: the body, shot and dumped by the road, the bomb with the warnings phoned through too late, the reactions, the condemnations, the retaliations. These are part of the recognizable vocabularies and image archives of political assassination and its aftermath. Nowhere is politics written on the body more clearly than in violent attack. Violence is a language, a sign system employing a number of recognizable figures and structures. What is truly frightening is the thought that textual, cinematographic, and televisual entertainment may well be prior in the minds of those who actually pull the triggers, or who set the timing devices. This was terrifyingly articulated by the killers who, just prior to spraying with bullets the customers of The Rising Sun Bar at Greysteel, shouted 'trick or treat!'.

What is largely absent in these poems (with the exception of 'Station Island') is any awareness of what might seem obvious: that these bodies are specular images, that they are circulated through diverse media. Of course, they find their addressees in understandable and predictable ways – through reading newspapers, by watching the TV news – but this economy of images of which *the poetic production is part* is nowhere evident in the poetry itself. Why might this be? Something perhaps to do with the loss of the real and the scandal this presents to the idea of the lyric poem? Or poetry's inability to establish the real, or to mark itself out from the precession of simulacra as an authenticated object of presence and punctuality? In the face of this silence, it is useful to remember the connections between death and the photograph made by Roland Barthes in *Camera Lucida*.[17] In the encounter with the photograph the viewer enters into, according to Barthes, 'flat Death'. While the photograph produces strong effects of presence ('I was really there when that was taken') it is, in fact, prone to the degradations of time, of light, of damage, of relocation and loss. Furthermore, the photograph sometimes becomes a form of refuse: it is placed in the drawer, or the wastebasket, or simply kept in its envelope. When the photograph is replicated (potentially *ad infinitum*) within mechanical and electronic media systems, any notion of authenticity (relating either to its referent or its own material presence) is put into question. The problems of representation are, of course, exacerbated exponentially in the action of the eye passing over the image, and the other images and texts which surround it. The implications of all this for the poetry are clear. The silent/silenced encounter with the photographic image in these poems can produce nothing but insubstantiality, belatedness, dispersion. In the face of this, 'flat Death' may be recuperable by recourse to the presence of the Word, or to the next best thing: the fully achieved poem.

Death in these poems is the site/moment in which the violence of the failed entity of the North is played out time and again in all its monotonous *grotesquerie*. But yet the links between the assaulted and dispersed body and the social formation are problematic in the majority of these poems, and in other poems of atrocity. There *may* be a tendency to refuse the political message written on the body, which goes more or less like this: see our work, read the body, understand its message, we've written the message on the body for you to understand and then we've posted it into the systems of media reproduction to be read, to make its demands to be read. The assaulted body defines the political culture. As Elizabeth Bronfen, referring to Foucault's 'Right of Death and Power over Life' writes: 'death is at once the locus and the instrument of power: that is, an independent power inheres in death itself, but other forms of power rely on death to disclose and enforce themselves'.[18] There are of course differences, as I've shown, in how the various poems approach this question.

There is also the question of the poem as ritual. Certainly in 'The Strand' and 'The Linen Workers' ritual allows death its dignity, while at the same time undoing death, transforming it into allegory. In most cultures death is formalized, sanctioned, even, through ritual. Death as fundamental challenge to order, civilization, reason, meaning is tamed through ritual. But can ritual diffuse death's power? Can ritual's beauty, its theatre, compensate for the terrible non-signification of death, its utter blankness?

There is, finally, the important question of witness, of testimony. There is the question of who represents the corpse. In poetry, elegy can be read as epitaph, as recording the life in writing. The images remembered in poems of atrocity have something to do with the human body re-membered, in opposition to the prior dis-memberment. Poetry reveals and sometimes flies from the horror of the deathly body, the horror articulated by Kristeva in terms of abjection:

> as in true theatre, without makeup or masks [. . .] corpses *show me* what I permanently thrust aside in order to live. These body fluids, this defilement, this shit are what life withstands, hardly and with difficulty [. . .]. [T]he corpse, the most sickening of

> wastes, is a border that has encroached upon everything. It is no longer I who expel, 'I' is expelled. The border has become an object [. . .]. The corpse seen without God and outside of science, is the utmost of abjection. It is death infecting life. Abject. It is something rejected from which one does not part, from which one does not protect oneself as from an object. Imaginary uncanniness and real threat, it beckons to us and ends up engulfing us.[19]

In the face of sickening abjection, presence may be restored by poetry which does not simply make a contribution to resolution, but is a form of resolution itself.[20] The poems I have discussed are as much engaged in a consideration of poetry's place, of poetry's agency (or its lack of agency in the hard world of political violence) as they are to do with the messy political, social and personal affront of the assaulted and dispersed material body.

Notes

1. See L. Mills, 'I Won't Go Back to It: Irish Women Poets and the Iconic Feminine', *The Feminist Review*, 50 (1995), 69–88; C. Wills, *Improprieties: Politics and Sexuality in Northern Irish Poetry* (Oxford: Clarendon, 1993), pp. 49–77; E. Longley, 'From Cathleen to Anorexia: The Breakdown of Irelands' in *The Living Stream: Literature and Revisionism in Ireland* (Newcastle Upon Tyne: Bloodaxe, 1994), pp. 173–95; G. Meaney, 'History Gasps: Myth in Contemporary Irish Women's Poetry' in *Poetry in Contemporary Irish Literature*, ed. M. Kenneally (Gerrards Cross: Colin Smythe, 1995), pp. 99–113.
2. M. Foucault, *Discipline and Punish: The Birth of the Prison* (Harmondsworth: Penguin, 1979), pp. 3–31.
3. M. Foucault, *Discipline and Punish*, p. 5.
4. See J. Derrida, *Cinders* (Lincoln: Nebraska University Press, 1991).
5. See J. Kristeva, *Powers of Horror: An Essay on Abjection* (New York: Columbia University Press, 1982), pp. 3–4.
6. R. James, 'Beheading' in *Death and Representation*, eds S.W. Goodwin and E. Bronfen (Baltimore and London: The Johns Hopkins University Press, 1993), pp. 242–62. Before the guillotine it was only the aristocracy who were beheaded; not anyone convicted of a traitorous act could lose their heads. Now commoners as well as representations of the *ancien régime* would have the opportunity of being led to the guillotine.
7. M. Longley, *Poems 1963–1983* (Harmondsworth: Penguin, 1986), p. 149.

8. This is not of course the first time the two poems have been considered as a pair. I justify my revisitation on the grounds that insufficient attention has been paid to the poems' differing construction and metaphorization of the body, and in the dialogic relationships between the two texts.
9. S. Heaney, *Field Work* (London: Faber, 1979), p. 17.
10. S. Heaney, *Station Island* (London: Faber, 1984), p. 81.
11. C. Carson, *The Irish for No* (Newcastle Upon Tyne: Bloodaxe, 1987), p. 36.
12. For a more extensive discussion of the use of the field within Irish nationalist and Northern Irish loyalist discourses see my 'Fields for the Faction Fights: Poetry, Icons, Nationalisms' in *Contemporary Writing and National Identity*, eds T. Hill and W. Hughes (Bath: Sulis Press, 1995), pp. 121–8.
13. M. Longley, *Poems 1963–1983*, p. 198.
14. P. Muldoon, *Quoof* (London: Faber, 1983), p. 28.
15. See A. Bradley, *Requiem for a Spy: The Killing of Robert Nairac* (Cork: Mercier, 1992).
16. Quoted in A. Bradley, *Requiem for a Spy: The Killing of Robert Nairac*, p. 148.
17. R. Barthes, *Camera Lucida: Reflections on Photography* (London: Vintage, 1982), pp. 92–4.
18. See Bronfen's 'Introduction' to *Death and Representation*, p. 5.
19. J. Kristeva, *Powers of Horror: An Essay on Abjection*, pp. 3–4.
20. See David Lloyd's critique (based on similar grounds) of Heaney's poetry in '"Pap for the dispossessed": Seamus Heaney and the Poetics of Identity' in his *Anomalous States: Irish Writing and the Post-Colonial Moment* (Dublin: Lilliput, 1993), pp. 13–40.

11

Questioning the Frame: Hybridity, Ireland and the Institution

Richard Kirkland

> **Institution** is one of several examples (cf. CULTURE, SOCIETY, EDUCATION) of a noun of action or process which became, at a certain stage, a general and abstract noun describing something apparently objective and systematic; in fact, in the modern sense, an **institution.**[1]
>
> (Raymond Williams)

> It's a terrifying notion that history is a process which is working to articulate an idea, to express that idea in an institution.[2]
>
> (Tom Paulin)

INTRODUCTION: INSTITUTIONS AND IDENTITIES

The paradoxical relationship of the institution to history constitutes an uncomfortable intersection for cultural theory. As set against Tom Paulin's anxiety about history as 'process', that seamless progression of events leading ultimately to an expression of institutional totalitarianism, Raymond Williams's sense of the 'apparently objective' status of the institution allows for a moment of potential realization. In this model the concept of the institution reads itself as foreclosing; a black hole absorbing the light of materialist historiography and giving back nothing but its own self-evident eternity. How then, in the face of such pervasive constructions, to chart the history of institutions themselves? Williams's sharp perception that the concept of the institution is itself institutionalized tells us much about the tautologous rhetoric that surrounds it but little about how to overcome such strategies. Indeed, with this the suspicion emerges that it is in such terms, as a symbol of monolithic cultural formation denying the possibility of historical method, that the institution is most often invoked within Irish cultural theory. Such usage has a rhetorical emphasis. The institution as monolith can function as part of an opposition which emphasizes the break into more disruptive discourses and vigorous modes of analysis. In this it remains of course beyond analysis; a monument to its own permanence. It will be my contention in this essay that the rise of the post-colonial concept of hybridity as an evaluative criteria of identity in Irish cultural theory is a phenomenon located centrally at this point of contradiction and that analyses of such instances allow a greater understanding of the ideologies that surround the institution itself. While tracing this development it is then encouraging to take into account Gayatri Chakravorty Spivak's sense of crisis as being 'the moment at which you feel that your presuppositions of an enterprise are disproved by the enterprise itself' if only because of the proviso she adds: 'These are not necessarily moments of weakness'.[3] By tracing the usage of the concept of hybridity and the heterogeneous in a number of recent and important studies of Irish culture I intend to explore the shifting negotiations between the individual critical act and the institutional position that enables that utterance. While this raises difficult issues of complicity (an accusation which can of course be levelled at this essay as well) it also suggests that hybridity can be read as a form of containment that can allow the play of the heterogeneous while containing it within certain, largely unexamined, methodologies. Readings of Irish culture in terms of hybridity are deeply implicated in the process of the institution and yet are marked by a concomitant desire to make such implication appear as discreet as possible. However, taking account of Spivak's awareness, we may choose not to see this as a moment of weakness, but rather as a moment of (as yet unrealized) potential within the discursive practices of Irish studies.

This tendency then can be understood as a highly specific emergent cultural phenomenon but this should not be to deny the larger resonances of the development. At the time of writing the faltering peace process in Northern Ireland has stalled at a point of irreducible difference as the recognition of 'diversity' (and the secular construction of the pluralist subject that this word suggests) comes into conflict with narratives that in themselves are subversive of such relativistic interpretations. This represents a significant moment not just because it has heralded a return to violence but also because it signifies the limits of a government policy, codified since 1985, that has underwritten the creation of (or modified) many quasi-institutional structures[4] based on a pluralist notion of the state. I have considered elsewhere[5] the way in which literary criticism and, within this, a particular reading of the poetic artefact, has provided much of the theoretical apparatus for this interpretation but for the purposes of this essay it is enough to note that it is through a radicalized notion of tradition as plural, diverse and performative that this agenda has gained its specific momentum. The notion of a 'cultural tradition' as an expression of identity relinquishes the idea of a homogeneous society and allows instead the celebration of a number of different (if carefully delineated) traditions. In turn the expression of these beliefs is commodified under the sign of 'diversity'. As Roland Barthes has noted in relation to the 'privation of history': 'Nothing is produced, nothing is chosen: all one has to do is possess these new objects from which all soiling trace of origin or choice has been removed'.[6] The significance of this transformation is that it recognizes the diversity of identities, and yet in so doing seeks to limit the play of that identity within the strict Orange/Green framework it wishes (simultaneously) to subvert.

In this way, it can be seen that models of cultural diversity and institutional forms often have an uneasy coexistence in Ireland and such anxiety can also be found in oppositional intellectual formations. The relative absence (until recently) of hybridity as a means of analysing Irish identity indicated a wariness about the dangers of a possible cultural relativism unable to do anything more than compare and contrast. This tendency is most clearly demonstrated by the pamphlets produced by the Field Day Theatre Company and their related work. As Field Day was instigated in response to a crisis which, according to Seamus Deane, 'had made the necessity of a reappraisal of Ireland's political and cultural situation explicit and urgent',[7] so the characteristic response of its pamphlets to this crisis was to employ a strictly comparative or binary method. The immediate implication of this strategy was to focus analyses of the situation on the British/Irish polarity, an approach encapsulated by the title of Deane's pamphlet *Civilians and Barbarians* from 1983. For this reason, division within Ireland was perceived at the level of the nation rather than at the level of the individual; indeed the appearance of any hybridized identities at the level of the individual more often than not suggested a betrayal rather than a possibility. To an extent, the reasons for this approach lie in the oppositional politics of Field Day itself. As Deane notes:

> A commitment towards comprehending the system is what Field Day is about and, what's more, I recognize our failures. In fact, we could not *but* fail, given all the limitations of the situation with which we started, given the limitations of the individuals in Field Day. [. . .] Of course, it can only be an attempt at any given stage, and every attempt, like the Field Day attempt, is culture-bound and time-bound, and therefore subject to the same limitations other subjects have been.[8]

The critical project of Field Day is one that seeks to live through the oppositions and contradictions of the present. The Orange/Green binarism may be near exhausted and politically foreclosed and yet it is only by repeatedly encountering this in its different forms that a dialectical analysis may begin. The critic Terry Eagleton has responded to this reading in the most sustained and complex way both through his Field Day pamphlet *Nationalism: Irony and Commitment*[9] and his recent influential book *Heathcliff and the Great Hunger: Studies in Irish Culture.*[10] Again in these works we can find a reluctance to engage with the possibilities of identity as hybridized and instead a determination to 'grasp the present under the sign of its internal contradictions' which, in this instance, means living through 'the present's spurious repleteness'.[11] For Eagleton then 'oppositional politics' are 'ineluctably parasitic on their antagonists'. Just as the State defines identity in monolithic and homogeneous ways, so any counter-reading must begin at that same point, using what is available and operating under the sign of irony. In turn, as *Heathcliff and the Great Hunger* demonstrates in its analysis of radical Irish Republican women,[12] the contradictions of a figure like Constance Markiewicz are not read in terms of political hybridity but rather are subsumed in her passionate adherence to an essentially coherent Irish republicanism; a strategic reading in this case 'ineluctably parasitic' on revisionist models of the same figure.[13] For Field Day, Eagleton and, as we shall see, Declan Kiberd, oppositional readings are then figured in terms of strategic necessity. Totalized and oppressive readings of identity as singular and determined are challenged using essentially the same methodology as the only way of encountering a mutilated and fallen present.

HYBRIDITY AND THE MONOLITHIC INSTITUTION

What this suggests is that the recent number of critical works which read Irish culture as one informed by the concept of hybridity signify a decisive shift in the critical direction of Irish studies. Although in terms of British and Irish cultural studies one can argue that this is not a radical development, the absence of 'hybridity' from Williams's classic codification of cultural vocabulary *Keywords*[14] of 1983 signifies a more recent intensification of such analyses. Moving beyond Field Day's binary models of analysis, the use of hybridity as a concept represents a greater confidence in the status of the individual as a potential site of investigation. In turn, this tendency suggests a greater willingness to accept readings of Ireland as a post-colonial location and to employ modes of critical inquiry appropriate to that status. This has not been an uncontested transition and it is perhaps no surprise that it has been within literary criticism of Irish texts, and not from specifically post-colonial frameworks, where the possibilities inherent to hybridity were first explored as evaluative criteria. Two recent books on the subject of modern British and Irish poetry, Alan Robinson's *Instabilities in Contemporary British Poetry* and Clair Wills's *Improprieties: Politics and Sexuality in Northern Irish Poetry*,[15] foreground their approach in their titles and, in turn, perceive their subjects as being in some way destabilized or improper. As neither work fully theorizes this focus they both find it necessary to invoke the existence of a concomitant stability or propriety in opposition to which such radicalized concepts derive authority. This becomes a necessary and inevitable precondition as the assumption that modern poetics are *inherently* transgressive or unstable (as both these books come close to suggesting) simultaneously deprives the organizing concept of its effective force. Indeed, to accede to such a principle creates only the possibility of engaging with a critical practice capable of little more than celebrating a strictly non-dialectic heterogeneity. For this reason, and in order to protect the nominal terms of the opposition from outright collapse, the texts invoke other forms of monolithic cultural activity although in practice their treatment is typified mostly by the silence that surrounds them. Wills's introduction to her otherwise brilliant study, *Improprieties*, provides an interesting illustration of this:

> However, rather than explore the contours of a specifically Northern Irish tradition into which the poets may fit more properly, this study focuses on the improper and the anomalous. I emphasize the ways in which the poetry refuses to be contained either within the boundaries of nation-states, or in the available aesthetic categories and theoretical paradigms of current literary discourse. Impropriety characterizes not only the sense of place or home offered in the poetry, and the disruption of 'traditional' poetic form, but perhaps more obviously the sexual narratives the poets tell.[16]

As that qualification 'more obviously' may suggest, the actual location of the 'propriety' that the poetry is seen to dismiss is found in the more covert stabilities of the monolithic institution which seeks to contain through the 'available' categories and paradigms of literary study, and which asserts, in the face of an inherently transgressive poetry, the undefined although pervasive ideal of '"traditional" poetic form'. In turn, the decision to explore the 'improper' at the expense of a 'specifically Northern Irish tradition' assumes not only the existence of the latter but also its status as a containing and homogenizing entity; an assertion of dubious validity if one is to credit the extent to which the existence of Northern Ireland itself may equally be seen as 'anomalous'. In its desire to establish transgression, the methodology of 'impropriety' seeks to create an identity for itself in opposition to the totalizing structures of current critical frameworks, while, in actuality, its assertion of a new paradigm leaves it securely within those frameworks of institutional complicity it seeks to dismiss. This is not, one could argue, a matter of methodology, but rather a problem of rhetoric. The desire to express dissent coupled with a reluctance to consider the interaction of critical frameworks and institutional forms allows the operation of a rhetorical strategy which enables criticism to escape from its status as criticism and instead to be aligned with the anomalies of the object of its study; in this case modern poetic discourse. This is only significant because at no time does this progression ever actually move beyond the final claims of the institution it seeks to displace and discredit. It is through this Gramscian model of ideology that the institution replicates itself, totalizes the field of critical possibilities available, and renders itself as an object remote from the concerns of the individual critical act.

What I am suggesting then is that there is nothing anomalous about the critical strategies that Wills's introduction employs. Indeed, such frameworks can be seen as symptomatic of the way that Irish literary criticism of poetry has succeeded in subtending the crisis that was seen to exist within the discipline during the 1970s and early 1980s. By celebrating, and in effect being seen to elevate, the heterogeneity of poetic discourse above that of the *critical act as a methodology*, the individual critical utterance can perceive of itself as inherently transgressive and/or liberated while ignoring the mechanisms of hierarchy that allow it to establish such criteria. It is in these terms that the critical act can establish its own role as both insurgent and dissenting. Through a metonymic expression of the power of the institution as confined to a homogenizing, post-Leavisite ideal of form and tradition, other aspects of the crisis that have a more definite material base (such as the disappearance of any idea of an audience beyond the institution) can be more easily overlooked. There is, of course, a marked irony implicit to this act of collective amnesia. The pedagogical basis of New Criticism entailed that (whatever else it may have become) it did have the capacity within itself to recognize both the efficacies and limitations of the institution as an integral part of its own activities; a possibility that is now only signified by its absence. In place of this there becomes apparent a dissociated critical practice that reproduces itself by way of a constant process of bifurcation; a continual reapplication of the homogeneity/heterogeneity opposition that allows the critical act to dream of itself as liberated by locating the notionally homogenous entirely within a discourse of power.

For this reason the current opposition between the discourses of the homogenous and heterogeneous can be most easily understood by a return to the New-Critical reading act. By functioning as a pedagogical process, the assimilative urge of New Criticism, expressed as the aspiration to achieve an agreed standard of taste, was naturally homogenizing in its procedures. However, as with all attempts to assimilate or integrate the inferior subject, this was simultaneously an impossible desire as the fulfilment of the process would not only reveal the totalized limits of the structure but would also hybridize the previous ideal. As David Lloyd, a critic of Irish culture who has engaged perceptively with this dilemma, has noted in relation to the attempted assimilation of the colonial subject, the completion of the process has to be 'ever-withheld'.[17] This then constitutes the reverse of the tendency we have already considered. If, for Wills, heterogeneity defines itself through the always-absent figure of the homogenous, so then the putative stability/homogeneity of the New Critical agenda had to be reinforced precisely because its methodology revealed such striking cultural fissures. To put it another way, the degree to which the stability of the project was insisted upon[18] was in precise correlation to the continual reinvention of the poetic standard of taste by 'bad' subjects. In this way Wills's evocation of '"traditional" poetic form' carries with it its own internal tensions and what may look a liberation becomes, instead, another form of servitude.

ARTICULATING THE HYBRID IDENTITY

If this, to a large extent, suggests an impasse, then a rearticulation of the dilemma through the frameworks of recent post-colonial theory becomes necessary. Certainly it is practically impossible to trace the rise of the hybrid within contemporary cultural theory without acknowledging the concomitant need, as Homi Bhabha comments, to 'think beyond narratives of originary and initial subjectivities and to focus on those moments or processes that are produced in the articulation of cultural differences'.[19] This suggests that within post-colonial criticism (at least in its early formations)[20] the idea of the hybrid arises from the meeting of cultures which have been, in themselves, often posited as stable and homogeneous. In this context the hybrid is perceived as essentially marginal or 'liminal'. This is a crucial distinction for while it plays on the efficacies of the institution as a centred formation it also, as Spivak recognizes,[21] accounts for the self-recognized subjectivity of that position. The emphasis on the process of cultural formation (what Spivak terms the 'mechanics'[22]) in opposition to its authenticity necessitates this movement to the borders of signification. It is ironic that it is at the point at which this awareness comes up against a perceived crisis in the role of the institution that this agenda gains its force. The overall progression in recent cultural theory then is one which has moved beyond evocations of the hybrid as a way of destabilizing the authentic to a position that finds all cultural formations *essentially* hybridized (with all the paradoxical instabilities that such a conjunction suggests). In turn, authenticity becomes a ghosted presence haunting the hybrid formation, always at once removed from itself and recognizable only by its absence.

It is through this awareness and within analyses of colonized representations of subject positions that the hybrid has gained its political energy. Moreover, and perhaps more importantly for this argument, it has also been within these debates that the hybrid formation has become an absolute concept not inherently beholden to an oppositional monolith. This has occurred with the recognition that the hybrid formation (perceived in terms of discourse, identity and institution) is not the result of a meeting of two cultures but rather is the product of a crucial *ambivalence* existing at a point within the efficacies of colonial discourse itself. This is significant in that it does not posit the existence of the hybrid formation in opposition to a monolithic colonial power, or indeed a monolithic pre-colonized cultural identity. Rather this approach finds that it is at the moment of interaction that the essentially divided nature of colonial discourse is revealed. Thus, in its ambivalence, the unitary assertion of that discourse will always be simultaneously (and inevitably) heterogeneous. For Bhabha this constitutes a crucial distinction for it entails that what we can understand as the construction of subjectivities within colonialist relations is also (and inevitably) a 'persistent *questioning* of the frame'.[23]

It is through this formulation that hybridity forces us to address the institutional basis, or in this case 'frame', of any critical utterance. In turn, it has the striking effect of seriously problematizing models of colonial interaction based on theories of assimilation; foregrounding the impossibility of assimilation just as it destabilizes the putative constructions of fixed colonialist identity on which this is based. The 'ever-withheld' nature of fully assimilated citizenship gains a presence not just for the colonized subject but also for the colonizer who, in constructing the presence of authenticity, simultaneously reveals both its ambivalence and its failure ever to connect with itself. As Bhabha insists:

> Cultures come to be represented by processes of iteration and translation through which their meanings are very vicariously addressed to – *through* – an Other. This erases any essentialist claims for the inherent authenticity or purity of cultures which, when inscribed in the naturalistic sign of symbolic consciousness frequently become political arguments for the hierarchy and ascendancy of powerful cultures. It is in this hybrid gap, which produces no relief, that the colonial subject *takes place*, its subaltern position inscribed in the space of iteration [. . .] .[24]

This awareness enables the hybrid to become, not simply a point of interaction, but a point of transformation: a state of being *inbetween* that can never develop a unitary identity: it exists only as '*something else besides*'.[25] It is within this construction that the full resonances of the subaltern formation within post-colonial criticism are properly revealed. Rather than a classification, the subaltern becomes, as Spivak suggests, 'truly situational':[26] at once both Gramsci's censored utterance utilizing the methodology of his six point plan in 'Notes on Italian History',[27] that which does not conform to class analyses, and the unutterable counter to the totalizing agendas of teleological epistemes that locate themselves within a notionally centred logic of knowledge.

However, although this construction is useful it does not account for the ways in which this awareness has made itself present within the formation of the institution – a structure within cultural theory often perceived as deeply validated by the process of authenticity. Indeed, any account of the role of hybridity within institutional forms has to take cognizance of Spivak's clear suspicion of, even hostility to, the claims for the hybrid that are made within academic institutions.[28] It is at this point that the rise of the hybrid as a formation *desired* by its practitioners comes into conflict with its stubborn residual resistance to assimilation. In this context, as Stephen Slemon observes, post-colonialism operates mostly as an object of desire for a particular critical practice as it 'has the power to confer political legitimacy onto specific forms of institutionalised labour, especially on ones that are troubled by their mediated position within the apparatus of institutional power'.[29] This, however, is not without its problems and one can empathize with Lloyd's shrewd assertion that 'the fact that the subaltern cannot speak in our voice is a problem only insofar as the post-colonial intellectual retains the nostalgia for the universal position occupied by the intellectual in the narrative of representation'.[30] In turn the danger remains that in evoking the subaltern category within Irish cultural studies we merely buttress the prevailing academic discourse against its other by restricting the play of the hybrid to a containing metaphor. In this codification stability is reasserted and the discourse returns to a model predicated on the symbiotic relationship of the homogenous to the heterogeneous; a progression that comfortably forecloses issues of representation within the realm of the unknowable. Through this manoeuvre the subaltern is legitimized by its metaphoric function. Representing absolute hybridity, it can exist without agency and can only destabilize the totalizing agendas of the nation by offering itself only as a form of excess.

What we can find then in a consideration of the use of 'hybridity' in recent Irish cultural and literary criticism is a repetition, in a new language, of the kinds of debates surrounding identity that have previously been rehearsed (and possibly exhausted). In turn, such identitarian readings restrict the play of the hybrid within previously valorized models of Irish cultural formation. Luke Gibbons's 'Unapproved Roads: Ireland and Post-Colonial Identity'[31] associates the rise of hybridity with the fourth stage of Thomas McEvilley's model of cultural formation; that of the post-colonial phase or 'the stage ushered in by the generation born after the departure of the colonizing forces, which is less concerned with opposition to the colonial legacy'.[32] For Gibbons this is a moment of potential but one that can lead to the possibility of what he terms 'free play',[33] something marked more by a historical ambivalence rather than a productive interchange. Citing Ella Shohat and Robert Stam's awareness that a 'celebration of syncretism and hybridity per se, if not articulated with questions of historical hegemonies, risks sanctifying the fait accompli of colonial violence',[34] Gibbons adopts a historical narrative of oppression, beginning naturally with Edmund Spenser and moving through the sixteenth century and onto Edmund Burke (all within six lines). The intention of this is to reclaim the hybrid formation as something other than a mere celebration of a politically heterogeneous identity. This desire represents a laudable aim and yet it engenders other qualifications that necessitate this now familiar 'Edmund to Edmund' model of Irish history. Firstly, it is part of Gibbons's purpose to correct what he perceives as the 'essentialist myth that racist attitudes were already present in Irish emigrants'[35] as a means of explaining Irish complicity with colonial oppression in the United States. This interchange, however, is not seen as an example of hybridity in itself but rather a strategic relocation of an identity in the face of a white supremacy that reinforces, rather than questions, Irish identity as a post-colonial phenomenon. This desire to (re)place Irish experience within the frame of the post-colonial model leads then, not only to the historically foreshortened readings that give momentum to the essay, but also (in the same way as Wills's analysis) to a rhetorical mode of slightly celebratory criticism:

> Yet it is only when hybridity becomes truly reciprocal rather than hierarchical that the encounter with the culture of the colonizer ceases to be detrimental to one's development.
>
> Another way of negotiating identity through an exchange with the other is to make provision, not just for 'vertical' mobility from the periphery to the centre, but for 'lateral' journeys along the margins which short-circuit the colonial divide. This is the rational for the present welcome cultural exchange between Irish and Mexican culture in the 'Distant Relations' exhibition of the Irish Museum of Modern Art.[36]

It is around the notional 'truly reciprocal' that the strategies of closure that Gibbons is emphasizing gain momentum. Apart from an uneasiness about whose 'truly' this might represent (who, after all, is valorizing this awareness?), one can also identify at this point the re-emergence of authenticity as a valorizing concept. This is reinforced by the teleological (and slightly coy) phrase 'detrimental to one's development' which foregrounds a determined individualism that sits uncomfortably with the instability of identity that Gibbons had previously cited as an integral part of the post-colonial condition. These vagaries are mirrored by the essay's reluctance to be specific about the nature of colonial oppression itself. The margin/centre divide that the passage concentrates on conflates British colonialism and Spanish colonialism under the sign, as we are later informed, of 'global powers'. The reductiveness of this conflation not only generalizes the actual motives, and more crucially, the *effect* of colonization but also tilts the essay dangerously towards a celebration of oppression in a manner that comes close to the celebration of hybridity that the essay had previously warned the reader to avoid. For these reasons then, 'Unapproved Roads: Ireland and Post-Colonial Identity' shares with Wills's introduction the tendency towards overt rhetorical or celebratory strategies as a way of subtending contradiction. This is because it does not allow the recognition of the hybridized identity to question the frame of the relationships between subaltern, institution and nation. Similarly, it shares with the recent work of Kiberd a stated belief in cultural historicization while highlighting (albeit unconsciously) the selectivity that inevitably intrudes when institutions and hybridity meet. Read in this way, we can place such frameworks within Lloyd's sense of the 'nostalgia for the universal position'; a moment of theoretical crisis as the frame of representation becomes visible.

In Kiberd's *Inventing Ireland: The Literature of the Modern Nation*,[37] his previous work for Field Day is significantly repositioned in terms of hybridity. While in his 1984 Field Day pamphlet *Anglo Irish Attitudes*,[38] Kiberd had contrasted Oscar Wilde and George Bernard Shaw in terms of the dominant *national* stereotypes available to them, in *Inventing Ireland* such stereotypes are complicated by Ireland's post-colonial status and the hybrid formations thereby revealed. By placing Ireland within the remit of post-colonial experience, the '"mixed" nature of the experience of Irish people'[39] emerges as an important structural principle but with this, in the introduction to the work, another opposition surfaces which reminds the reader of Kiberd's earlier binarist thinking:

> Were the Irish a hybrid people, as the artists generally claimed, exponents of multiple selfhood and modern authenticity? Or were they a pure, unitary race, dedicated to defending a romantic notion of integrity? These discussions anticipated many others which would be heard across the 'Third World': in Ireland, as elsewhere, artists celebrated the hybridity of the national experience, even as they lamented the underdevelopment which seemed to be found alongside such cultural richness. At the level of practical politics, the 'green' and 'orange' essentialists seized control, and protected their singular versions of identity on either side of a patrolled border, but the pluralist philosophy espoused by the artists may yet contain the shape of the future.[40]

Present here is another version of hybrid experience as beholden to the example set by the aesthetic artefact; a tendency that can be identified in the work of The Cultural Traditions Group and Wills's reading of impropriety. In this instance Irish artists have a prophetic function and yet one which operates at a level remote from 'practical politics'. Hybridity, in turn, is 'celebrated' as an alternative to the monolithic formation and is seen to be *in itself*, a worthwhile and/or liberating phenomenon. This returns us to the conflation of hybridity and pluralism and a reading of the experience of post-colonialism as one which does not replicate the colonial but rather disperses and relativizes experience. The 'shape of the future' that such a pluralist vision may offer is given substance in the final chapter of the book as the green flag that was once draped around Cathleen ní Houlihan's shoulders is transformed into 'a quilt of many patches and colours, all beautiful, all distinct, yet all connected too'.[41] In Kiberd's model, Ireland will outgrow the oppositions which once sustained it and, informed by the example of art, will become a site of celebration, of distinctive individualism. Again, as with Gibbons's thinking, the recognition of hybridity is seen as the moment of liberation and the final stage of a teleological narrative yet to be fulfilled. For this reason, it is of no surprise that celebration is seen as the natural response: the fallen present, gripped by essentialism and scarred by partition, will eventually pass away and hybridity will be the defining character of a new structure of feeling. However, while *Inventing Ireland* welcomes this transition, the prophetic nature of the vision locates the point of utterance as caught in a nostalgia for the 'singular versions of identity' which simultaneously validates its critique.

CONCLUSION: SUBALTERN STUDIES AND IRELAND

The difficulty which Irish post-colonial criticism faces then can be articulated by a return to one of Bhabha's formulations: the distinction between relativist cultural diversity[42] as located in the institution and cultural difference as a violation of previously mapped cultural territories.[43] While cultural diversity has often been expressed as an ideal model of social formation (at least within the West) it is necessary to place such expression in the context of the overarching institution which, within its own mechanics, has the capacity to contain just as it can allow a nominal expression of free play. 'The finally universal claims of the hegemonic institutions within which conflicting and contradictory interests are negotiated',[44] as Lloyd expresses it, can articulate the hybrid just as it represses it. Such a contradiction is as crucial as it is precise and it is at this point that the revisionary nature of theory comes into conflict with its institutional status; a dilemma developed interestingly by Bhabha:

> The continual reference to the horizon to other cultures which I have mentioned earlier is ambivalent. It is a site of citation, but it is also a sign that such critical theory cannot forever sustain its position in the academy as the adversarial cutting edge of Western idealism. What is required is to demonstrate another territory of translation, another testimony of analytical argument, a different engagement in the politics of and around cultural domination.

While this involves breaking with telelogical notions of the hybrid as it is constituted within the academy it also, and more importantly, necessitates a breaking with relativist structures of engagement and perceiving cultural difference as an '*enunciative* category'[45] emerging from the hybrid gap to which I have already made reference. Recognizing cultural difference as a project predicated on the *construction* of the Other rather than as a play of oppositions destabilizes the colonial binarism just as it demands another mode of representation emerging (as Bhabha insists) at the level of the sign and capable of recognizing its own complicities.

These criticisms should be taken seriously for if the formation of the subaltern is to structure future post-colonial readings of Irish culture so one should attend to Spivak's belief that the intellectual 'must pay more attention to Gramsci and not focus on the work going on in India'.[46] This is not just an example of cultural protectionism on her part (although we can locate aspects of this thinking elsewhere in her work) but an awareness that can negotiate some of the difficulties of 'easy transferability'[47] (as Lloyd puts it) that bedevil post-colonial theory and which explain, in part, the continued attraction of the anachronistic approach termed 'new literatures in English'. For Lloyd, Gramsci 'offers a model in which a given conceptual apparatus gains in complexity according to the levels of specificity with which it is applied',[48] and it is through a critique of the conflict between hegemony and counter-hegemony within state institutions that this specificity gains its theoretical energy. In turn, and more contentiously, this approach may also involve a reappraisal of currently discredited Althusserian readings of the subject and their relation to Gramsci's structural frameworks of hegemony: a possibility that Bhabha has already recognized. As he comments in relation to the difficulties I have outlined above: 'Althusser's critique of the temporal structure of the Hegelian-Marxist expressive totality, despite its functionalist limitations, opens up the possibilities of thinking the relations of production in a time of differential histories'.[49]

Despite this, it is at present difficult to envisage Irish Cultural Studies critics (re)turning to Althusserian materialism even if such an approach would enable a locational and temporal critique of the institution to emerge. However, it is important to take cognizance of both Spivak's and Bhabha's reservations as a greater concentration on the Gramscian concept of the subaltern prevents the term moving into the silenced territory of the passive. Although Gramsci's sense of the subaltern as a grouping which seeks affiliation to dominant formations in order 'to influence the programmes of these formations [and . . .] to press claims of their own',[50] contains within itself a certain deterministic or teleological trajectory, it also reinvigorates subaltern consciousness as something at war with itself, something that can be both subversive and complicit in its 'active or passive affiliations'.[51] This is a necessary development if Irish Studies is to avoid pietistic readings of the Other as a site of pure disempowerment. A history which is, in Gramsci's terms, 'fragmented and episodic',[52] is at least a history that can be reconstituted; an act that allows the mechanics of oppression to be approached with a contextual specificity far from constructions of oppressive commonality. In this way the subject position of the subaltern is subversive only in the manner to which it denies the ethical purity of the liminal grouping. Perhaps this is the lesson to be learnt from analyses of the subaltern undertaken in India. From an Irish institutional perspective the post-colonial framework of the hybrid as it is emerging often appears totalizing and contextually insensitive due to an inability to recognize the full epistemological instability it engenders. Ironically this is an impasse that has both its genesis and its conclusion in the extensions of an ethical criticism deriving from within the institution itself. An awareness of the hybrid, the heterogeneous and the anomalous should not be the catalyst for celebration but rather should instigate a considered process of rereading to assess just how far the frames of representation themselves need to be re-evaluated. While this may indeed suggest that the Orange/Green binarism by which Irish identity has been structured has long since been unworkable, it may also prompt the dismantling of the discreet discursive practices of Irish Studies itself.

Notes

1. R. Williams, *Keywords: A Vocabulary of Culture and Society* (London: Fontana, 1983), p. 168.
2. T. Paulin in *Viewpoints: Poets in Conversation with John Haffenden* (London: Faber, 1981), p. 166.
3. G.C. Spivak, 'Negotiating the Structures of Violence' in *The Post-Colonial Critic: Interviews, Strategies, Dialogues* (London: Routledge, 1990), p. 138.
4. For instance (and in no particular order): The Cultural Traditions Group, Education for Mutual Understanding, The Community Relations Council, The Central Community Relations Unit, and, it can be argued, The Arts Council of Northern Ireland.
5. R. Kirkland, *Literature in Culture in Northern Ireland Since 1965: Moments of Danger* (London: Longman, 1996), pp. 85–120.
6. R. Barthes, *Mythologies* (London: Paladin, 1973), p. 151.
7. S. Deane, et al., *Ireland's Field Day* (London: Hutchinson, 1985). p. vii.
8. S. Deane, 'Canon Fodder: Literary Mythologies in Ireland', in *Styles of Belonging: The Cultural Identities of Ulster*, eds Jean Lundy and Aodán Mac Póilin (Belfast: Lagan Press, 1992), p. 25.
9. T. Eagleton, *Nationalism: Irony and Commitment* (Derry: Field Day, 1988).
10. T. Eagleton, *Heathcliff and the Great Hunger: Studies in Irish Culture* (London: Verso, 1995).
11. T. Eagleton, *Nationalism: Irony and Commitment*, p. 7.
12. T. Eagleton, *Heathcliff and the Great Hunger*, pp. 291–7.
13. R.F. Foster in *Paddy and Mr Punch: Connections in Irish and English History* (London: Penguin, 1993) p. 304, concentrates on Markiewicz's own sense that, despite herself, she was fully in tune with the ideology of Englishness; a tendency coherent with Foster's sense of the 'borrowings of identity' that typified the Treaty debates.
14. R. Williams, *Keywords*.
15. Respectively A. Robinson, *Instabilities in Contemporary British Poetry* (Basingstoke: Macmillan, 1988) and C. Wills, *Improprieties: Politics and Sexuality in Northern Irish Poetry* (Oxford: Oxford University Press, 1993).

16. C. Wills, *Improprieties*, p. 3.
17. D. Lloyd, *Anomalous States: Irish Writing and the Post-Colonial Moment* (Dublin: Lilliput Press, 1993), p. 113.
18. For an example of such insistence see F.R. Leavis's 'How to Teach Reading: A Primer for Ezra Pound' in *Education and the University: A Sketch for an 'English School'* (London: Chatto and Windus, 1948).
19. H.K. Bhabha, *The Location of Culture* (London: Routledge, 1994), p. 1.
20. For instance F. Fanon's *Black Skin, White Masks* (London: Pluto Press, 1991).
21. G.C. Spivak, 'Can the Subaltern Speak?' in *Marxism and the Interpretation of Culture*, ed. C. Nelson and L. Grossberg (London: Macmillan, 1988), pp. 271–2.
22. G.C. Spivak, 'Can the Subaltern Speak?', p. 294.
23. H.K. Bhabha, 'Interrogating Identity: The Postcolonial Prerogative' in *Anatomy of Racism*, ed. D.T. Goldberg (Minneapolis: University of Minnesota Press, 1990), p. 189.
24. H.K. Bhabha, *The Location of Culture*, pp. 58–9.
25. H.K. Bhabha, *The Location of Culture*, p. 28.
26. G.C. Spivak, 'Negotiating the Structures of Violence', p. 141.
27. A. Gramsci, *Selections From the Prison Notebooks* (London: Lawrence and Wishart, 1971), p. 52.
28. Such instances are numerous but one can again refer to the opening of G.C. Spivak, 'Can the Subaltern Speak?' (p. 271) as a suitable example.
29. S. Slemon, 'The Scramble for Post-Colonialism' in *De-Scribing Empire: Post-Colonialism and Textuality*, eds C. Tiffin and A. Lawson (London: Routledge, 1994), p. 17.
30. D. Lloyd, *Anomalous States*, p. 124.
31. L. Gibbons, *Transformations in Irish Culture* (Cork: Cork University Press/Field Day, 1996), pp. 171–80.
32. L. Gibbons, *Transformations in Irish Culture*, p. 172.
33. L. Gibbons, *Transformations in Irish Culture*, p. 172.
34. E. Shohat and R. Stam, *Unthinking Eurocentricism: Multiculturalism and the Media* (New York: Routledge, 1994), p. 42, cited in *Transformations in Irish Culture*, p. 177.
35. L. Gibbons, *Transformations in Irish Culture*, p. 175.
36. L. Gibbons, *Transformations in Irish Culture*, p. 180.
37. D. Kiberd, *Inventing Ireland: The Literature of the Modern Nation* (London: Random House, 1995).
38. S. Deane, et al., *Ireland's Field Day*, pp. 83–105.
39. D. Kiberd, *Inventing Ireland*, p. 5.
40. D. Kiberd, *Inventing Ireland*, p. 7.
41. D. Kiberd, *Inventing Ireland*, p. 653.
42. In considering this phrase I am reminded of the Cultures of Ireland Group, a classically institutional formation, whose conference proceedings are entitled *Culture in Ireland: Division or Diversity?*, ed. E. Longley (Belfast: Institute of Irish Studies, 1991).
43. H.K. Bhabha, *The Location of Culture*, p. 60.
44. D. Lloyd, *Anomalous States*, p. 9.

45. H.K. Bhabha, *The Location of Culture*, p. 60.
46. G.C.Spivak, 'Negotiating the Structures of Violence', p. 142.
47. D. Lloyd, *Anomalous States* p. 9.
48. D. Lloyd, *Anomalous States*, p. 9.
49. H.K. Bhabha, *The Location of Culture*, p. 31.
50. A. Gramsci, *Selections From the Prison Notebooks*, p. 52.
51. A. Gramsci, *Selections From the Prison Notebooks*, p. 52.
52. A. Gramsci, *Selections From the Prison Notebooks*, p. 55.

Bibliography

Abrams, M.H., *The Mirror and the Lamp: Romantic Theory and the Critical Tradition* (Oxford: Oxford University Press, 1953)

Achebe, C., *Hopes and Impediments: Selected Essays, 1965–87* (London: Heinemann, 1988)

Acherson, N., 'Troops Out, If the Nationalists Lower Their Sights', *The Independent on Sunday*, 19 January 1992, p. 28

Adamson, I., *The Cruthin: The Ancient Kindred* (Belfast: Pretani, 1974)

Adorno, T., *The Jargon of Authenticity* (London: Routledge and Kegan Paul, [1964] 1986)

Altieri, J., 'Style and Purpose in Maria Edgeworth's Fiction', *Nineteenth-Century Fiction*, 23 (1968), 265–78

Anderson, B., *Imagined Communities: Reflections on the Origin and Spread of Nationalism* (London: Verso, 1983)

Anderson, J., 'Nationalisms in a Disunited Kingdom' in *The Political Geography of Contemporary Britain*, ed. J. Mohan (London: Macmillan, 1989), pp. 35–50

Anderson, P., *In the Tracks of Historical Materialism* (London: Verso, 1983)

Andrews, E., 'Tom Paulin: Underground Resistance Fighter' in *Poetry in Contemporary Irish Literature*, ed. M. Kenneally (Gerrards Cross: Colin Smythe, 1995), pp. 338–41

anonymous, ed., *Thomas Davis: Essays and Poems with a Centenary Memoir by Eamon de Valera* (Dublin: Gill and Son Ltd, 1945)

Anthias, F. and Yuval-Davis, N., *Racialised Boundaries: Race, Nation, Colour and Class and the Anti-Racist Struggle* (London: Routledge, 1992)

Archer, J.A., *The Irish in Britain* (London: Routledge and Kegan Paul, 1963)

Arnold, M., *Culture and Anarchy* (London: Macmillan, 1869)

Ashcroft, B., Griffiths, G. and Tiffin, H., eds, *The Post-Colonial Studies Reader* (London: Routledge, 1995)

Attridge, D. and Ferrer, D., eds, *Post-Structuralist Joyce: Essays from the French* (Cambridge: Cambridge University Press, 1984)

Auden, W.H., *The Enchafèd Flood, or, The Romantic Iconography of the Sea* (London: Faber, 1951)

Balibar, E. and Wallerstein, I., *Race and Nation* (New York, Sage, 1991)

Barrell, J., *The Idea of Landscape and the Sense of Place 1730–1840* (Cambridge: Cambridge University Press, 1972)

Barthes, R., 'Criticism as Language' in *Twentieth-Century Literary Criticism*, ed. D. Lodge (Harlow: Longman, 1972), pp. 647–51

——, *Mythologies* (London: Paladin, 1973)

——, *Camera Lucida: Reflections on Photography* (London: Vintage, 1982)

Baudrillard, J., *Simulations*, trans. P. Foss, P. Patton and P. Beitchman (New York: Semiotext(e), 1983)

Bauman, Z., *Life in Fragments* (London: Blackwell, 1995)
Beale, J., *Women in Ireland: Voices of Change* (London: Macmillan, 1986)
Beckett, J.C., 'The Irish Writer and his Public in the Nineteenth Century', *Yearbook of English Studies*, 11 (1981), 102–16
Beckett, S., 'Dante . . . Bruno. Vico . . . Joyce' in *Our Exagmination Round His Factification For Incamination of Work in Progress* (London: Faber and Faber, [1929] 1961), pp. 3–22
Bell, D., 'Ireland Without Frontiers? The Challenge of the Communications Revolution' in *Across the Frontiers: Ireland in the 1990s*, ed. R. Kearney (Dublin: Wolfhound, 1988), pp. 219–30
Bender, B., ed., *Landscape, Politics and Perspectives* (Providence and Oxford: Berg, 1993)
Benjamin, W., 'The Task of the Translator' in *Illuminations: Essays and Reflections*, ed. H. Arendt and trans. H. Zohn (New York: Shocken Books, 1968), pp. 69–82
——, 'Edward Fuchs, Collector and Historian' in *One Way Street and Other Writings* (London: Verso, 1985), pp. 349–88
Bennett, T., 'Texts, Readers, Reading Formations', *Literature and History*, 9: 2 (1983), 214–27
——, *Outside Literature* (London: Routledge, 1990)
Berger, J. and Mohr, J., *A Seventh Man* (Harmondsworth: Pelican, 1975)
Bhabha, H.K., 'Representation and the Colonial Text: A Critical Exploration of Some Forms of Mimeticism' in *The Theory of Reading*, ed. F. Gloversmith (Brighton: Harvester Press, 1984), pp. 93–122
——, Signs Taken for Wonders: Questions of Ambivalence and Authority Under a Tree Outside Delhi, May 1817', *Critical Inquiry*, 12 (1985), 144–64
——, ed., *Nation and Narration* (London: Routledge, 1990)
——, 'Interrogating Identity: The Postcolonial Prerogative' in *Anatomy of Racism*, ed. D.T. Goldberg (Minneapolis: University of Minnesota Press, 1990), pp. 183–209
——, *The Location of Culture* (London: Routledge, 1994)
Bolger, D., *The Journey Home* (Harmondsworth: Penguin, 1990)
——, *The Woman's Daughter* (Harmondsworth: Penguin, 1991)
——, *A Dublin Quartet* (Harmondsworth: Penguin, 1992)
Bolton, R., 'The Truth Behind the Treaty', *The Guardian*, 13 January 1992, p. 23
Bowcott, O., 'IRA Aims for the Treasury', *The Guardian*, 22 December 1992, p. 2
Bradley, A., *Requiem for a Spy: The Killing of Robert Nairac* (Cork: Mercier Press, 1992)
Brah, A., 'Difference, Diversity and Differentiation' in *'Race', Culture and Difference*, eds J. Donald and A Rattansi (London: Sage, 1992), pp. 126–48
Braidotti, R., *Nomadic Subjects: Embodiment and Sexual Difference in Contemporary Feminist Theory* (New York: Columbia University Press, 1994)
Brown, T., *Northern Voices* (Dublin: Gill and Macmillan, 1975)
——, *Ireland: A Social and Cultural History, 1922–85* (London: Fontana, 1986)
——, *Ireland's Literature* (Gigginstown: Lilliput Press, 1988)

Butler, D., *The Trouble With Reporting Northern Ireland* (Aldershot: Avebury, 1995)
Butler, J., *Gender Trouble: Feminism and the Subversion of Identity* (London: Routledge, 1990)
Butler, M., *Romantics, Rebels and Reactionaries: English Literature and Its Background 1760–1830* (Oxford: Oxford University Press, 1981)
Cairns, D. and Richards, S., 'Discourses of Opposition and Resistance in Late Nineteenth and Early Twentieth Century Ireland', *Text and Context*, 2: 1 (1988), 76–84
Callaghan, D., 'An Interview with Seamus Deane', *Social Text*, 38 (1994), 39–50
Carson, C., *The Irish for No* (Newcastle Upon Tyne: Bloodaxe, 1987)
Carter, E., Donald, J. and Squires, J., eds, *Space and Place: Theories of Identities and Location* (London: Lawrence and Wishart, 1993)
Cashmore, E.E., *A Dictionary of Race Relations* (London: Routledge, 1984)
Castles, S., et al., *Here for Good* (London: Pluto, 1984)
Caulfield, B. and Bhat, A., 'The Irish in Britain: Intermarriage and Fertility Levels, 1971–1976', *New Community*, 9 (1981), 73–83
Chambers, I., 'Narratives on Nationalism: Being British' in *Space and Place: Theories of Identity and Location*, eds E. Carter, J. Donald and J. Squires (London: Lawrence and Wishart, 1993)
Cheyfitz, E., *The Poetics of Imperialism: Translation and Colonization from 'The Tempest' to 'Tarzan'* (New York and London: Oxford University Press, 1991)
Cohen, P., 'The Perversions of Inheritance: Studies in the Making of Multi-Racist Britain' in *Multi-Racist Britain*, eds P. Cohen and H. Bains (London: Macmillan, 1988), pp. 9–118
Colley, L., *Britons: Forging the Nation, 1707–1837* (London: Pimlico, 1992)
Colum, P., intro., *The Complete Grimm's Fairy Tales* (London: Routledge, 1975 [1943])
Coogan, T.P., *Michael Collins: A Biography* (London: Hutchinson, 1990)
Corcoran, N., 'Strange Letters: Reading and Writing in Recent Irish Poetry' in *Irish Writing: Exile and Subversion*, eds P. Hyland and N. Sammells (London: Macmillan, 1991), pp. 234–47
——, ed., *The Chosen Ground: Essays in the Contemporary Poetry of Northern Ireland* (Bridgend: Seren Books, 1992)
——, *English Poetry Since 1940* (London: Longman, 1993)
Corkery, D., *Synge and Anglo-Irish Literature: A Study* (Cork: Cork University Press, 1931)
Corry, P., [review of *The Treaty*], *The Morning Star*, 15 January 1992, p. 4
Crawford, R., *Devolving English Literature* (Oxford: Clarendon, 1993)
Curtis, L.P., *Anglo-Saxons and Celts: A Study of Anti-Irish Prejudice in Victorian England* (Connecticut: University of Bridgeport, 1968)
—— *Apes and Angels: The Irishman in Victorian Caricature* (Washington: Smithsonian Institution Press, 1971)
Curtis, L., *Nothing But the Same Old Story: The Roots of Anti-Irish Racism* (London: Information on Ireland, 1984)
——, *Ireland: The Propaganda War* (London: Pluto Press, 1984)
Curtis, L. and Jempson, M., *Interference on the Airwaves: Ireland, the Media*

and the Broadcasting Ban (London: Campaign for Press and Broadcasting Freedom, 1993)

Daily Mail, Cartoon, 12 July, 1972, p. 11

—— 'Who's Taking the Mickey', 8 June 1994, p. 1

Daily Telegraph, 'Question: Why Can't They Make Icecubes in Ireland?', 9 June 1994, p. 17

Davis, G., 'Little Irelands' in *The Irish in Britain 1815–1939*, eds R. Swift and S. Gilley, (London: Pinter, 1989), pp. 104–33

Dawe, G., 'A Gritty Prod Baroque' in *A Real Life Elsewhere* (Belfast: Lagan, 1993), pp. 71–87

Deane, S., 'Fiction and Politics: The Nineteenth-Century National Character', *Gaeliana*, 6 (1984), 77–103

——, 'Remembering the Irish Future', *The Crane Bag*, 8:1 (1984), 81–6

——, 'Heroic Styles: The Tradition of an Idea' in *Ireland's Field Day*, eds Field Day Theatre Company (London: Hutchinson, 1985), pp. 45–58

——, 'Introduction', *Nationalism, Colonialism and Literature* (Minneapolis: University of Minneapolis Press, 1990), pp. 3–19

——, 'Wherever Green is Read' in *Revising the Rising*, eds M. Ní Dhonnchadha and T. Dorgan (Derry: Field Day Theatre Company, 1991), pp. 91–105

——, 'Cannon Fodder: Literary Mythologies in Ireland' in *Styles of Belonging: The Cultural Identities of Ulster*, eds. J. Lundy and A. Mac Póilin (Belfast: Lagan Press, 1992), pp. 22–32

Derrida, J., *Of Grammatology*, trans. G.C. Spivak (Baltimore: The Johns Hopkins University Press, 1976 [1967])

——, *Positions* (London: Athlone, 1981)

——, 'Des Tours de Babel' in *Difference in Translation*, ed. and trans. J.F. Graham (Ithaca and London: Cornell University Press, 1992), pp. 165–207

——, *Cinders* (Lincoln: Nebraska University Press, 1991)

——, 'The Deconstruction of Actuality: An Interview with Jacques Derrida', *Radical Philosophy: A Journal of Socialist and Feminist Philosophy*, 68 (1994), 28–41

Devlin, A., *After Easter* (London: Faber and Faber, 1994)

Di San Lazarro, *Klee: His Life and Work*, trans. S. Hood (London: Thames and Hudson, 1964)

Dirlick, A., 'The Postcolonial Aura: Third World Criticism in the Age of Global Captialism', *Critical Inquiry*, 20 (1994), 328–56

Dollimore, J., *Sexual Dissidence: Augustine to Wilde, Freud to Foucault* (Oxford: Clarendon Press, 1991)

Dreyfus, H.L. and Rabinow, P., 'What is Maturity? Habermas and Foucault on "What is Enlightenment?"' in *Foucault: A Critical Reader*, ed. D.C. Hoy (Oxford: Basil Blackwell, 1986), pp. 109–22

Duckworth, A.M., 'Literature and Landscape' in *Encyclopaedia of Literature and Criticism*, eds M. Coyle, P. Garside, M. Kelsall and J. Peck (London: Routledge, 1990), pp. 1018–19

Dunne, T., '"A gentleman's estate should be a moral school": Edgeworthstown in Fact and Fiction' in *Longford: Essays in County History*, eds R. Gillespie and G. Moran (Dublin: Lilliput, 1991), pp. 89–114

Dwyer, T.R., *Michael Collins: The Man Who Won the War* (Dublin: Mercier, 1990)
Eagleton, T., *The Function of Criticism: From The Spectator to Post-Structuralism* (London: Verso, 1984)
——, *Nationalism: Irony and Commitment* (Derry: Field Day, 1988)
——, *Heathcliff and the Great Hunger: Studies in Irish Culture* (London: Verso, 1995)
East Anglian Daily Times, 'Disbelief Over Grant to Research Prejudice', 24 January 1994, p. 9
Edgeworth, M., 'The Grateful Negro' in *Maria Edgeworth: Tales and Novels*, 10 vols (Hildesheim: Georg Olms, 1969 [1893]), II
——, *'Castle Rackrent' and 'Ennui'*, ed. M. Butler (Harmondsworth: Penguin, 1992)
——, *Ormond* (Belfast: Appletree Press, 1992)
Edgeworth, R., *Poetry Explained for the Use of Young People* (London, 1802)
Edgeworth, R.L. and Edgeworth, M., *Essay on Irish Bulls* in *Maria Edgeworth: Tales and Novels*, 10 vols (Hildesheim: Georg Olms, 1969 [1893]), IV
Eglinton, J., 'National Drama and Contemporary Life' in *Literary Ideals in Ireland*, eds J. Eglinton et al. (London: T. Fisher Unwin, 1899; rept. New York: Lemma Publishing Corporation, 1973), pp. 23–7
Elliott, M., *Watchmen in Sion: The Protestant Idea of Liberty* (Derry: Field Day, 1985)
Ellman, R., *Yeats: The Man and the Masks* (New York: Thornton, 1979)
Engels, F., *The Condition of the Working Class in England in 1844* (Stanford: Stanford University Press, 1959)
Everest, K., *English Romantic Poetry: An Introduction to the Historical Context and the Literary Scene* (Milton Keynes: Open University Press, 1990)
Fabian, J., *Time and the Other: How Anthropology Makes Its Object* (New York: Colombia University Press, 1983)
Family, screenplay by Roddy Doyle. Dir. Michael Winterbottom. BBC 1, May 1994
Fanon, F., *Black Skins, White Masks* (London: Pluto Press, [1952] 1986)
——, *The Wretched of the Earth* (Harmondsworth: Penguin, [1961] 1990)
Fennell, D., *Nice People and Rednecks: Ireland in the 1980s* (Dublin: Gill and Macmillan, 1986)
Ferguson, S., 'Hardiman's *Irish Minstrelsy*, Part 1', *Dublin University Magazine*, 3: 16 (1834), 465–77
——, 'Hardiman's *Irish Minstrelsy*, Part 2', *Dublin University Magazine*, 4: 20 (1834), 152–67
——, 'Hardiman's *Irish Minstrelsy*, Part 3', *Dublin University Magazine*, 4: 22 (1834), 447–67
——, 'Hardiman's *Irish Minstrelsy*, Part 4', *Dublin University Magazine*, 4: 23 (1834), 514–42
Flanagan, T., *The Irish Novelists 1800–1850* (New York: Columbia University Press, 1959)
——, *The Year of the French* (New York: Holt, Rheinhart and Winston, 1979)
Fortnight, 299–301 (1991)
Foster, R.F., *Paddy and Mr Punch: Connections in Irish and British History* (London: Allen Lane, 1993)

Foucault, M., *Discipline and Punish: The Birth of the Prison* (New York: Vintage, 1979)
——, 'The Order of Discourse' in *Untying the Text*, ed. R. Young (London: Routledge and Kegan Paul, 1981), pp. 48–78
——, 'Of Other Spaces', *Diacritics*, 16 (1986), 22–7
——, *The Archaeology of Knowledge* (London: Routledge, 1989)
Gallagher, T., 'The Catholic Irish in Scotland: In Search of Identity' in *Irish Immigrants and Scottish Society in the Nineteenth and Twentieth Centuries*, ed. T. Devine (Edinburgh: John McDonald, 1991), pp. 19–43
Garvin, T., 'The Politics of Denial and of Cultural Defence: The Referenda of 1983 and 1986 in Context', *The Irish Review*, 3 (1988), 1–7
Gibbons, L., 'Montage, Modernism and the City', *The Irish Review*, 10 (1991), 1–6
——, '"A Shadowy Narrator": History, Art and Romantic Nationalism in Ireland 1750–1850' in *Ideology and the Historians*, Historical Studies XVII, ed. C. Brady (Dublin: Lillput, 1991), pp. 99–127
——, *Transformations in Irish Culture* (Cork: Cork University Press/Field Day, 1996)
Gilbert, S. and Gubar, S., *The Madwoman in the Attic: The Woman Writer and the Nineteenth-Century Literary Imagination* (New Haven and London: Yale University Press, 1979)
Gilley, S., 'English Attitudes to the Irish in England 1780–1900' in *Immigrants and Minorities in British Society*, ed. C. Holmes (London: George Allen and Unwin, 1978), pp. 81–110
Gilroy, P., *There Ain't No Black in the Union Jack* (London: Hutchinson, 1987)
Golomb, J., *In Search of Authenticity: From Kierkegaard to Camus* (London: Routledge, 1995)
Graham, C., '"Liminal Spaces": Post-Colonial Theories and Irish Culture', *The Irish Review*, 8 (1994)
Gramsci, A., *Selections from the Prison Notebooks* (London: Lawrence and Wishart, 1971)
Greater London Council, *Report on the Prevention of Terrorism Act in London and Report on Consultation with the Irish Community* (Greater London Council Ethnic Minorities Unit, 1984)
Griffiths, G., 'The Myth of Authenticity: Representation, Discourse and Practice' in *De-Scribing Empire: Post-Colonialism and Textuality*, eds C. Tiffin and A. Lawson (London: Routledge, 1994), pp. 70–85
Guardian, 'Scots of the Second City Suffer an Ethnic Setback', 15 February 1986, p. 3
——, 'Industrial Tribunal Rules Irish Jokes Racist', 8 June 1994, p. 1
Haffenden, J., *Viewpoints: Poets in Conversation with John Haffenden* (London: Faber, 1981)
Hall, S., 'When Was "The Post-Colonial"? Thinking at the Limit' in *The Post-Colonial Question: Common Skies, Divided Horizons*, eds I. Chambers and L. Curti (London: Routledge, 1996), pp. 242–60
Hardy, T., *Selected Poems*, ed. and intro. D. Wright (Harmondsworth: Penguin, 1978)
Harris, R., *The Nearest Place That Wasn't Ireland* (Ames, Iowa: Iowa State University Press, 1994)

Heaney, S., *Door into the Dark* (London: Faber, 1969)
——, *Wintering Out* (London: Faber, 1972)
——, *North* (London: Faber, 1975)
——, *Field Work* (London: Faber, 1979)
——, *Station Island* (London: Faber, 1984)
——, *Preoccupations: Selected Prose 1968–1978* (London: Faber, 1987)
——, 'An Open Letter' in *Ireland's Field Day*, eds Field Day Theatre Company (London: Hutchinson, 1985), pp. 23–9
——, 'Place and Displacement: Reflections on Some Recent Poetry from Northern Ireland' in *Contemporary Irish Poetry: A Collection of Critical Essays*, ed. E. Andrews (London: Macmillan, 1992), pp. 124–44
Hear My Song, dir. Peter Chelsom, Miramax films, 1991
Hechter. M., *Internal Colonialism: The Celtic Fringe in British National Development* (Berkeley: University of California Press, 1975)
Heidegger, M., 'Building Dwelling Thinking' in *Basic Writings*, ed. D.F. Krell (London: Routledge and Kegan Paul, 1978), pp. 323–39
Herron, T., 'Fields for the Faction Fights: Poetry, Icons, Nationalism' in *Contemporary Writing and National Identity*, eds T. Hill and W. Hughes (Bath: Sulis Press, 1995), pp. 121–8
Hickman, M., 'A Study of the Incorporation of the Irish in Britain with Special Reference to Catholic State Education: Involving a Comparison of Attitudes of Pupils and Teachers in Selected Secondary Schools in London and Liverpool' (Ph.D. dissertation, University of London Institute of Education, 1990)
——, *Religion, Class and Identity: The State, the Catholic Church and the Education of the Irish in Britain* (London: Avebury, 1995)
——, 'The Irish in Britain: Racism, Incorporation and Identity', *Irish Studies Review*, 10 (1995), 16–19
Hickman, M. and Walter, B., 'Deconstructing Whiteness: Irish Women in Britain', *Feminist Review*, 49 (1995), 5–19
Hill, J., 'Images of Violence' in *Cinema and Ireland*, eds K. Rockett, L. Gibbons and J. Hill (London: Routledge, 1988), pp. 147–93
Hillyard, P., *Suspect Community: People's Experience of the Prevention of Terrorism Act in Britain* (London: Pluto Press, 1993)
Hughes, E., 'Question and Answer with Tom Paulin', *Irish Literary Supplement*, Fall 1988, 32
——, 'Sent to Coventry: Emigrations and Autobiography' in *Returning to Ourselves: Papers from the John Hewitt International Summer School*, ed. E. Patten (Belfast: Lagan, 1995), pp. 99–113
Hyde, D., 'The Necessity for De-Anglicising Ireland' in *The Revival of Irish Literature: Addresses by Sir Charles Gavan Duffy, Dr George Sigerson, Dr Douglas Hyde* (London: T. Fisher Unwin, 1984; rept. New York: Lemma Publishing, 1973), pp. 117–61
Into the West, dir. Mike Newell, Majestic Films, 1992
Ireland, McConnell's Advertising Ltd., *c.* 1994
Irish Post, 'Catholic Loyalty at a High Level Still', 26 December 1992, p. 7
——, 'How Close are the British to the Irish?', 17 December 1994, p. 7
——, 'The "British Irish" and Catholicism', 28 January 1995, p. 7
——, 'Recognition of Ethnicity', 3 June 1995, p. 2

ITC Programme Code (London: ITC, 1993)
James, R., 'Beheading' in *Death and Representation*, eds S.W. Goodwin and E. Bronfen (Baltimore and London: The Johns Hopkins University Press, 1993), pp. 242–62
Jameson, F., *Marxism and Form* (Princeton: Princeton University Press, 1971)
——, 'Cognitive Mapping' in *Marxism and the Interpretation of Culture*, eds C. Nelson and L. Greenberg (Urbana and Chicago: University of Illinois Press, 1988), pp. 347–60
Jones, Sir W., 'The Mahomedan Law of Succession to the Property of Inestates' in *The Works of Sir William Jones* (London, 1749), III
Joyce, J., *Ulysses* (Oxford: Oxford University Press, [1922] 1993)
Joyriders, dir. A. Walsh, Little Bird Films, 1988
Kearney, R., 'Myth and Motherland' in *Ireland's Field Day*, eds Field Day Theatre Company (London: Hutchinson, 1985), pp. 61–80
——, *The Irish Mind: Exploring Intellectual Traditions* (Dublin: Wolfhound, 1985)
——, ed., *Across the Frontiers: Ireland in the 1990s* (Dublin: Wolfhound, 1988)
——, *Transitions: Narratives in Modern Irish Culture* (Manchester: Manchester University Press, 1988)
——, 'Postmodernity and Nationalism: A European Perspective', *Modern Fiction Studies*, 38: 3 (1992), 581–93
—— *Postnationalist Ireland: Politics, Culture, Philosophy* (London: Routledge, 1996)
Keenan, S., 'The Treaty', *Film Ireland*, 27 (1992), 6–7
Kells, M., *Ethnic Identity Amongst Young Irish Middle Class Migrants in London* (London: University of North London Press, Irish Studies Centre Occasional Papers Series 6, 1995)
Kerr, P., 'F is for Fake' in *Understanding Television* (London: Routledge, 1990), pp. 74–87
Kiberd, D., 'Inventing Irelands', *The Crane Bag*, 8: 1 (1984), 11–23
——, 'The Elephant of Revolutionary Forgetfulness' in *Revising the Rising*, eds Máirín Ní Dhonnchadha and Theo Dorgan (Derry: Field Day Theatre Company, 1991), pp. 1–20
——, *Inventing Ireland: The Literature of the Modern Nation* (London: Jonathan Cape, 1995)
Kiernan, V., *The Lords of Humankind* (Harmondsworth: Penguin, 1972)
Kinsella, T., 'The Irish Writer' in W.B. Yeats and T. Kinsella, *Davis, Mangan, Ferguson? Tradition and the Irish Writer* (Dublin: The Dolmen Press, 1970), pp. 57–70
Kirkaldy, J., 'English Newspaper Images of Northern Ireland, 1968–73: An Historical Study in Stereotypes and Prejudices' (Ph.D. thesis, University of New South Wales, 1979)
Kirkland, R., *Literature and Culture in Northern Ireland Since 1965: Moments of Danger* (London: Longman, 1996)
Kowaleski-Wallace, E., *Their Father's Daughter: Hannah More, Maria Edgeworth and Patriarchal Company* (New York and Oxford: Oxford University Press, 1991)

Kowarzik, U., *Developing a Community Response: the Service Needs of the Irish Community in Britain* (London: Action Group for Irish Youth and the Federation of Irish Societies, 1994)

Kristeva, J., *Powers of Horror: An Essay on Abjection* (New York: Columbia University Press, 1982)

Last, R., [review of *The Treaty*], *The Daily Telegraph*, 16 January 1992, p. 15

Leavis, F.R., 'How to Teach Reading: A Primer for Ezra Pound' in *Education and the University: A Sketch for an 'English School'* (London: Chatto and Windus, 1948)

Lebow, N., 'British Historians and Irish History', *Eiré-Ireland*, 8: 4 (1973), 3–38

Lecky, W.E.H., *History of Ireland in the Eighteenth Century*, 5 vols (London, 1892)

Lennon, M., McAdam, M. and O'Brien, J., *Across the Water: Irish Women's Lives in Britain* (London: Virago, 1988)

Lennon, M. and Diski, R., *The Treaty* (London: Thames TV Screen Guide, 1991)

Lees, L., *Exiles of Erin: Irish Migrants in Victorian London* (Manchester: Manchester University Press, 1979)

Lloyd, D., *Nationalism and Minor Literature: James Clarence Mangan and the Emergence of Irish Cultural Nationalism* (Berkeley: University of California Press, 1987)

——, *Anomalous States: Irish Writing and the Post-Colonial Moment* (Dublin: Lilliput, 1993)

Longley, E., '"When did you last see your father?": Perceptions of the Past in Northern Irish Writing, 1965–1985' in *Cultural Contexts and Literary Idioms in Contemporary Irish Literature*, ed. M. Kenneally (Gerrards Cross: Colin Smythe, 1988), pp. 88–112

——, ed., *Culture in Ireland: Division or Diversity?* (Belfast: Institute of Irish Studies, 1991)

——, 'The Aesthetic and the Territorial' in *Contemporary Irish Poetry. A Collection of Critical Essays*, ed. E. Andrews (London: Macmillan, 1992)

——, *The Living Stream: Literature and Revisionism in Ireland* (Newcastle Upon Tyne: Bloodaxe, 1994)

Longley, M., *Poems 1963–1983* (Harmondsworth: Penguin, 1986)

Love Lies Bleeding, dir. M. Winterbottom, Screenplay by R. Bennett, BBC, 1993

Lundy, J. and A. Mac Póilin, eds, *Styles of Belonging: The Cultural Identities of Ulster* (Belfast: Lagan Press, 1988)

MacAnna, F., 'The Dublin Renaissance: An Essay on Modern Dublin and Dublin Writers', *The Irish Review*, 10 (Spring, 1991), 14–30

Mac Aonghusa, P., and Ó Réagáin, eds, *The Best of Pearse* (Cork: Mercier Press, 1967)

MacCarthy, B.G., *The Later Women Novelists 1744–1818* (Cork and Oxford: Cork University Press, 1947)

MacGill, P., *Songs of the Dead End* (London: Yearbook Press, 1914)

MacGowan, S., 'The Sick Bed of Cuchulain', *Rum, Sodomy and the Lash*, Stiff Records, 1985

MacKenzie, S., and Rose, D., 'Industrial Change, the Domestic Economy and Home Life' in *Redundant Spaces? Social Change and Industrial Decline in Cities and Regions*, eds J. Anderson, S. Duncan and R. Hudson (London: Academic Press, 1983), pp. 155–200

Mackintosh, D., 'The Comparative Anthropology of England and Wales', *Anthropology Review Journal*, 4 (1868), 15–16

MacLaughlin, J., 'Place, Politics and Culture in Nation-building Ulster', *Canadian Review of Studies in Nationalism*, 20: 4 (1993)

——, 'Defending the Frontiers: The Political Geography of Race and Racism in the European Community' in *The Political Geography of the New World Order* (London: Bellhaven Press, 1993)

——, *Historical and Recent Irish Emigration* (London: University of North London Press, 1994)

——, *Ireland: The Emigrant Nursery and the World Economy* (Cork: Cork University Press, 1994)

MacNeice, L., *The Collected Poems*, ed. E.R. Dodds (London: Faber, 1979)

Mallie, E., 'Thatcher Opened Secret Channel to IRA in 1990', *The Observer*, 21 April 1996, p. 1

Man of Aran, dir. R. Flaherty, 1934

Marcuse, H., *Eros and Civilisation: A Philosophical Inquiry into Freud* (London: Allen Lane The Penguin Press, 1969)

Marx, K., *Capital* (London: Lawrence and Wishart, 1961)

Marx, K. and Engels, F., *Selected Works* (Moscow: Moscow Press, 1975)

Mayhew, H. and Binney, J., *The Criminal Prisons of London* (London: Charles Griffin, 1862)

McCormack, W.J., 'Maria Edgeworth' in *The Field Day Anthology of Irish Writing*, ed. S. Deane (Derry: Field Day, 1991), I, pp. 1011–13

McCrone, D., *Understanding Scotland: The Sociology of a Stateless Nation* (London: Routledge, 1992)

McDonald, P., 'Michael Longley's Homes' in *The Chosen Ground: Essays in the Contemporary Poetry of Northern Ireland*, ed. N. Corcoran (Bridgend: Seren Books, 1992), pp. 65–83

——, History and Poetry: Derek Mahon and Tom Paulin' in *Contemporary Irish Poetry: A Collection of Critical Essays*, ed. E. Andrews (London: Macmillan, 1992), pp. 86–106

McGann, J., *The Romantic Ideology: A Critical Investigation* (London and Chicago: University of Chicago Press, 1983)

McKittrick, D., *Endgame: The Search for Peace in Northern Ireland* (Belfast: Blackstaff, 1994)

Meaney, G., 'History Gasps: Myth in Contemporary Irish Women's Poetry' in *Poetry in Contemporary Irish Literature*, ed. M. Kenneally (Gerrards Cross: Colin Smythe, 1995), pp. 99–113

Melville, H., *Moby Dick* (Harmondsworth: Penguin, 1972 [1851])

Memmi, A., *The Colonizer and the Colonized* (London: Souvenir Press, 1974)

Mercier, V., *Modern Irish Literature: Sources and Founders* (Oxford: Clarendon Press, 1994)

Miles, R., *Capitalism and Unfree Labour* (London: Tavistock, 1987)

Miles, R., *Racism After 'Race Relations'* (London: Routledge, 1993)

Miller, D., *Don't Mention the War: Northern Ireland, Propaganda and the Media* (London: Pluto Press, 1994)

Mills, L., 'I Won't Go Back to It: Irish Women Poets and the Iconic Feminine', *The Feminist Review*, 50 (1995), 69–88
Moi, T., *Sexual/Textual Politics* (London: Methuen, 1985)
Montague, J., *The Rough Field* (Dublin: Dolmen, 1979)
Moore, G., 'Literature and the Irish Language' in *Ideals in Ireland*, ed. Lady Gregory (London: At the Unicorn VII Cecil Court, 1901), pp. 45–51
Morley, D., and Robins, K., 'No Place Like Heimat: Images of Home(land) in European Culture' in *Space & Place: Theories of Identity and Location*, eds J. Donald and J. Squires (London: Lawrence and Wishart, 1993), pp. 3–31
Mortimer, A., '*Castle Rackrent* and its Historical Contexts', *Etudes Irlandaises*, 9 (1984), 107–23
Muldoon, P., *Mules* (London: Faber, 1977)
——, *Quoof* (London: Faber, 1983)
Murphy, T., *Conversations on a Homecoming* (Dublin: Gallery Press, 1986)
Nairn, T., *The Break-Up of Britain: Crisis and Neo-Nationalism* (London: New Left Books, 1977)
——, *The Enchanted Glass* (London: Radius Press, 1988)
Nandy, A., *The Intimate Enemy: Loss and Recovery of Self Under Colonialism* (Delhi: Oxford University Press, 1983)
Nash, C., 'Remapping and Renaming: New Cartographies of Identity, Gender and Landscape in Ireland', *Feminist Review*, 44 (1993), 39–57
Neal, F., *Sectarian Violence: The Liverpool Experience 1819–1914* (Manchester: Manchester University Press, 1988)
Nietzsche, F., 'On the Uses and Disadvantages of History for Life' in *Untimely Meditations* (Cambridge: Cambridge University Press, 1983), pp. 59–123
Niranjana, T., *Siting Translation: History, Post-Structuralism and the Colonial Context* (Berkeley and Oxford: University of California Press, 1992)
Nolan, E., *James Joyce and Nationalism* (London: Routledge, 1994)
O'Brien, G., 'Aspects of the Novelist', *The Irish Review*, 10 (Spring 1991), 113–18
O'Brien Johnson, T., and Cairns, D., *Gender in Irish Writing* (Milton Keynes: Open University Press, 1991)
O'Connor, F., 'The Future of Irish Literature', *Horizon*, 5: 25 (1942), 55–63
O'Dowd, L., 'Town and Country in Irish Ideology', *Canadian Journal of Irish Studies*, 12: 2 (1987), 43–53
O' Faolain, J., *No Country for Young Men* (New York: Carroll and Graf, 1980)
O'Faolain, S., 'Yeats and the Younger Generation', *Horizon*, 5: 25 (1942), 43–54
——, 'This is Your Magazine' in *The Best from the Bell*, ed. S. McMahon (Dublin: The O'Brien Press, 1978), pp. 13–16
——, *The Irish* (Harmondsworth: Penguin, 1980)
Office of Population Censuses and Surveys, *1991 Census Ethnic Group and Country of Birth* (London: Her Majesty's Stationery Office, 1993)
O'Flynn, J., *Identity Crisis: Access to Benefits and ID Checks* (London: Action Group for Irish Youth, 1993)

O'Leary, P., 'Anti-Irish Riots in Wales', *Llafur: Journal of Welsh Labour History*, 5 (1991), 27–36

O'Loughlin, M., 'Cuchulainn' in *The Inherited Boundaries: Younger Poets of the Republic of Ireland* (Dublin: Dolmen Press, 1986), pp. 122–3

——, 'The Irish Lesson' in *The Inherited Boundaries*, p. 125

——, 'On Hearing Michael Hartnett Read his Poetry in Irish' in *The Inherited Boundaries*, pp. 139–40

Olwig, K.R., 'Sexual Cosmology: Nation and Landscape at the Conceptual Interstices of Nature and Culture; or What Does Landscape Really Mean?' in *Landscape, Politics and Perspectives*, ed. B. Bender (Providence and Oxford: Berg, 1993), pp. 307–43

OPCS, Census, Britain. Ethnic Group and Country of Birth Tables (1993)

Osmond, J., *The Divided Kingdom* (London: Constable, 1988)

O'Toole, F., 'Going West: The Country Versus the City in Irish Writing', *The Crane Bag*, 9:2 (1985), 111–16

——, 'Island of Saints and Silicon: Literature and Social Change in Contemporary Ireland' in *Cultural Contexts and Literary Idioms in Contemporary Irish Literature*, ed. Michael Kenneally (Gerrards Cross: Colin Smythe, 1988), pp. 11–35

——, *Black Hole, Green Card: The Disappearance of Ireland* (Dublin: New Island Books, 1994)

Owen, D., 'Irish-Born People in Great Britain: Settlement Patterns and Socio-Economic Circumstances', *University of Warwick: Census Statistical Paper*, 9 (1995)

Paget, D., *True Stories? Documentary-Drama on Radio, Screen and Stage* (Manchester: Manchester University Press, 1990)

Pajaczkowska, C. and Young, L., 'Racism, Representation and Psychoanalysis' in *'Race', Culture and Difference*, eds J. Donald and A. Rattansi (London: Sage, 1992), pp. 198–219

Parry, B., 'Resistance Theory/Theorising Resistance or Two Cheers for Nativism' in *Colonial Discourse/Postcolonial Theory*, eds F. Barker, P. Hulme and M. Iversen (Manchester: Manchester University Press, 1993), pp. 172–96

Paulin, T., *Thomas Hardy: The Poetry of Perception* (London: Macmillan, 1975)

——, *A State of Justice* (London: Faber, 1977)

——, 'Living Out of London – VII', *London Magazine* (April/May 1979), 83–8

——, *The Strange Museum* (London: Faber, 1980)

——, *Ireland and the English Crisis* (Newcastle Upon Tyne: Bloodaxe, 1984)

——, *Liberty Tree* (London: Faber, 1983

——, *Fivemiletown* (London: Faber, 1987)

——, 'Introduction: Northern Protestant Oratory and Writing, 1791–1985' in *The Field Day Anthology of Irish Writing*, 3 vols, ed. S. Deane (Derry: Field Day, 1991), Vol. 3, p. 315

——, *Minotaur* (London: Faber, 1992)

——, *Walking a Line* (London: Faber, 1994)

——, 'Milton – One of Us' in *Power and the Throne*, ed. and intro. A. Barnett (London: Vintage in association with Charter 88, 1994)

Peach, C., ed., *Ethnicity in the 1991 Census*, Volume 2 (London: HMSO, 1996)
Pearse, P., 'The Spiritual Nation' in *The Best of Pearse*, eds P. Mac Aonghusa and L. Ó Réagáin (Cork: Mercier Press, 1967)
Penman, A., [review of *The Treaty*], *Today*, 16 January 1992, p. 30
Pettitt, L., 'Situation Tragedy? The "Troubles" in British Television Drama', *Irish Studies Review*, 1 (1992), 20–2
——, 'A Camera-Woven Tapestry of the Troubles', *Irish Studies Review*, 8 (1994), 54–6
Phelan, B., 'Writing the Treaty' in *Thames Screen Guide*, eds M. Lennon and R. Diski (London: Thames TV, 1991), pp. 20–2
Pieterse, J.N., 'White Negroes' in *Gender, Race and Class in Media* (London: Sage, 1992)
Pooley, C., 'Segregation or Integration? The Residential Experience of the Irish in Mid-Victorian Britain' in *The Irish in Britain 1815–1939*, eds R. Swift and S. Gilley (London: Pinter, 1989)
Producer's Guidelines (London: BBC, 1989)
Rattansi, A., 'Changing the Subject? Racism, Culture and Education' in *'Race', Culture and Difference*, eds J. Donald and A. Rattansi (London: Sage, 1992), pp. 11–48
Rayner, J., 'In at the Birth of a Nation', *The Times*, 11 January 1992, p. 3
Redfield, J.W., *Comparative Physiognomy* (London: Grenville and Company, 1852)
Report of Poor Removal (London: William and Clowes, 1884)
Report on the Prevention of Terrorism Act and Report on Consultation with the Irish Community (London: Greater London Council, Ethnic Minorities Unit, 1984)
Report on the Sanitary Condition of the Labouring Population of Scotland (1842)
Report on the State of the Irish Poor in Great Britain (London: Macmillan and Co., 1836)
Robinson, A., *Instabilities in Contemporary British Poetry* (Basingstoke: Macmillan, 1988)
Rockett, K., Gibbons, L., Hill, J., *Cinema and Ireland* (London: Routledge, 1988)
Rose, E. and associates, *Colour and Citizenship* (Oxford: For the Institute of Race Relations by Oxford University Press, 1969)
Rushdie, S., *Imaginary Homelands: Essays and Criticism 1981–1991* (London: Penguin, 1992)
Saghal, G. and Yuval-Davis, N., *Refusing Holy Orders: Women and Fundamentalism in Britain* (London: Virago, 1992)
Said, E.W., *Orientalism* (London: Routledge and Kegan Paul, 1978)
——, *The World, the Text and the Critic* (London: Vintage, 1983)
——, 'Foucault and the Imagination of Power' in *Foucault: A Critical Reader*, ed. D.C. Hoy (Oxford: Basil Blackwell, 1986), pp. 149–56
——, *Culture & Imperialism* (London: Chatto & Windus, 1993)
Sangari, K., 'The Politics of the Possible' in *The Post-Colonial Studies Reader*, eds B. Ashcroft, G. Griffiths and H. Tiffin (London: Routledge, 1995), pp. 143–7
Schwarz, B., 'Conquerers of Truth: Reflections on Postcolonial Theory'

in *The Expansion of England: Race, Ethnicity and Cultural History*, ed. B. Schwarz (London: Routledge, 1996), pp. 9–31

Seth, S., 'Nationalism in/and Modernity' in *The State in Transition: Reimagining Political Space*, eds J.A. Camilleri, A.P. Jarvis and A.J. Paolini (Boulder and London: Lynne Rienner Publishers, 1995), pp. 41–59

Sheeran, P.F., 'Colonists and Colonized: Some Aspects of Anglo-Irish Literature from Swift to Joyce', *Yearbook of English Studies*, 13 (1983), 97–115

Shohat, E, and Stam, R., *Unthinking Eurocentricism: Multiculturalism and the Media* (New York: Routledge, 1994)

Sinfield, A., 'Subculture and Dissidence: Stating the Queer/Queering the State', Opening Plenary at 'Citizenship and Cultural Frontiers', Conference at Staffordshire University, 14–17 September 1994

Slemon, S., 'The Scramble for Post-Colonialism' in *De-Scribing Empire: Post-Colonialism and Textuality*, eds C. Tiffin and A. Lawson (London: Routledge, 1994), pp. 15–32.

Sloan, B., *The Pioneers of Anglo-Irish Fiction 1800–1850* (Totowa, New Jersey: Barnes and Noble, 1986)

Smith, A., *An Inquiry into the Nature and Causes of The Wealth of Nations*, eds R.H. Campbell, A.S. Skinner and W.B. Todd, 2 vols (Oxford: Clarendon, 1976)

Smith, P., *Discerning the Subject* (Minneapolis: University of Minnesota Press, 1988)

Smyth, G., 'Writing About Writing and National Identity' in *Contemporary Writing and National Identity*, eds T. Hill and W. Hughes (Bath: Sulis Press, 1995), pp. 8–17

——, '"The natural course of things": Matthew Arnold, Celticism and the English Poetic Tradition', *Journal of Victorian Culture*, 1: 1 (Spring 1996), 35–53

Snyder, E.D., *The Celtic Revival in English Literature 1760–1800* (Cambridge: Harvard University Press, 1923)

Sommer, D., *Foundational Fictions: The National Romances of Latin America* (Berkeley, Los Angeles and London: University of California Press, 1991)

Spivak, G.C., 'Imperialism and Sexual Difference', *Oxford Literary Review*, 8 (1986), 225–40

——, *In Other Worlds: Essays in Cultural Politics* (London: Routledge, 1988)

——, *The Post-Colonial Critic: Interviews, Strategies, Dialogues*, ed. S. Harasym (London: Routledge, 1990)

——, 'Can the Subaltern Speak?' in *Colonial Discourse and Post-Colonial Theory: A Reader*, eds P. Williams and L. Chrisman (Hemel Hempstead: Harvester Wheatsheaf, 1993), pp. 66–111

Stavenhagen, R., *Agrarian Problems and Peasant Movements in Latin America* (New York: Doubleday, 1962)

Stephenson, A., 'Regarding Postmodernism – A Conversation with Fredric Jameson' in *Universal Abandon? The Politics of Postmodernism*, ed. A. Ross (Minneapolis: University of Minneapolis, 1988), pp. 3–30

Storkey, M., *London's Ethnic Minorities: One City Many Communities. An Analysis of the 1991 Census Results* (London: London Research Centre, 1994)

Subaltern Studies I–VI, ed. R. Guha (Delhi: Oxford University Press, 1982–89)

Subaltern Studies VII, eds P. Chatterjee and G. Pandey (Delhi: Oxford University Press, 1992)

Suleri, S., 'The Rhetoric of English India' in *The Post-Colonial Studies Reader*, eds B. Ashcroft, G. Griffiths and H. Tiffin (London: Routledge, 1995), pp. 111–13

Sun, 'The Irish Joke's On Us', 9 June 1994, p. 9

Sunday Times, 'Is a Holiday in Ireland Safe?', 4 June 1972, p. 44

Sutherland, K., 'Fictional Economies: Adam Smith, Walter Scott and the Nineteenth-Century Novel', *NLH*, 54 (1987), 97–127

Swift, R., 'Crime and the Irish in Nineteenth-Century Britain' in *The Irish in Britain 1815–1939*, eds R. Swift and S. Gilley (London: Pinter, 1989), pp. 163–82

Synge, J.M., *The Aran Islands* in *J.M. Synge: Collected Works*, Vol. II, ed. A. Price (London: Oxford University Press, 1966)

The Treaty, dir. J. Lewis, Merlin Films International, 1991

Thompson, E.P., *The Making of the English Working Class* (Harmondsworth: Penguin, 1968)

Under the Shadow of the Gun: The Return of Michael Collins, dir. D. Kerr, Written by F. O'Toole, BBC, 1995

Ussher, A. and van Metzgradt, C., 'An Interpretation of Grimm's Fairy Tales: 2, The Greatest Fairy Tale', *The Dublin Magazine* (April–June 1950), 11–15

Wallerstein, I., *Geopolitics and Geoculture* (New York: Cambridge University Press, 1991)

Walshaw, R., *Migration to and from the British Isles* (London: Jonathan Cape, 1941)

Walter, B., 'The Geography of Irish Migration to Britain, with Special Reference to Luton and Bolton' (D.Phil. thesis, University of Oxford, 1979)

——, 'Tradition and Ethnic Interaction: Second Wave Irish Settlement in Luton and Bolton' in *Geography and Ethnic Pluralism*, eds C. Clarke, D. Ley and C. Peach (London: George Allen and Unwin, 1984), pp. 258–83

——, 'Ethnicity and Irish Residential Segregation', *Transactions of the Institute of British Geographers*, 11 (1986), 131–46

——, *Irish Women in London: the Ealing Dimension*, 2nd edn (London: Women's Unit, London Borough of Ealing, 1989)

——, 'Gender and Irish Migration to Britain', *Anglia Geography Working Paper 4* (1989)

——, 'Gender and Recent Irish Migration to Britain' in *Contemporary Irish Migration*, ed. R. King (Dublin: Geographical Society of Ireland, Special Publications 6, 1991), pp. 11–20

——, 'Irishness, Gender and Place', *Environment and Planning D: Society and Space*, 13 (1995), 35–50

Waters, J., *Jiving at the Crossroads* (Belfast: Blackstaff Press, 1991)

——, *Race of Angels: The Genesis of U2* (London: Fourth Estate, 1994)

Weekes, A.O., *Irish Women Writers: An Uncharted Tradition* (Lexington, Kentucky: University of Kentucky Press, 1990)

White, J., *The Worst Street in North London: Campbell Bunk, Islington Between the Wars* (London: Routledge and Kegan Paul, 1986)

Williams, P. and Chrisman, L., eds, *Colonial Discourse and Post-Colonial Theory: A Reader* (Hemel Hempstead: Harvester Wheatsheaf, 1993)

Williams, R., *Keywords: A Vocabulary of Culture and Society* (London: Fontana, 1983)

——, *The Country and the City* (London: Hogarth, [1973] 1985)

Wills, C., *Improprieties: Politics and Sexuality in Northern Irish Poetry* (Oxford: Clarendon, 1993)

Wolfe, T., *The Painted Word* (New York: Bantam, 1976)

Wordsworth, W., *The Prelude: A Parallel Text*, ed. J.C. Maxwell (Harmondsworth: Penguin, 1971)

Yeats, W.B., *Fairy and Folk Tales of the of the Irish Peasantry* (1888) in *Fairy and Folk Tales of Ireland* (London: Picador, 1973), pp. 3–294

Young, G.M., *Victorian England* (Oxford: Oxford University Press, 1969)

Young, R., ed., *Untying the Text* (London: Routledge, 1981)

Young, R.J.C., *White Mythologies: Writing History and the West* (London: Routledge, 1990)

——, *Colonial Desire: Hybridity in Theory, Culture and Race* (London: Routledge, 1995)

Index